Foundations of ASP.NET AJAX

Robin Pars, Laurence Moroney, and John Grieb

Apress®

Foundations of ASP.NET AJAX

Copyright © 2007 by Robin Pars, Laurence Moroney, and John Grieb

ISBN-13 (pbk): 978-1-59059-828-3

ISBN-10 (pbk): 1-59059-828-8

Trademarked names may appear in this book. Rather than use a trademark symbol with every occurrence of a trademarked name, we use the names only in an editorial fashion and to the benefit of the trademark owner, with no intention of infringement of the trademark.

Lead Editor: Ewan Buckingham
Technical Reviewers: Andy Olsen, Fabio Claudio Ferracchiati
Editorial Board: Steve Anglin, Ewan Buckingham, Tony Campbell, Gary Cornell, Jonathan Gennick, Jason Gilmore, Kevin Goff, Jonathan Hassell, Matthew Moodie, Joseph Ottinger, Jeffrey Pepper, Ben Renow-Clarke, Dominic Shakeshaft, Matt Wade, Tom Welsh
Project Manager: Beth Christmas
Copy Editor: Julie McNamee
Associate Production Director: Kari Brooks-Copony
Production Editor: Janet Vail
Compositor: Gina Rexrode
Proofreader: Lisa Hamilton
Indexer: Broccoli Information Management
Cover Designer: Kurt Krames
Manufacturing Director: Tom Debolski

Distributed to the book trade worldwide by Springer-Verlag New York, Inc., 233 Spring Street, 6th Floor, New York, NY 10013. Phone 1-800-SPRINGER, fax 201-348-4505, e-mail orders-ny@springer-sbm.com, or visit http://www.springeronline.com.

For information on translations, please contact Apress directly at 2855 Telegraph Avenue, Suite 600, Berkeley, CA 94705. Phone 510-549-5930, fax 510-549-5939, e-mail info@apress.com, or visit http://www.apress.com.

The information in this book is distributed on an "as is" basis, without warranty. Although every precaution has been taken in the preparation of this work, neither the author(s) nor Apress shall have any liability to any person or entity with respect to any loss or damage caused or alleged to be caused directly or indirectly by the information contained in this work.

The source code for this book is available to readers at http://www.apress.com.

I would like to dedicate this book to the memory of Steve Irwin. May the world have more people as knowledgeable, genuine, enthusiastic, benevolent, and compassionate as him.

—Robin Pars

*This book is dedicated to Rebecca, my wonderful wife and constant supporter.
I just don't know what I would do without her.
Also to Claudia and Christopher, the greatest daughter and son a guy could ask for!*

—Laurence Moroney

Contents at a Glance

Contents

About the Authors

 **ROBIN PARS** has more than 12 years of IT development experience as a developer and architect. He has been working with ASP.NET since the initial release of the ASP+ runtime in the summer of 2000. Robin holds a B.Sc. degree in Computer Science from the University of California along with nearly a dozen IT certifications. He has also been a coauthor or a contributing author to seven other technical books.

 **LAURENCE MORONEY** is a technology evangelist at Microsoft, where he specializes in the technologies for the next generation of the Web. He has been amazed at how things have progressed since *Foundations of Atlas* (the predecessor of this book) was published. It is a better time than ever to be into technology, and the power that we have at our fingertips with technologies such at ASP.NET AJAX, Silverlight, and .NET 3.x is making work fun again! Laurence's blog is at `http://blogs.msdn.com/webnext`.

JOHN GRIEB lives on Long Island, New York, and works for Reuters as a technical specialist. He is currently the lead developer of a project to migrate Reuters Messaging to Microsoft Live Communication Server 2005. Prior to that, he spent several years in Reuter's Microsoft R&D Group and Innovation Lab, gaining experience in a broad range of cutting-edge Microsoft technologies by participating in many of Microsoft's beta programs and developing prototypes demonstrating how they could be applied to Reuter's own products and services.

About the Technical Reviewers

 **ANDY OLSEN** is a freelance developer and consultant based in the UK. Andy has been working with .NET since Beta 1 days and has co-authored and reviewed several books for Apress covering C#, Visual Basic, ASP.NET, and other topics. Andy is a keen football and rugby fan and enjoys running and skiing (badly). Andy lives by the seaside in Swansea with his wife Jayne and children Emily and Thomas, who have just discovered the thrills of surfing and look much cooler than he ever will!

FABIO CLAUDIO FERRACCHIATI is a senior consultant and a senior analyst/developer using Microsoft technologies. He works for Brain Force (www.brainforce.com) in its Italian branch (www.brainforce.it). He is a Microsoft Certified Solution Developer for .NET, a Microsoft Certified Application Developer for .NET, a Microsoft Certified Professional, and a prolific author and technical reviewer. Over the past 10 years, he's written articles for Italian and international magazines and coauthored more than 10 books on a variety of computer topics. You can read his LINQ blog at www.ferracchiati.com.

Acknowledgments

First and foremost, thanks to everyone at Apress who helped make this book possible including Ewan Buckingham, Julie McNamee, and Janet Vail. I especially would like to thank the wonderful Beth Christmas for her continuing patience and understanding. I'd also like to extend a big thank you to Andy Olson for his excellent technical reviews done with great diligence and attention to detail.

Above all, I would like to thank Ted Kasten and Katja Svetina for their patience and incessant warm support throughout this long and arduous project.

Robin Pars

Introduction

AJAX is fast becoming a de facto standard for developing responsive and rich web applications. This evolutionary step in the user experience is being used in more and more web applications from Outlook Web Access to Google maps and beyond.

But how do you write AJAX applications? Not too long ago, you had to be a JavaScript expert and use tools that are not as sophisticated as those used in standard ASP.NET development. As such, it had been difficult and time-consuming to develop, debug, and maintain AJAX applications despite their innate user friendliness. However, as the popularity and use of AJAX web applications rose, so did a number of frameworks designed to ease AJAX development by providing more out-of-the-box functionality. A few of those packages had been somewhat geared toward developers working with ASP.NET.

After a long beta period, in early 2007, Microsoft officially released the ASP.NET AJAX Extensions, which include a set of client- and server-side controls and functionality leveraging some of the existing technologies in ASP.NET. This release also included the ASP.NET AJAX Toolkit, which contains a set of control extenders that offer enhanced UI effects and built-in AJAX capabilities that can be used on a page with very little development effort. With this release, Microsoft brought about major productivity leaps to AJAX development in the world of ASP.NET.

With ASP.NET AJAX, you can easily convert your existing ASP.NET applications to AJAX applications, and you can add sophisticated user interface elements such as drag and drop, networking, and browser compatibility layers, with simple declarative programming (or, if you prefer to use JavaScript, you can do that too).

This book is a primer on this technology. It introduces you to ASP.NET AJAX, explores some of the main features and controls, and takes you into how to build AJAX applications quickly and simply, taking advantage of the IDE productivity offered by Visual Studio.

It's going to be a fun ride, and by the end of it, you'll be an expert in Web 2.0 and hungry to start developing for it.

Who This Book Is For

This book is for anyone interested in developing next-generation web application interfaces that make the most of AJAX-style asynchronous functionality. Anyone who has ever coded a web page will understand the latency problems associated with postbacks and maintaining state and will be able to gain valuable new tools for their programming arsenal by reading this book.

Some knowledge and prior experience with ASP.NET, C#, or Visual Basic .NET will be helpful to properly understand and follow along with this book.

Prerequisites

You'll need Visual Studio 2005 or Visual Studio 2008; any edition is fine. If you are using Visual Studio 2005, you will also need the ASP.NET AJAX Extensions and the ASP.NET AJAX Toolkit, which can be downloaded from `http://ajax.asp.net`.

■ ■ ■

CHAPTER 1

Introducing AJAX

Welcome to *Foundations of ASP.NET AJAX*. This book is intended to get you up and running with the new framework from Microsoft that allows you to build Web 2.0 applications that implement AJAX functionality. If you've been working in the field of web technology, you know AJAX is hard to avoid—and even harder to implement. Microsoft has thrown its hat into the AJAX arena by doing what it does best—giving you, the developer, a framework and the tools that allow you to build highly interactive and personalized solutions that satisfy your web-based business requirements and users' experiences more quickly and easily than previously possible.

This chapter brings you up-to-date on web application technology with a brief overview of computing history from its huge mainframe origins to today's powerful desktop PCs and the global reach provided by the World Wide Web. It's the beginning of what I hope will be an enjoyable and informative ride.

Delving into the History of Web Application Technology

After the popularity of office productivity applications exploded, and as people began using these applications daily, they required even faster and more sophisticated platforms, which caused the client to continue to evolve exponentially.

It's important to note that the more sophisticated applications were *disconnected* applications. Office productivity suites, desktop-publishing applications, games, and the like were all distributed, installed, and run on the client via a fixed medium such as a floppy disk or CD-ROM. In other words, they weren't connected in any way.

The other breed of application, which was evolving much more slowly, was the *connected* application, where a graphical front end wrapped a basic, text-based communication with a back-end server for online applications such as e-mail. CompuServe was one of the largest online providers, and despite the innovative abstraction of its simple back end to make for a more user-centric, graphical experience along the lines of the heavy desktop applications, its underlying old-school model was still apparent. Remember the old Go commands? Despite the buttons on the screen that allowed a user to enter communities, these simply issued a Go <communityname> command behind the scenes on your behalf.

Although this approach was excellent and provided a rich online experience, it had
to be written and maintained specifically for each platform; so for a multiplatform experience, the vendor had to write a client application for Windows, Unix, Apple, and all
other operating systems and variants.

In the early 1990s, however, a huge innovation happened: the web browser.

This innovation began the slow merger of these two application types (connected
and disconnected)—a merger that still continues today. We all know the web browser by
now, and it is arguably the most ubiquitous application used on modern computers,
displacing solitaire and the word processor for this storied achievement!

But the web browser ultimately became much more than just a new means for
abstracting the textual nature of client/server network communication. It became an
abstraction on top of the operating system on which applications could be written and
executed (see Figure 1-1). This was, and is, important. As long as applications are written
to the specification defined by that abstraction, they should be able to run anywhere
without further intervention or installation on behalf of the application developer. Of
course, the browser had to be present on the system, but the value proposition of having
a web browser available to the operating system was extremely important and ultimately
launched many well-known legal battles.

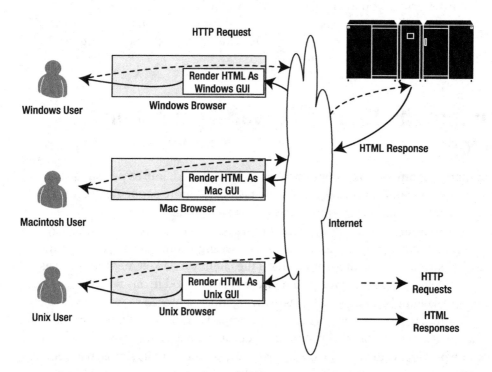

Figure 1-1. *Web browser–based request/response architecture*

Probably, the problem with this abstraction was that it was relatively simple and not originally designed or implemented for anything more complex than laying out and formatting text and graphics. I am, of course, referring to Hypertext Markup Language (HTML). This specification, implemented by a browser, meant that simple text could be placed on a web server, downloaded from a server, interpreted by a browser, and laid out in a far more pleasing way than simple green-on-black on a page, giving the user a better experience. More importantly, however, it could generate a whole new breed of application developers; all a developer had to do to create an online, connected application with a graphical experience was to generate it as HTML, and the browser would do the rest. You wouldn't need the resources of a CompuServe or an America Online to build an application that rendered the text for you! All you had to do was generate HTML, either by coding it directly or writing a server-side application (called Common Gateway Interface, usually written in the C/C++ language) that would generate it for you. Although the Internet had been around for a long time, it was just now starting to come of age.

And guess what happened? The cycle began again.

Everybody jumped on the browser bandwagon, and Common Gateway Interface (CGI) applications, running on a server and delivering content to browsers, were hot. The user experience, with the only interaction being postbacks to the server (similar to computer terminals, only prettier), soon became too limiting due to server responsiveness, huge network loads, and so on, and new technologies began to emerge to improve the user experience.

Enter Java and the applet. Java applications run on top of the Java Virtual Machine (JVM). A *Java applet* is a special kind of Java application that runs in a browser; the browser provides the JVM for the applet. In other words, the Java applet runs in a virtual machine (the JVM) on top of another virtual machine (the browser) on top of a virtual machine (the operating system) on top of a real machine (the underlying hardware). This provided a greater abstraction and introduced a new platform that developers could code to and have even richer applications running within the browser. This was important because it increased complex client-side functionality implemented in a modern, OO (object-oriented) programming language. Enhanced graphical operations (e.g., graphs), client-side processing of business rules possibly, multithreading, and so on used the same simple transport mechanisms of the Internet, but again without requiring the resources of a huge company writing their own GUI platform on which to do it. Probably, Java applets suffered from constraints; namely, to achieve a cross-platform experience, developers had to follow a lowest common denominator approach. The clearest example of this was in its support for the mouse. Apple computers supported one button, the Microsoft Windows operating system supported two, and many Unix platforms supported three. As such, Java applets could support only one button, and many Unix users found themselves two buttons short!

The Java applets run in a security sandbox and therefore cannot access local resources such as the file system or databases, and they cannot create new outbound connections to new URLs on the server (because this could be potentially dangerous). This lack of access to corporate resources led to Java spreading to the server side: server-side Java applications called *servlets* generate HTML pages dynamically and have access to enterprise resources (such as corporate databases, message queues, user information, etc.) because the servlet runs in a more secure server-side environment.

The JVM and language evolved to become a server-side implementation and a great replacement for CGI applications on the server. In addition to this, web browsers continued to evolve and became even more flexible with the introduction of the Document Object Model (DOM) and Dynamic HTML (DHTML) support. Scripting support was added to the browser with the development of JavaScript (unrelated to Java despite its name) and VBScript. To handle these scripting languages, interpreters were plugged into the browser. An extensible browser architecture proved to be a powerful feature.

Thanks to extensibility, applications such as Macromedia Flash added a new virtual machine on top of the browser, allowing for even more flexible and intense applications. The extensible browser then brought about ActiveX technology on the Windows platform, whereby Windows application functionality could be run within the browser when using Microsoft browsers (or alternative ones with a plug-in that supported ActiveX). This powerful solution enabled native functionality to be accessible from networked applications (see Figure 1-2). This got around the restrictions imposed by the security sandbox and lowest common denominator approach of the JVM, but ultimately, this led to problems in the same vein as distributing client-only applications; specifically, a heavy configuration of the desktop, was necessary to get them to work. Although this configuration could be automated to a certain degree, it resulted in two show-stopping points for many.

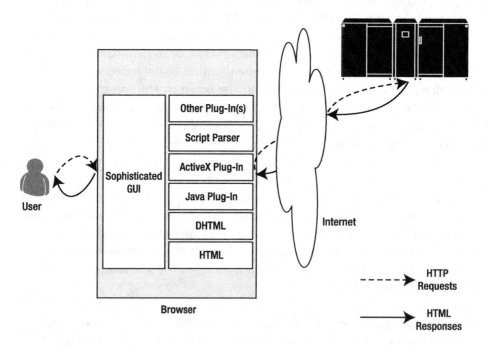

Figure 1-2. *Sophisticated browser architecture*

First, it didn't always work, as the nature of the configuration, changing the Windows registry, often failed—or worse, broke other applications. ActiveX controls were rarely self-contained and usually installed runtime support files. Different versions of these support files could easily be installed on top of each other—a common occurrence leading to broken applications (called DLL Hell).

The second problem was security. A user's computer, when connected to the Internet, could effectively allow code, written by anybody, to run. The ActiveX technology was fully native, not restricted by the Java or HTML sandboxes (more about these in a moment); therefore, users could innocently go to a web page that downloaded an ActiveX control and wrought havoc or stole vital information from their systems. As such, many users refused to use them, and many corporate administrators even disallowed them from use within the enterprise. The virtual nature of Java and HTML—where applications and pages were coded to work on a specific virtual machine—offered better security; these machines couldn't do anything malicious and, therefore, applications written to run on them couldn't either. Users were effectively safe, although limited in the scope of what they could do.

At the end of the 1990s, Microsoft unveiled the successor to ActiveX (among others) in its .NET Framework. This framework would form Microsoft's strategic positioning for many years to come. Like Java, it provided a virtual machine (the Common Language Runtime [CLR]) on which applications would run. These applications could do only what the CLR allowed and were called *managed* applications. The .NET Framework was much more sophisticated than the JVM, allowing for desktop and server-side web applications with differing levels of functionality (depending on which was used). This was part of "managing" the code. With the .NET Framework came a new language, C#, but this wasn't the only language that could be used with .NET because it was a multilanguage, single-runtime platform that provided great flexibility.

The .NET Framework was revolutionary because it united the client-application experience and connected-application experience with a common runtime that ActiveX had tried but ultimately failed to accomplish. Because the same platform was used to write both types of applications, the result was that the user experience would be similar across both (see Figure 1-3). Coupled with the emergence of Extensible Markup Language (XML), a language similar to HTML but specialized for handling data instead of presentation, web application development was finally coming of age.

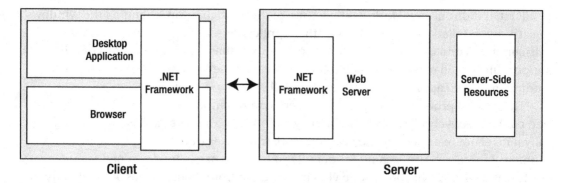

Figure 1-3. *The .NET Framework provides consistent browser, desktop, and server application programming interfaces (APIs).*

Thus, the pendulum has swung back toward the thin client/fat server approach. Ironically, the thin client is probably fatter than the original servers because it's an operating system that can support a browser that is extended to support XML (through parsers), scripting (through interpreters), and other plug-ins, as well as Java and .NET virtual machines! With all these runtime elements available to developers and a consistent server-side API (through the .NET Framework or server-side Java), rich, high-performing applications built using the client/server model are now possible.

Thin Client Applications Save the Day

In the summer of 2001, I had my first "wow" experience with the power of what could be done with a browser-based interface using scripting, DHTML, and asynchronous XML. I was working for a product development group in a large financial services company in New York and was invited by one of their Chief Technical Office (CTO) teams to take a look at their new prototype of a zero-footprint technology for delivering financial information, both streaming and static. They claimed they could stream news, quotes, and charts to a browser with no installation necessary at the desktop, and they could do it in such a manner that it met all the requirements of a typical client. In those days, the biggest support problems were in the installation, maintenance, and support of heavy Component Object Model (COM) desktop applications, and this would wipe them all out in a single blow.

Naturally I was skeptical, but I went to see it anyway. It was a prototype, but it worked. And it largely preserved the user experience that you'd expect from a heavier application with drag-and-drop functionality; streaming updates to news, quotes, and charts; and advanced visualization of data. If anything, it was almost superior to the heavy desktops we were using!

And, it was all built in DHTML, JavaScript, DHTML behaviors, and a lot of server-side functionality using Microsoft-based server products. It was pretty revolutionary.

In fact, it was too revolutionary—and it was too hard for management to take a risk on it because it was so beyond their understanding of how applications *should* work and how the market would accept it. (To be fair, part of their decision was based on my report of concerns about how well the streaming part would scale, but that was nothing that couldn't be fixed!)

But then something terrible happened: September 11, 2001. On that fateful day, a group of individuals turned airliners into missiles, crashing into the World Trade Center and the Pentagon, and killing thousands of people. Part of all this destruction was the loss of many data distribution centers that our company ran for the Wall Street community. With the country having a "get-up-and-running" attitude and wanting the attack to have as little impact on day-to-day affairs as possible, the pressure was on our company to start providing news, quotes, charts, and all the other information that traders needed to get the stock market up and running. The effort to build new data centers and switch the Wall Street users over to them by having staff reconfigure each desktop one by one would take weeks.

The CTO group, with its zero-footprint implementation, ran a T3 line to the machines in the lab that was hosting the application, opening them to the Internet; set up a Domain Name System (DNS) server; and were off and running in a matter of hours. Any trader—from anywhere—could open Internet Explorer, point it at a URL, and start working…no technical expertise required!

Thanks to an innovative use of technology, a business need was met—and that is what our business is all about. Thanks to this experience, and what that group did, I was hooked. I realized the future again belonged to the thin client, and massive opportunities existed for developers and companies that could successfully exploit it.

AJAX Enters the Picture

AJAX, which stands for Asynchronous JavaScript and XML or Asynchronous Java and XML (depending on who you ask), is a technique that has received a lot of attention recently because it has been used with great success by companies such as Amazon and Google. The key word here is *asynchronous* because, despite all the great technologies available in the browser for delivering and running applications, the ultimate model of the browser is still the synchronous request/response model. This means that when an operation occurs in the web page, the browser sends a request to the server waiting for its response. For example, clicking the Checkout button within an HTML page of an e-commerce application consists of calling the web server to process the order and waiting for its response. As such, duplicating the quick refresh and frequent updates provided by desktop applications is hard to achieve. The typical web application involves a refresh cycle where a postback is sent to the server, and the response from the server is re-rendered. In other words, the server returns a complete page of HTML to be rendered by the browser, which looks kind of clunky compared to desktop apps. This is a drawback to this type of architecture because the round-trip to and from the server is expensive in user time and bandwidth cost, particularly for applications that require intensive updates.

What is interesting about the AJAX approach is that there is really nothing new about it. The core technology—the `XMLHttpRequest` object—has been around since 1999 with Internet Explorer, when it was implemented as an ActiveX plug-in. This is a standard JavaScript object recognized by contemporary browsers, which provides the asynchronous postback capabilities upon which AJAX applications rely. More recently, it has been added to the Mozilla Firefox, Opera, and Safari browsers, increasing its ubiquity, and has been covered in a World Wide Web Consortium (W3C) specification (DOM Load and Save). With the high popularity of web applications that use the `XMLHttpRequest` object, such as Google Local, Flickr, and Amazon A9, it is fast becoming a de facto standard.

The nice part about the `XMLHttpRequest` object is that it doesn't require any proprietary or additional software or hardware to enable richer applications. The functionality is built right into the browser. As such, it is server agnostic. Except for needing to make some minor changes to your browser security settings, you can use it straightaway, leveraging coding styles and languages you already know.

To see an example of how it works, refer to Google Local (see Figure 1-4). As you use the mouse to drag the map around the screen, the sections of the map that were previously hidden come into view quickly; this is because they were cached on your initial viewing of the map. Now, as you are looking at a new section (by dragging the mouse), the sections bordering the current one are downloading in the background, as are the relevant satellite photographs for the section of map you are viewing.

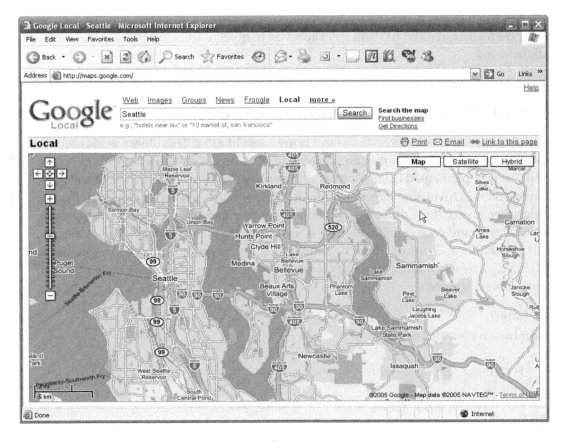

Figure 1-4. *Google Local uses AJAX extensively.*

This background downloading, using the XMLHttpRequest object, makes using Google Local such a smooth and rewarding experience. Remember, nothing is *new* here; it's just that having the XMLHttpRequest object built into the browser that can do this asynchronously makes it possible to develop applications like this.

Note For full details on how to develop in AJAX, check out *Foundations of AJAX* (Apress, 2005).

You will be looking at AJAX from a high level in this book and delving more deeply into how Microsoft ASP.NET AJAX will allow you to quickly and easily build AJAX-enabled applications.

Using the XMLHttpRequest Object

As mentioned, the XMLHttpRequest object is the heart of AJAX. This object sends requests to the server and processes the responses from it. In versions of Internet Explorer prior to IE7, it is implemented using ActiveX, whereas in other browsers, such as Mozilla Firefox, Safari, Opera, and Internet Explorer 7, it is a native JavaScript object. Unfortunately, because of these differences, you need to write JavaScript code that inspects the browser type and creates an instance of it using the correct technology.

Thankfully, this process is a little simpler than the spaghetti code you may remember having to write when using JavaScript functions that heavily used DOM, which had to work across browsers:

```
var xmlHttp;
function createXMLHttpRequest()
{
    if (window.ActiveXObject)
    {
        xmlHttp = new ActiveXObject("Microsoft.XMLHTTP");
    }
    else if (window.XMLHttpRequest)
    {
        xmlHttp = new XMLHttpRequest();
    }
}
```

In this case, the code is simple. If the browser doesn't support ActiveX objects, the window.ActiveXObject property will be null, and, therefore, the xmlHttp variable will be set to a new instance of the native JavaScript XMLHttpRequest object; otherwise, a new instance of the Microsoft.XMLHTTP ActiveX Object will be created.

Now that you have an XMLHttpRequest object at your beck and call, you can start playing with its methods and properties. Some of the more common methods you can use are discussed in the next few paragraphs.

The open method initializes your request by setting up the call to your server. It takes two required arguments (the Hypertext Transfer Protocol [HTTP] command such as GET, POST, or PUT, and the URL of the resource you are calling) and three optional arguments (a boolean indicating whether you want the call to be asynchronous, which defaults to true, and strings for the username and password if required by the server for security). It returns void.

```
xmlHttp.open("GET" , "theURL" , true , "MyUserName" , "MyPassword");
```

The send method issues the request to the server. It is passed a single parameter containing the relevant content. Had the original request been declared as asynchronous (using the boolean flag mentioned earlier), the method would immediately return; otherwise, this method would block until the synchronous response was received. The content parameter (which is optional) can be a DOM object, an input stream, or a string.

```
xmlHttp.send("Hello Server");
```

The setRequestHeader method takes two parameters: a string for the header and a string for the value. It sets the specified HTTP header value with the supplied string.

```
xmlHttp.setRequestHeader("Referrer","AGreatBook");
```

The getAllResponseHeaders method returns a string containing the complete set of response headers from the XMLHttpRequest object after the HTTP response has come back and containing their associated values. Examples of HTTP headers are "Content-Length" and "Date". This is a complement to the getResponseHeader method, which takes a parameter representing the name of the specific header you are interested in. The method returns the value of the header as a string.

```
var strCL;
strCL = xmlHttp.getResponseHeader("Content-Length");
```

In addition to supporting these methods, the XMLHttpRequest object supports a number of properties, as listed in Table 1-1.

Table 1-1. *The Standard Set of Properties for* XMLHttpRequest

Property	Description
onreadystatechange	Specifies the name of the JavaScript function that the XMLHttpRequest object should call whenever the state of the XMLHttpRequest object changes
readyState	The current state of the request (0=uninitialized, 1=loading, 2=loaded, 3=interactive, and 4=complete)
responseText	The response from the server as a string
responseXML	The response from the server as XML
status	The HTTP status code returned by the server (for example, "404" for Not Found or "200" for OK)
statusText	The text version of the HTTP status code (for example, "Not Found")

Using Visual Studio 2005

Throughout this book, you'll be using Visual Studio 2005 to develop AJAX applications using ASP.NET AJAX. Several editions of this application are available to satisfy different needs.

You can download the free edition, Visual Web Developer 2005 Express, from the Microsoft Developer Network (http://msdn.microsoft.com/vstudio/express/vwd). From this page, you can also navigate to the downloads for the other Express editions, including ones for C#, VB .NET, Visual J#, and C++ development.

You can use any edition of Visual Studio 2005, including Standard, Professional, or one of the flavors of Team Edition, to build and run the samples included in this book.

If you are following along with the figures in this book, you'll see they have been captured on a development system that uses the Visual Studio 2005 Team Edition for Software Developers.

Seeing a Simple Example in Action

Understanding how this technology all fits together is best shown using a simple example. In this case, suppose you have a client application that uses JavaScript and an XMLHttpRequest object to issue a server request to perform the simple addition of two integers. As the user types the values into the text boxes on the client, the page calls the server to have it add the two values and return a result, which it displays in a third text box. You can see the application in action in Figure 1-5.

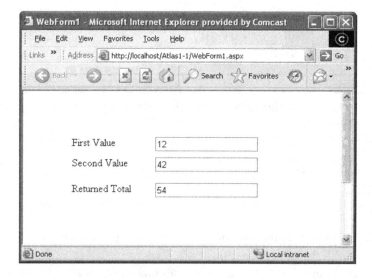

Figure 1-5. *The AJAX addition client*

To create this client, start Visual Studio 2005, create a new web site, edit the page Default.aspx, and set its content to be the same as Listing 1-1.

Listing 1-1. *Creating Your First AJAX Application*

```
<%@ Page language="C#" CodeFile="Default.aspx.cs" AutoEventWireup="false"
Inherits="_Default" %>

<!DOCTYPE HTML PUBLIC "-//W3C//DTD HTML 4.0 Transitional//EN" >
<HTML>
  <HEAD>
  <title>WebForm1</title>
  <script language="javascript">
    var xmlHttp;

    function createXMLHttpRequest() {
        if (window.ActiveXObject) {
            xmlHttp = new ActiveXObject("Microsoft.XMLHTTP");
        }
        else if (window.XMLHttpRequest) {
            xmlHttp = new XMLHttpRequest();
        }
    }

    function updateTotal() {
        frm = document.forms[0];
        url="Default2.aspx?A=" + frm.elements['A'].value +
            "&B=" + frm.elements['B'].value;
        xmlHttp.open("GET",url,true);
        xmlHttp.onreadystatechange=doUpdate;
        xmlHttp.send();
        return false;
    }

    function doUpdate() {
        if (xmlHttp.readyState==4 && xmlHttp.status == 200) {
                document.forms[0].elements['TOT'].value=xmlHttp.responseText;
        }
    }

}
  </script>
  </HEAD>
```

```
<body onload="createXMLHttpRequest();">
      <form>
      <TABLE height="143" cellSpacing="0" cellPadding="0"
                  width="300" border="0" >
            <TR vAlign="top">
                  <TD height="32">First Value</TD>
                  <TD><INPUT type="text" id="A" value="0"
                                   onkeyup="updateTotal();"></TD>
            </TR>
            <TR vAlign="top">
                  <TD height="32">Second Value</TD>
                  <TD><INPUT type="text" id="B" value="0"
                                   onkeyup="updateTotal();"></TD>
            </TR>
            <TR vAlign="top">
                  <TD height="23">Returned Total</TD>
                  <TD><INPUT type="text" id="TOT" value="0"></TD>
            </TR>
      </TABLE>
      </form>
   </body>
</HTML>
```

When the web page loads, the createXMLHttpRequest function is called (as a result of setting the onload event handler in the body tag) to create the XMLHttpRequest object. After that, whenever a key is pressed in the A or B text boxes, the updateTotal function is called (by trapping the onkeyup event on the two text boxes).

The updateTotal function takes the values of A and B from their form elements and uses them to build the URL to *Default2.aspx*, which will look something like Default2.aspx?A=8&B=3. It then calls the open method on XMLHttpRequest, passing it this URL and indicating that this will be an asynchronous process. Next, it specifies the doUpdate function to handle the readystate changes on the XMLHttpRequest object.

To get this application to work, add a new C# web form to the project, and leave the default name of *Default2.aspx*. In the page designer, delete all of the HTML so that the page contains just the ASPX Page directive:

```
<%@ Page language="C#"
    CodeFile="Default2.aspx.cs"
    AutoEventWireup="true"
    Inherits="Default2" %>
```

Then add the following code to the C# code file's Page_Load method (you can add it by double-clicking the *Default.aspx* page when it is shown in the design window of Visual Studio 2005):

```
int a = 0;
int b = 0;
if (Request.QueryString["A"] != null)
{
        a = Convert.ToInt16(Request.QueryString["A"].ToString());
}
if (Request.QueryString["B"] != null)
{
        b = Convert.ToInt16(Request.QueryString["B"].ToString());
}

Response.Write(a+b);
```

This handles the asynchronous request from the page *Default.aspx*, getting the values of A and B, and writing the sum to the response buffer. When the XMLHttpRequest object receives the response from *Default2.aspx*, it calls the doUpdate function, which checks to see if the value of the readyState property is equal to "4," indicating that the request has been completed. If the value is equal to "4," the function updates the INPUT field named TOT with the value returned by *Default2.aspx*, which is stored in the XMLHttpRequest object's responseText property.

Summary

In this chapter, you were given a brief history of the methodologies of building user interfaces that send data to servers for processing and the constantly swinging pendulum from thin client to fat client. You were brought up-to-date on what the newest trend in this development is—web-based thin clients with rich functionality—thanks to the asynchrony delivered by the XMLHttpRequest object, which is the core of AJAX. You then built a simple example that demonstrated how it works. This example was very basic and barely scratched the surface of what can be done with AJAX. However, it demonstrated one of the drawbacks of using this methodology; namely, that it requires a lot of scripting. JavaScript, although powerful, is tedious to write and onerous to debug and manage when compared to languages such as C#, VB .NET, and Java. As such, the application benefits you receive by using an AJAX approach may be more than offset by the application development getting bogged down in thousands (or more) lines of JavaScript.

With this problem in mind, Microsoft integrated the power of AJAX with the productivity of ASP.NET 2.0 and Visual Studio 2005 to develop ASP.NET AJAX.

In the next chapter, you'll be introduced to the wonderful world of ASP.NET AJAX. You will look at its architecture, learn how it allows you to use Visual Studio 2005 and ASP.NET 2.0 server controls to generate client-side code, and see how this can give you the best of AJAX while avoiding the worst of it.

CHAPTER 2

■ ■ ■

Taking AJAX to the Next Level

In Chapter 1, you were introduced to the basics of how AJAX works and saw a code example on how AJAX can be used to build a web page that responds to user input asynchronously. In this chapter, you will be introduced to Microsoft's ASP.NET AJAX, which allows you to build AJAX applications more easily and manage their development, deployment, and debugging using Visual Studio 2005.

ASP.NET AJAX consists of two different pieces. The first is a set of script files, collectively named the Microsoft AJAX Library, which gets deployed to the client. These files implement a number of JavaScript classes that provide common functions and an object-oriented programming framework.

The other piece of ASP.NET AJAX is the ASP.NET 2.0 AJAX Extensions, which includes a set of server controls that allows you to add AJAX functionality to a web page by simply dragging and dropping controls onto the Visual Studio 2005 page designer. Through the use of these server controls, developers can deliver AJAX functionality to the client without doing much hand-coding because the server-side ASP.NET controls generate the required HTML and JavaScript. This feature is one of the fundamental underpinnings of ASP.NET and is essential to understanding the AJAX Extensions.

In this chapter, you will first be introduced to how ASP.NET server controls work. After that, you'll be given an overview of the ASP.NET AJAX architecture, taken on a tour of the AJAX Library, and shown how the AJAX Extensions integrate with ASP.NET 2.0.

Introducing ASP.NET 2.0 Server Controls

Understanding the ASP.NET 2.0 AJAX Extensions and how they are architected first requires an understanding of what ASP.NET 2.0 server controls are and how they work. Server controls are a fundamental part of the ASP.NET framework. At their core, *server controls* are .NET Framework classes that provide visual elements on a web form as well as the functionality that these elements offer. An example of this is a drop-down list box control. ASP.NET provides a server-side ListBox control that renders a list box as HTML elements on the web page. When the web page is returned to the browser, the browser displays the list box to the user. When the user selects an item in the list box, you can run client-side JavaScript to handle the event locally. Alternatively (or additionally), you can arrange for a postback to the server to happen; server-side code can handle the user's selection and perform some related server-side operation (such as populating another part of the web page with data relating to the user's selection). Deciding how much functionality to place client-side (in JavaScript) and server-side (e.g., in C#) is one of the key design issues you have to address when implementing AJAX applications. We'll discuss this more later.

Some of the server controls are straightforward and map closely to standard HTML tags, effectively providing a server-side implementation of those tags. Others are larger-scale abstractions that encapsulate complex GUI tasks such as a calendar or grid. It's important to note that the server controls are not ActiveX controls or Java applets; the control's server-side code generates a combination of HTML (to display the control) and JavaScript (to provide the client-side functionality of the code), which is rendered in the client's browser.

Several types of server controls exist:

HTML server controls: These classes wrap standard HTML tags. Within the ASP.NET web page (usually with the *.aspx* file extension), the HTML tags have a `runat="server"` attribute added to them. An example is the `HtmlAnchor` control, which is a server-side representation of the `<a>`, or anchor, tag. This type of control gives the developer the ability to access the tag's properties from the server-side code. If you add an element such as the following to your ASPX page, your code-behind class will have an instance variable of the same name:

```
<a id="myLink" runat="server" href="MyOtherPage.aspx">Click me</a>
```

In this example, the code-behind class will have an instance variable named `myLink`, which is an instance of the `HtmlAnchor` class. You can use this instance variable to get or set properties on the hyperlink tag.

Web controls: These classes duplicate the functionality of basic HTML tags but have methods and properties that have been standardized across the entire set of web controls, making it easier for developers to use them. Usually web controls are prefixed by `asp:`, such as `<asp:HyperLink>`. With custom web controls, however, you can choose the prefix as well. Many of them are analogous to HTML server controls (e.g., the hyperlink) but have methods and properties that are designed to be used by .NET developers using C# or VB. NET. These controls also expose properties useful to set the standard HTML attributes that ordinary HTML tags have. These properties don't have the same HTML tag attributes, but they are very similar. For example, the NavigateUrl property of the HyperLink web server control will be rendered as the href attribute of the <a> HTML tag. These controls make it easier to develop web applications for those developers who are not used to hand-coding HTML.

Rich controls: This special set of web control is complex and generates large amounts of HTML and JavaScript. An example of this is the calendar control.

Validation controls: These controls validate user input against a predetermined criteria, such as a telephone number or a ZIP code. Should the validation fail, they encapsulate the logic to display an error on the web page.

Data controls: The data controls link to data sources, such as databases or web services, and display the data that they provide. They include controls such as grids and lists and support advanced features such as using templates, editing, sorting, paginating, and filtering.

Navigation controls: These display site map paths (bread crumb trails) and menus to allow users to navigate a site.

Login controls: These have built-in support for forms authentication, providing a set of web controls for the authentication process in your web sites.

Web part controls: These allow you to build a modular user interface (UI) within the browser that provides the user with the ability to modify the content and appearance of a web page. These controls have been created to be used with Microsoft Share Point 2003 and then have been included in ASP.NET 2.0.

Mobile controls: These are for applications that render web content on portable devices such as personal digital assistants (PDAs) and smart phones.

The power of server controls is best demonstrated by example. Fire up Visual Studio 2005, and create a new ASP.NET web site called AJAX2. Drag a calendar from the Standard Controls tab of the Toolbox to the design surface of the *Default.aspx* page that was created for you by Visual Studio. You should have something that resembles Figure 2-1.

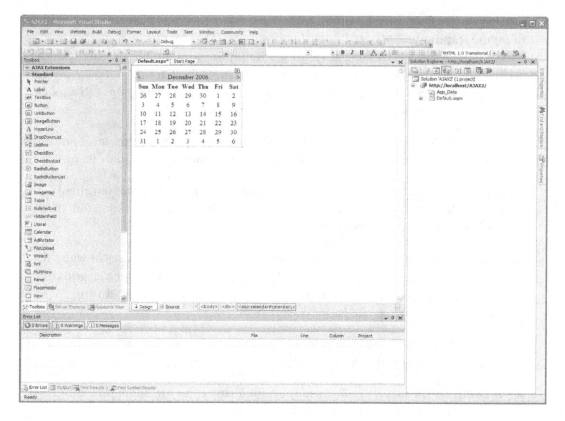

Figure 2-1. *Adding a calendar to the default form*

If you change to source view, you will see very straightforward markup, and there isn't a whole lot of it—certainly not enough to render the calendar, much less the interactivity of selecting dates and paging backward and forward through the months. You can see the markup in Figure 2-2.

Figure 2-2. *Inspecting the markup for the calendar page*

The implementation of the calendar is encapsulated within the asp:Calender tag:

```
<asp:Calendar ID="Calendar1" runat="Server"></asp:Calendar>
```

Visual Studio invokes code within the Calendar server control class to create the visual representation in the designer view of the integrated development environment (IDE). Similarly, at runtime, the ASP.NET engine detects the <asp:Calendar> tag and invokes code within the Calendar server control class to generate the HTML necessary to render the calendar in the browser and the JavaScript that provides its functionality. Figure 2-3 shows the page being rendered in Internet Explorer.

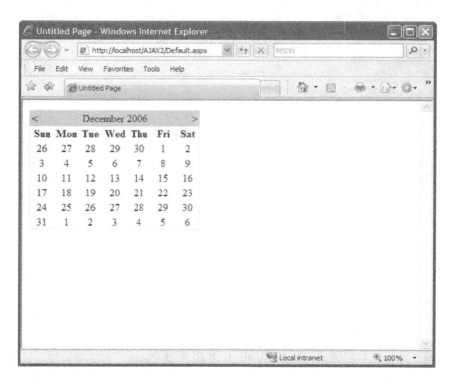

Figure 2-3. *Viewing the calendar page in a browser*

By clicking the Browser's View ➤ Source menu item, you can inspect the combination of HTML and JavaScript that was generated by the server control (see Figure 2-4). You can see that it is vastly different from what was shown at design time in Figure 2-2. The `<asp:Calendar>` tag has been replaced by a `<div>` tag that encapsulates the HTML. This lays out the calendar as a table—showing the days, dates, and month; and the JavaScript that handles the links to move forward and backward by month.

Figure 2-4. *Viewing the client-side code behind the calendar page*

This is an example of the power of server-side controls, and it is with controls such as these that you can deliver AJAX functionality to the browser without overly complex hand-coding, as demonstrated in Chapter 1. You will also be able to take advantage of using a professional IDE so that you can debug and manage your AJAX pages as easily as standard web forms or Windows applications.

These two concepts have been the premier design goals of ASP.NET AJAX. It is well understood that creating AJAX-based web applications can be complex and requires extensive knowledge of client-side script, which is slow to develop and debug. Microsoft has reinvented how AJAX applications can be developed by allowing web developers to use the same familiar productivity features and IDE of Visual Studio 2005 that they use to develop standard web applications.

Synchronous vs. Asynchronous Web Applications

One of the biggest limitations of web applications has always been that they are not dynamic and responsive. For example, consider the case of implementing a simple financial portal. When you change the company you want to inspect, several areas of the page update to display the new company's information. Consider the scenario where the user decides he wants to see more detailed information on the current company and clicks the button to retrieve it. You want this new information to appear on the same page but don't want to refresh the whole page to get it—you just want it to appear. Even if the round-trip to the web server is fast, the entire page will "blink" as the new data is rendered. The browser will clear and redraw the entire page, even though most of it doesn't change.

Using AJAX, you can implement a solution that simply displays a visual indicator that the data is being loaded while it is being retrieved in the background. Although the operation of retrieving and displaying the data takes about the same amount of time, the second example provides a much more dynamic look and feel. The user is still in control while the data is being retrieved. At any time, he can enter the code for a new company and retrieve its information without waiting for the first company's data to be loaded.

AJAX applications typically use HTML, JavaScript, and the associated technologies DHTML and Cascading Style Sheets (CSS) to build UIs. When the interfaces need to change dynamically, a call to the server is usually made using the XMLHttpRequest object. The server returns new HTML markup for the bit of the page that needs to be updated, which gets inserted into the DOM and re-rendered by the browser.

Part of the problem with this approach is that it doesn't provide a clean separation of the presentation and the business logic. The server that manages the data also generates the UI, and the presentation layer (e.g., the browser) dumbly inserts what the server dispatches to it. For example, the server could generate HTML markup for a table that displays data for the company selected by the user. Of course, the server could simply send the data instead of the HTML markup, but it is generally more onerous to have JavaScript parse data and generate the HTML than it is to generate the HTML on the server side where you can use the power of Visual Studio and C# or VB .NET—or indeed Java and any Java IDE.

ASP.NET AJAX follows the model in which the data is managed on the server, where it belongs, and the presentation, after the initial rendering, is handled by the components and controls that run within the browser. Controls and components are higher-level abstractions that fall into two categories:

- *Components* are reusable building blocks that can be created programmatically using client-side script.

- *Controls* are server controls, which are rendered as HTML and the JavaScript that provides the functionality of the UI.

Introducing the ASP.NET AJAX Architecture

The ASP.NET AJAX architecture, which is illustrated in Figure 2-5, consists of two major pieces. First is the Microsoft AJAX Library, which makes developing the client-side functionality of AJAX web applications easier and less time consuming. It has core classes that extend JavaScript to support object-oriented (OO) scripting represented by the Core Services block. It also consists of a base class library, which provides classes that offer extended error handling among other things. There is a network layer (represented by the Networking block in Figure 2-5) that provides asynchronous communication with web and application services, and a UI layer that supports capabilities such as controls and behaviors (the Components block). Finally, it is supported across multiple types of browsers through the use of a browser compatibility layer—the Browser Compatibility block in Figure 2-5—that sits at the bottom layer of the script library. It supports most modern browsers, including Mozilla/Firefox, Safari, Opera, and, of course, Internet Explorer. The Microsoft AJAX Library is covered in detail in Chapter 3.

Second are the ASP.NET 2.0 AJAX Extensions, which provide a server development platform that integrates AJAX and ASP.NET 2.0. Together, they provide a powerful programming model that allows the development of AJAX functionality using the same mechanism that is already in place for developing standard ASP.NET web applications. This eliminates much of the tedious and burdensome scripting associated with the development of AJAX applications today. Finally, it makes it very easy to AJAX-enable your existing ASP.NET applications. The ASP.NET 2.0 AJAX Extensions are discussed in detail in Chapter 4.

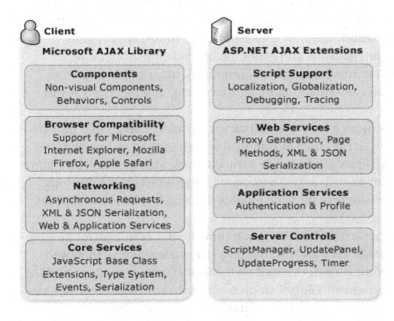

Figure 2-5. *The ASP.NET AJAX architecture*

With the ASP.NET 2.0 AJAX Extensions, the process of developing an AJAX application is similar to what is done today to build an ASP.NET web forms application. Server controls generate the HTML UI as well as the JavaScript functionality, and the AJAX-enabled pages run within the browser by leveraging the AJAX Library. The result is rich client-side functionality within the browser. These server controls can also connect directly to ASP.NET Web Services using JavaScript service proxies to provide a richer experience on the client.

This architecture allows for increased productivity because server controls generate much of the code, which enables you to write fewer lines of JavaScript code. It allows for the clean separation of content, style, behavior, and application logic. A typical design pattern of an ASP.NET AJAX application involves it consuming web services directly from the client without requiring postbacks to the web server. Not only do postbacks slow down an application, but they also complicate the application design, implementation, and deployment. In fact, if you don't use the AJAX functionalities, you have to post the page back to the server (for example, because the user clicks the button where you have inserted the code to call the Web Service method). The page is loaded again and then the button click event handler is called. In the event handler code, there is the creation of the object from the proxy class referenced to the web service. When the method is called, another HTTP request is accomplished. When using AJAX, just the last operation is done, and a lot of time and TCP traffic is saved.

An Overview of the AJAX Library

The AJAX Library provides a powerful JavaScript programming model with a rich type system. JavaScript supports the basic concept of classes but doesn't offer many of the constructs needed for OO programming, nor does it provide a robust type system. To allow developers to create more readable and maintainable code, the AJAX Library extends JavaScript to support namespaces, classes, interfaces, inheritance, and other artifacts that are usually associated with modern high-level languages such as C# and Java.

The AJAX Library also includes a Base Class Library with helper classes that provides additional functionality to JavaScript, such as extended error handling, debugging, and tracing. In the next version of Visual Studio (code named *Orcas*), Microsoft will be adding support for JavaScript developers such as doc comments, Intellisense, and debugging. The AJAX Library incorporates some of the functionality that will be needed to support this functionality.

One of the important aspects of ASP.NET is that it provides a mechanism for developers to globalize (i.e., date formats, etc.) and localize (i.e., string translations) their web applications to support different languages based on the user's browser setting. The AJAX Library also provides this mechanism. Globalization is supported through the Base Class Library's Sys.CultureInfo class and the localFormat method on the number, date, and string types. Localization is supported through a combination of the Sys.CultureInfo class and the ability to load JavaScript files at runtime: By having a set of equivalent JavaScript files in different languages, you can load the one that is applicable.

The ASP.NET AJAX installation package, which can be downloaded from http://www.asp.net/ajax/, includes both the client-side and server-side portions. However, the AJAX Library is also offered as an independent download. The client-side portion of ASP.NET AJAX can be used independently of the server-side portion, which means you can develop AJAX applications using the Microsoft AJAX Library and host them on non-Microsoft web servers. However, it is important to note that although the AJAX Library can be used without the ASP.NET 2.0 AJAX Extensions, there are aspects of the library that work in conjunction with ASP.NET 2.0 to make client-side development even easier and more productive. An example of this is the ability to leverage the ScriptManager server control to make the retrieval of the correct version of a localized JavaScript file automatic.

The Microsoft AJAX Library and Web Services

The AJAX Library has a client-side networking stack built upon the XMLHttpRequest object that provides access to server-based functionality. Although designed to access ASP.NET ASMX (Active Server Methods) web services, it may also be used to access static web content. This functionality is supported via classes within the Sys.Net namespace. These classes, designed to work across all of the major browsers, abstract the use of the XMLHttpRequest object and provide a consistent programming model that allows you to build AJAX applications that access web resources regardless of the platform they are running on.

To simplify access to ASP.NET Web Services, ASP.NET AJAX provides a web services bridge, which allows services to be accessed directly from JavaScript via a function call. It does this by generating a JavaScript proxy that gets downloaded to the client when the service is invoked using a special URI. The proxy, which provides the interface between the client and the web service, is generated by an HTTP handler provided by the ASP.NET 2.0 AJAX Extensions and leverages the Sys.Net classes supplied by the AJAX Library. It is invoked by appending /js to the service URI like this: http://servername/servicename/service.asmx/js. By adding the HTML tag <script src="http://servername/servicename/service.asmx/js"></script> to a web page, the JavaScript is downloaded to the client, and the service can be invoked asynchronously by calling one of its methods using the format service.method(…).

So if you have wrapped or exposed your middleware as a web service using the .NET Framework, it can now be accessed asynchronously from the browser using ASP.NET AJAX. In the past, a web application would have to perform a postback to the server, which would access the web service on its behalf and then return the results to the web application all while the user waited for the web page to be refreshed. You'll see examples of this in Chapters 3 and 8.

JavaScript Object Notation (JSON)

To allow for a more efficient transfer of data and classes between web applications and web services, ASP.NET AJAX supports the JavaScript Object Notation (JSON) format. It is lighter weight than XML (Extensible Markup Language)/SOAP (Simple Object Access Protocol), and delivers a more consistent experience because of the implementation differences of XML/SOAP by the various browsers.

JSON is a text-based data-interchange format that represents data as a set of ordered name/value pairs. As an example, take a look at the following class definition, which stores a person's name and age:

```
Public class MyDetails
{
    Public string FirstName;
    Public string LastName;
    Public int Age;
}
```

A two-element array of this object is represented as follows:

```
{ MyDetails : [ { "FirstName" : "Landon", "LastName" : "Donovan", "Age" : "22"}
                { "FirstName" : "John", "LastName" : "Grieb", "Age" : "46"}
]
}
```

An Overview of the ASP.NET 2.0 AJAX Extensions

The ASP.NET 2.0 AJAX Extensions integrate AJAX and ASP.NET 2.0 by providing a set of AJAX server controls that can be dragged and dropped onto a web page in the same way as any ASP.NET 2.0 server control. Each server control encapsulates the rendering (HTML) and programming (JavaScript) that is necessary to perform its function. As you can imagine, this significantly reduces the amount of effort that is required to develop AJAX web applications.

The most powerful server control that the ASP.NET 2.0 AJAX Extensions provide is the UpdatePanel. By "wrapping" existing content from your current ASP.NET web applications within an UpdatePanel tag, the content can then be updated asynchronously from a user's browser without a complete page refresh. In other words, putting the current HTML of an ASP.NET page within the start and end UpdatePanel tags allows you to implement AJAX functionality without knowing anything about the XMLHttpRequest object or JavaScript. The significance of this cannot be overstated: existing web pages can easily be converted to AJAX applications through the use of asynchronous partial-page updates!

In addition to server controls, the ASP.NET 2.0 AJAX Extensions also provide infrastructural support such as the `Scripthandlerfactory` HTTP handler that was mentioned previously, which supports the creation of JavaScript proxies for ASP.NET Web Services. There is also an HTTP handler that caches and compresses the JavaScript files that make up the AJAX Library. Another piece of functionality that the AJAX Extensions provides is JSON serialization and deserialization.

ASP.NET 2.0 introduced a Membership service, which provides a forms authentication and user management framework, and a Profile service, which supports long-term storage of users' preferences and data. The ASP.NET 2.0 AJAX Extensions expose the authentication portion of the Membership service and the Provider service as web services. These services can be leveraged by the AJAX Library. The library's `Sys.Service.Authentication` class provides the ability to log users on to their site using forms authentication, without requiring a postback to the server. Similarly, the library's `Sys.Service.Profile` class provides for asynchronous storage and retrieval of user settings, such as the site theme. By avoiding postbacks to a web server, even while logging on to your web site, users will perceive your site as being dynamic rather than just another static web application.

Summary

A lot of this may not make much sense right now, but don't worry if you didn't understand all the details we've just discussed. As you work through the examples in this book and see how elegantly ASP.NET AJAX script interacts with the underlying HTML and understand how the server-side controls eliminate much of the manual scripting, it will become much clearer.

In this chapter, you were introduced to the overall architecture of ASP.NET AJAX, given a tour of the various features the architecture offers, and introduced to how it can empower the development of richer browser-based clients.

ASP.NET AJAX is based on two pillars. The first pillar is the client-portion, Microsoft's AJAX Library, which encapsulates many common functions, provides an object-oriented programming environment for JavaScript developers, and enables access to ASP.NET Web Services. The second pillar is the ASP.NET 2.0 AJAX Extensions, which is a set of server controls that implicitly generates the JavaScript code that is needed to implement your AJAX application on the client.

In the next chapter, you'll see in more detail how the AJAX Library makes writing the JavaScript portion of your AJAX applications much easier and how the different aspects of the library come together to provide a unified design and coding framework. You'll also get an overview of each of the library's namespaces and their associated classes and will learn about details of the object-oriented environment it provides, with features such as types, namespaces, and inheritance.

■ ■ ■

CHAPTER 3

The Microsoft AJAX Library: Making Client-Side JavaScript Easier

In the first two chapters, you began to get a sense of the power of AJAX and Microsoft's implementation: ASP.NET AJAX. In addition, you were shown how asynchronous JavaScript and XML can make ordinary web applications more interactive and responsive. Chapter 2 provided an overview of ASP.NET 2.0 and, in particular, server controls, which simplify web development by giving developers the ability to drag and drop rich controls such as calendars or data grids into web pages. By integrating AJAX with ASP.NET 2.0 and Visual Studio 2005, Microsoft has greatly simplified the process of developing, deploying, and debugging AJAX web applications. The second chapter also introduced the features of the client-side aspect of ASP.NET AJAX: the Microsoft AJAX Library. This chapter delves more deeply into the AJAX Library, demonstrating the object-oriented programming paradigm it overlays on JavaScript and then providing some examples of the different namespaces it offers.

JavaScript with the Microsoft AJAX Library

In the following sections, you'll learn how to program JavaScript using the Microsoft AJAX Library by creating your first ASP.NET AJAX-enabled application.

Downloading and Installing ASP.NET 2.0 AJAX Extension 1.0

To use the Microsoft AJAX Library in your web applications, you must first download the ASP.NET 2.0 AJAX framework from the ajax.asp.net web site. After clicking on the Download link, you can choose either the ASP.NET 2.0 AJAX Extension 1.0 or Microsoft AJAX Library options. Choose the first option because the Microsoft AJAX Library option contains just the client JavaScript components that are included in the full ASP.NET AJAX installation. On the other hand, besides the client JavaScript components, the ASP.NET 2.0 AJAX Extension 1.0 option also allows developers to use Visual Studio 2005 to create ASP.NET AJAX web applications easily. Moreover, the libraries contained in the ASP.NET AJAX Extension 1.0 are needed to use the ASP.NET AJAX Controls Kit.

After downloading the ASP.NET AJAX Extension 1.0 setup, you can simply run the executable and follow the easy wizard's steps. The installer will add all the necessary files and Visual Studio 2005 templates to use ASP.NET AJAX in your web applications.

Creating Your First AJAX Application

To get started, fire up Visual Studio 2005, and create a new AJAX web site by selecting File ➤ New Web Site and then selecting ASP.NET AJAX-Enabled Web Site from the New Web Site dialog box (see Figure 3-1).

When you click OK, Visual Studio 2005 creates a new solution for you that contains everything you need to get started with ASP.NET AJAX. You can see the structure it sets up in Figure 3-2. The web site is very straightforward; there is a default web page named *Default.aspx*, a *Web.config* file, and an empty *App_Data* folder that can be used to store any databases or data files used by the web site.

So what makes this an ASP.NET AJAX-enabled web site? Well, the work is all done for you behind the scenes. When ASP.NET AJAX is installed, the assembly that provides its functionality—*System.Web.Extensions*—was stored in the Microsoft .NET Global Assembly Cache (GAC). When you created your web site, a reference to this assembly was added to the web site's *Web.config* file. Several other additions were also made to the *Web.config* file, including several sections that are commented out, which may optionally be used to provide additional functionality such as the Profile and Authentication services. All of this will be covered in more detail in the next chapter when we dive into the ASP.NET 2.0 AJAX Extensions.

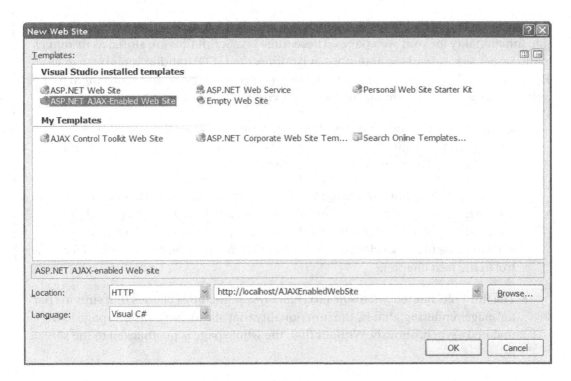

Figure 3-1. *Creating a new ASP.NET AJAX-enabled web site*

Note The web sites are created on HTTP because I have IIS installed on my development computer. If you don't have it, choose File System from the Location drop-down list, and specify a location somewhere on your hard disk. (It doesn't affect the example whether you use HTTP or the file system.)

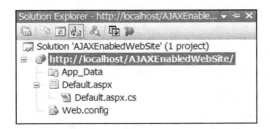

Figure 3-2. *Default ASP.NET AJAX-enabled web site solution structure*

The Microsoft AJAX Library contains three core JavaScript files that deliver client-side functionality for your web pages. These three JavaScript files are stored as resources in the System.Web.Extensions assembly. At runtime, the HTTP handler ScriptResourceHandler loads the files, caches them for future use, compresses them, and sends them to the web browser when they're requested. The files contain the following functionality:

- The primary file, named *MicrosoftAjax.js*, contains 90% of the Microsoft AJAX Library's functionality. It includes, among other things, the browser compatibility layer, the core JavaScript classes, and the Base Class Library.

- The second file, named *MicrosoftAjaxTimer.js*, contains classes needed to support the Timer server control. This control enables you to update either part of or an entire web page at regular intervals; for example, you might want to update the current value of stock prices every 30 seconds. You'll see how to use the Timer control in the next chapter.

- The third file, named *MicrosoftAjaxWebForms.js*, includes classes that support partial-page rendering, that is, the functionality that allows portions of a page to be updated asynchronously. Without that, the whole page is postbacked to the server.

Adding a Custom JavaScript Class

Now that you've created your AJAX-enabled web site, you will create your own JavaScript file that defines a namespace, which contains the class definition for a car. As you will see in the next few sections, the AJAX Library brings object-oriented programming (OOP) to JavaScript by providing namespaces, inheritance, interfaces, and other features. If you are familiar with the OO paradigm, then the advantages are obvious. If not, you will start to see how namespaces and inheritance make code simpler to write, debug, and understand.

To create the JavaScript file, right-click the project within Solution Explorer, and click on Add New Item (see Figure 3-3).

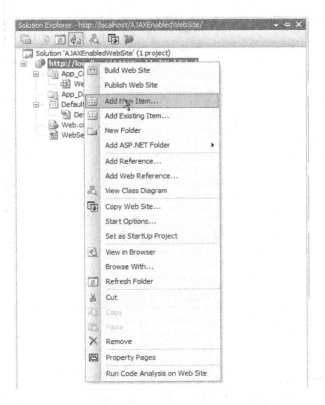

Figure 3-3. *Adding a new file to your solution*

In the dialog box that is displayed, select the JScript File template, and enter a name for the file. In this example, the name *AJAXBook.js* was used, but you may call it anything you like (see Figure 3-4).

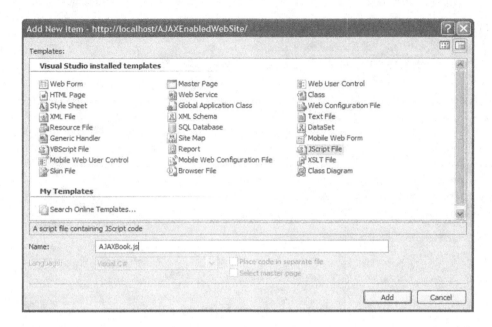

Figure 3-4. *Creating a new JavaScript file*

You can now add the code that implements the namespace AJAXBook and the class Car. When you use Visual Studio 2005 to create and edit JavaScript code, it provides syntax coloring to make the code easier to understand and maintain. Unfortunately, Visual Studio 2005 doesn't add Intellisense; in other words, when you say "Type," it doesn't bring up a list of members on the Type type.

Figure 3-5 shows the namespace AJAXBook and the class definition for Car in the editor.

```
AJAXBook  Open File (Ctrl+O)                                                                  ▼ ×

Type.registerNamespace("AJAXBook");

AJAXBook.Car = function(strMake, strModel, strYear)
{
    this._Make = strMake;
    this._Model = strModel;
    this._Year = strYear;
};

AJAXBook.Car.prototype =
{
    get_Make: function()
    {
        return this._Make;
    },

    get_Model: function()
    {
        return this._Model;
    },

    get_MakeandModel: function()
    {
        return this._Make + " " + this._Model;
    },

    get_Year: function()
    {
        return this._Year;
    },

    dispose: function()
    {
        alert("Bye");
    }
};

AJAXBook.Car.registerClass("AJAXBook.Car");
```

Figure 3-5. *Implementing your namespace and class in JavaScript*

You'll learn what all this syntax means later in this chapter, but it will make more sense if we run through the entire example first.

Using the AJAX Script Manager to Deliver Your Custom Class

To implement a web page that uses this class, add a new web form to the solution, and call it *TestAJAXBookNamespace.aspx* (see Figure 3-6).

Note The *Default.aspx* page already contains the ScriptManager server control, but we'll use a new page to show how to add the control to a new page.

To this web form, you will add an ASP.NET AJAX ScriptManager server control. This server-side control manages the downloading of the Microsoft AJAX Library JavaScript files to the client so that the support for your AJAX code will be available when the user opens the web page. In addition, it will load any of your custom JavaScript files. The easiest way to add the server control to your web page is by simply dragging and dropping it on the page designer.

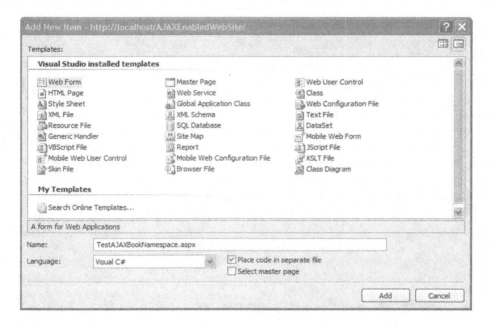

Figure 3-6. *Adding a web form to test your JavaScript*

You'll now see the suite of ASP.NET AJAX server controls in your Toolbox installed into Visual Studio 2005 (see Figure 3-7). Drag and drop the ScriptManager control onto the designer for *TestAJAXBookNamespace.aspx* (or whatever you called the web form). Also drag and drop (from the HTML tab) an Input (Button) control to the web page. You can see the result in Figure 3-8.

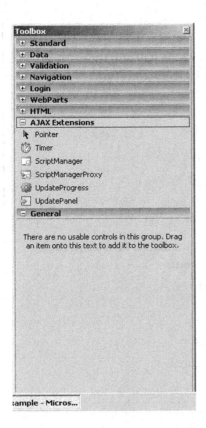

Figure 3-7. *The ASP.NET AJAX server control within the Toolbox*

Figure 3-8. *The* `ScriptManager` *server control and HTML button in the Visual Studio 2005 Designer*

Coding and Running the Application

If you double-click the button in the designer, Visual Studio 2005 will add the `onclick` attribute to the `<input type="button">` HTML element, set its value to `return Button1_onclick()`, and implement the stub of the function `Button1_onclick` inside a `<script>` element within the HTML head element.

You can then put the following script into this function:

```
var testCar = new AJAXBook.Car('Honda','Pilot','2005');
alert(testCar.get_MakeandModel());
alert(testCar.get_Year());
return false;
```

The last step is to tell the `ScriptManager` to download your custom JavaScript file by adding the following HTML inside the `<ScriptManager>` element:

```
<Scripts>
    <asp:ScriptReference Path="~/AJAXBook.js" />
</Scripts>
```

You can see the HTML of the complete web page in Figure 3-9.

```
TestAJAXBookNamespace.aspx*
Client Objects & Events                                           (No Events)

<%@ Page Language="C#" AutoEventWireup="true" CodeFile="TestAJAXBookNamespace.aspx.cs" Inherits="TestAJAXBookNamespace" %>

<!DOCTYPE html PUBLIC "-//W3C//DTD XHTML 1.0 Transitional//EN" "http://www.w3.org/TR/xhtml1/DTD/xhtml1-transitional.dtd">

<html xmlns="http://www.w3.org/1999/xhtml" >
<head runat="server">
    <title>Untitled Page</title>
<script language="javascript" type="text/javascript">
// <!CDATA[

function Button1_onclick() {
    var testCar = new AJAXBook.Car('Honda','Pilot','2005');
    alert(testCar.get_MakeandModel());
    alert(testCar.get_Year());
    return false;
}

// ]]>
</script>
</head>
<body>
    <form id="form1" runat="server">
    <div>
        <asp:ScriptManager ID="ScriptManager1" runat="server">
            <Scripts>
                <asp:ScriptReference Path="~/AJAXBook.js" />
            </Scripts>
        </asp:ScriptManager>

    </div>
        <input id="Button1" type="button" value="button" onclick="return Button1_onclick()" />
    </form>
</body>
</html>
```

Figure 3-9. *The HTML for your first ASP.NET AJAX web page*

Now run your application by pressing the F5 key. You'll be asked if you want to modify the *Web.config* file to enable debugging. After you click OK, your default web browser will open, and you'll see a pretty dull-looking web page with a single button that, when clicked, returns the values for the properties of make, model, and year for this instance of a Car object. In Figure 3-10, you can see the partial output of this application because just the first message box has been captured (after closing this message box, the other showing the year will be shown).

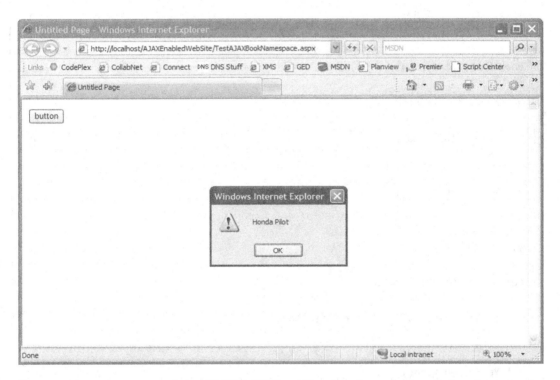

Figure 3-10. *Running your first ASP.NET AJAX application that uses JavaScript classes and namespaces*

Using Namespaces and Classes in JavaScript

The AJAX core classes (*MicrosoftAjax.js*) contain the facility to register namespaces and classes using the Type.registerNamespace and Type.registerClass methods. You can use these to build objects in JavaScript and assign them to the namespaces for clearer, easier-to-read, and easier-to-debug code. Listing 3-1 shows the definition of the Car class you used earlier. This class is registered to the AJAXBook namespace.

Listing 3-1. *Creating a Car Namespace*

```
Type.registerNamespace("AJAXBook");

AJAXBook.Car = function(strMake, strModel, strYear)
{
    this._Make = strMake;
    this._Model = strModel;
    this._Year = strYear;
};

AJAXBook.Car.prototype =
{
    get_Make: function()
    {
        return this._Make;
    },

    get_Model: function()
    {
        return this._Model;
    },

    get_MakeandModel: function()
    {
        return this._Make + " " + this._Model;
    },

    get_Year: function()
    {
        return this._Year;
    },

    dispose: function()
    {
        alert("Bye");
    }
};

AJAXBook.Car.registerClass("AJAXBook.Car");
```

In the code, the namespace `AJAXBook` is registered using the `Type.registerNamespace` method..registerNamespace command. Next, the class `Car` is implemented using the prototype model. In the prototype model, a class consists of two parts: the *constructor*, which initializes the private variables, and the *prototype*, which is used to declare the methods of the class and the *dispose* function in which you can perform any cleanup before your object is reclaimed. It is important to note that in the prototype model, the notion of private is handled by using variables that are prefixed with the underscore (_) character.

Finally, the class is registered to the namespace using the `AJAXBook.Car.registerClass` method, which, in this case, takes a single parameter: the fully qualified name of the class. Now any JavaScript that includes this JavaScript file will be able to create an instance of an `AJAXBook.Car` object by using script such as the following:

```
var testCar = new AJAXBook.Car('Honda', 'Pilot', '2005');
```

Your code can then invoke methods on this object in the usual manner:

```
alert(testCar.get_Year());
```

Using Inheritance in JavaScript

In the previous section, you registered your class using the `registerClass` method prototype that accepts only a single parameter. You can also include a second parameter that specifies the base class from which the class is *inheriting*. One of the goals of AJAX is to make your JavaScript easier to read and debug. Inheritance is a useful way to prevent replication of member variables and methods among your classes, thereby helping you to achieve this goal.

This is probably best demonstrated by example. Earlier you created a `Car` class for a generic car. Lots of different types of cars exist; for example, a sport utility vehicle (SUV) is different from a sports car in that it will usually have four-wheel drive (4WD), whereas the sports car will have only two-wheel drive. If you want to implement car classes where you will query if the car has the 4WD, it makes sense to have a subclass of `Car` called `SUV` that has a `4WD` property.

You can try this by adding the following code to the bottom of the JavaScript file you created earlier:

```
AJAXBook.SUV = function(strMake, strModel, strYear, strDriveType)
{
    AJAXBook.SUV.initializeBase(this, [strMake, strModel, strYear]);

    this._DriveType = strDriveType;
}
```

```
AJAXBook.SUV.prototype =
{
    get_DriveType: function()
    {
        return this._DriveType;
    },

    dispose: function()
    {
        alert("Disposing instance of class SUV");
    }
}
AJAXBook.SUV.registerClass("AJAXBook.SUV", AJAXBook.Car);
```

The earlier code implemented an AJAXBook.Car class that had a constructor that received three parameters to initialize the _Make, _Model, and _Year members on the Car object. This code now implements the SUV class. The SUV constructor takes the same parameters as the Car constructor, plus an additional parameter (strDriveType) that specifies the type of 4WD the vehicle will use.

The first line of the SUV constructor passes the make, model, and year up to the base class, so they can be initialized in the base class, thereby avoiding the need to duplicate them in the initialization code in the AJAXBook.SUV class. The SUV constructor then implements and initializes the single distinct property of the SUV class: _DriveType. The prototype of the class contains two methods: the first allows you to define the DriveType property, and the second, the Dispose method, just displays an alert that the memory of the class instance is being reclaimed. The last statement in the code shows how to use the registerClass method to register the SUV class in the AJAXBook namespace. The first parameter in the registerClass method, AJAXBook.SUV, specifies the fully qualified name of the new class. The second parameter in the registerClass method, AJAXBook.Car, specifies the base class. In other words, AJAXBook.SUV inherits from AJAXBook.Car.

To see the AJAXBook.SUV class in action, return to the web page you created earlier, and change the Button1_onclick script to match the following code:

```
function Button1_onclick()
{
    var testCar = new AJAXBook.Car('Honda','Pilot','2005');
    alert(testCar.get_MakeandModel());
    alert(testCar.get_Year());

    var testSUV = new AJAXBook.SUV('Honda','Pilot','2005','Active');
    alert("SUV Make and Model: " + testSUV.get_MakeandModel());
    alert(testSUV.get_Year());
```

```
    alert(testSUV.get_DriveType());

    return false;
}
```

We've added the creation of an instance of the class `AJAXBook.SUV` and invoked its methods `get_MakeandModel`, `get_Year`, and `get_DriveType`. The instance of the class `AJAXBook.SUV` contains the method `get_DriveType`, but the `get_MakeandModel` and `get_Year` methods are implemented by the base class `AJAXBook.Car` and inherited by the derived class `AJAXBook.SUV`. Run the application, and you'll see them in action (see Figure 3-11).

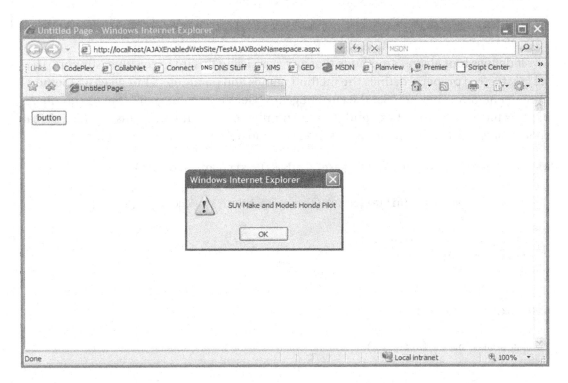

Figure 3-11. *Calling a method from the base class on the derived class*

Implementing Interfaces in JavaScript

The AJAX Library also adds support for interfaces to JavaScript. An interface is a contract—by implementing an interface, you state that you will implement a specific set of methods. Using interfaces allows you to implement a common set of methods across multiple classes with less room for error (e.g., leaving a method out in one of the classes).

As an example, consider the following case. There are two types of sports cars: a "real" sports car that has a stick shift (manual transmission) and an "imitation" sports car that has an automatic transmission.

Here is the code that defines the stick shift interface:

```
AJAXBook.IStickShift = function()
{
    this.get_GearCount = Function.abstractMethod;
    this.set_GearCount = Function.abstractMethod;
    this.get_CurrentGear = Function.abstractMethod;
    this.set_CurrentGear = Function.abstractMethod;
}
AJAXBook.IStickShift.registerInterface('AJAXBook.IStickShift');
```

It defines four abstract methods that any class using this interface must support. The abstractMethod property defines the method names and parameters but gives no method implementation. They are "Set the current gear," "Get the current gear," "Set the number of gears the transmission has," and "Get the number of gears the transmission has." A real sports car is one that implements this interface and, by definition, these methods:

```
AJAXBook.SportsCar = function(strMake, strModel, strYear, strGears)
{
    AJAXBook.SportsCar.initializeBase(this, [strMake, strModel, strYear]);

    this._GearCount = strGears;
    this._CurrentGear = 0;
}


AJAXBook.SportsCar.prototype =
{
    get_GearCount: function()
    {
        return this._GearCount;
    },

    set_GearCount: function(strGears)
    {
        this._GearCount = strGears;
    },

    get_CurrentGear: function()
    {
        return this._CurrentGear;
```

```
    },

    set_CurrentGear: function(strCurrentGear)
    {
        this._CurrentGear = strCurrentGear;
    },

    dispose: function()
    {
        alert("Disposing instance of class SportsCar");
    }
}


AJAXBook.SportsCar.registerClass("AJAXBook.SportsCar",
                                 AJAXBook.Car,
                                 AJAXBook.IStickShift);
```

In this case, the registerClass method call passes the fully qualified name of the class, the class it inherits from, and the interface it implements. You can implement more than one interface with your class simply by specifying each interface into the register-Class method and separating the interface's name by a comma.

Conversely, an imitation sports car is just a fancy-looking normal car, so its class definition would look like this:

```
AJAXBook.ImitationSportsCar  = function(strMake, strModel, strYear)
{
    AJAXBook.ImitationSportsCar.initializeBase(this, [strMake, strModel, strYear]);
}


AJAXBook.ImitationSportsCar.prototype =
{
  Dispose: function()
  {
    Alert("Disposing instance of class ImitationSportsCar");
  }
}


AJAXBook.ImitationSportsCar.registerClass(
                            "AJAXBook.ImitationSportsCar",
                            AJAXBook.Car);
```

Within your client-side JavaScript, you can check whether or not your class implements the IStickShift interface so that you can determine what kind of car it is and whether or not it implements the interface's methods prior to using them.

The following example uses the web page from earlier but changes the content of the button's onclick event handler to this:

```
function Button1_onclick()
{
        var testSportsCar = new AJAXBook.SportsCar('Porsche','999','2005','6');
        var testImitationSportsCar  =  new AJAXBook.ImitationSportsCar('Shorspe',
                              '123',
                              '2005');

        ProcessCar(testSportsCar);
        ProcessCar(testImitationSportsCar);

        return false;
}
```

This event handler calls a helper function named ProcessCar, which looks like this:

```
function ProcessCar(theCar)
{
        if(AJAXBook.IStickShift.isImplementedBy(theCar))
        {
            alert("Current Car: "
                        + theCar.get_MakeandModel()
                        + " This is a good sports car "
                        + " -- I can change gears with a stick shift.");

            theCar.set_CurrentGear(5);
            alert(theCar.get_MakeandModel()
                        + " is now cruising in gear number: "
                        + theCar.get_CurrentGear());
        }
        else
        {
            alert("Current Car: "
                        + theCar.get_MakeandModel()
                        + " This is an imitation sports car "
                        + " -- it's an automatic with a sleek body.");
        }
}
```

This method checks to see whether the car being passed is a "real" sports car. It does this by checking whether it implements the `IStickShift` interface using the method `AJAX-Book.IStickShift.isImplementedBy()`, which returns true only if the specified object is an instance of a class that implements the `IStickShift` interface. After it is determined that the car object implements the interface, then it is safe to call the methods `set_Current-Gear()` and `get_CurrentGear()`. If an attempt was made to call the methods and they didn't exist, an exception would be thrown.

You can see the application in action in Figure 3-12.

Figure 3-12. *Implementing the* `IStickShift` *interface*

Accessing Server Resources from JavaScript

A typical design pattern in web applications is consuming a web service and presenting the data it returns to the user. This forms a typical *n*-tier architecture, with the web service and the information it provides being a resource tier for your web application, which is the presentation tier. To consume the web service, you would normally require the web service to be invoked from the server because before the AJAX framework release, it wasn't possible to call it from the client side. This degrades the responsiveness of a web application because it first must issue a postback to the server and then wait for a response while the server-side code invokes the web service.

With ASP.NET AJAX, web applications can now invoke web services directly from the client. The AJAX Library supports client-side web service proxies, which make calling a web service as easy as calling a JavaScript function. To generate a client-side web service proxy, you need to specify a `<Services>` tag within the `<ScriptManager>` tag that was discussed earlier. Within the `<Services>` tag, you need to add a `<asp:ServiceReference>` tag for each web service you want to use.

Web services are ideally suited for business logic that needs to be used by a number of applications. In the following example, a web service is what calculates the value of a car based on its make, model, and how much it has depreciated in value. Depreciation is not something that can normally be calculated on the client because it is based on a complex formula that uses database lookups. For this example, the depreciation will simply be calculated as $2,000 in value for each year the car has aged.

First you need to add a new web service item to your Visual Studio 2005 project and name it *CarService.asmx*. Add a new WebMethod to the web service named getCarValue. You'll need to add the following using statements at the top of the code file to provide access to the ASP.NET 2.0 AJAX Extensions' attributes and keywords:

```
using System.Web.Script;
using System.Web.Script.Services;
```

Now here's the code for your getCarValue method:

```
[WebMethod]
public int getCarValue(string strCarMake,
string strCarModel,
int strCarYear)
{
    int nReturn = 0;
    if (strCarMake == "Honda")
    {
        if (strCarModel == "Pilot")
        {
            nReturn = 40000;
        }
        else
        {
            nReturn = 30000;
        }
    }
    else
    {
        nReturn = 20000;
    }

    int nDepreciation = (System.DateTime.Now.Year - strCarYear) * 2000;
    nReturn -= nDepreciation;

    return Math.Max(0, nReturn);
}
```

This crude calculation establishes the base value of a Honda at $30,000 (unless it is a Pilot, in which case, it is $40,000). Other makes of car have a base value of $20,000. Depreciation is then subtracted from the car's base value at $2,000 per year of age.

Finally, you need to add a [ScriptService] attribute to the web service declaration. By adding this tag to the web service, you're telling the ASP.NET 2.0 AJAX Extensions to create a proxy object for the web service so that it is accessible via JavaScript.

```
[ScriptService]
public class CarService : System.Web.Services.WebService
```

The web service is complete and ready to be invoked from the client; now it's time to create the web page that is going to call it. Open *Default.aspx* in the designer, and add a ScriptManager element to the page by dragging it from the Toolbox and dropping it onto the page designer. Now add three ASP.NET label controls, three HTML input (text) controls, and an HTML input (button) control to the web page. Label the three text fields "Make:", "Model:", and "Year:", and name them txtMake, txtModel, and txtYear. Set the text of the button to "Get Value". The web page should look like Figure 3-13.

Figure 3-13. *Designing the web service client application*

■**Note** By using the HTML Input button, the page does not have to be posted back when the button is clicked.

Next, go to the source view for this form, find the asp:ScriptManager tag, and add a <Services> tag inside of it. Within the <Services> tag, add an <asp:ServiceReference> tag with a Path attribute that points to the web service. This will cause the AJAX Library to generate a web service proxy at runtime. The HTML should look like this:

```
<asp:ScriptManager ID="ScriptManager1" runat="server">
    <Scripts>
        <asp:ScriptReference Path="~/AJAXBook.js" />
    </Scripts>
    <Services>
        <asp:ServiceReference Path="~/CarService.asmx" />
    </Services>
</asp:ScriptManager>
```

Next, you need to implement the button's onclick event handler, which will invoke the web service, via its proxy, and pass it the parameters entered in the text fields. In design view, double-click the button to create the event handler function. You will automatically be returned to the source view and will be inside the Button1_onclick function. Add the following code to this function:

```
requestValue = CarService.getCarValue(form1.txtMake.value,
    form1.txtModel.value,
    form1.txtYear.value,
    OnComplete,
    OnError);

return false;
```

In JavaScript, you refer to an HTML control by prefixing it with the name of the form that it is on. In this case, the form is called form1; therefore, you can get the value of the txtMake field using form1.txtMake.value.

To invoke a web service method via a proxy, you use the name of the web service, followed by a period, followed by the name of the web method you want to call. You pass parameters into the web method, and get the return value, just like for a normal function call. In this case, the web method is named getCarValue, and the service is called CarService, so the method that needs to be called is CarService.getCarValue. If the web service is defined within a namespace, then the name of the method would be prefixed by the namespace (e.g., if the namespace is MyServicesForAjaxApps, then the method name would be MyServicesForAjaxApps.CarService.getCarValue). If you are in doubt as to what to use, then look at the value of the Class attribute in the web service's .asmx file (see the <%@ WebService %> attribute at the start of the .asmx file) and use that appended with the name of the web method.

Now, the getCarValue web method only expects three parameters, but we've passed five parameters into the web service proxy. Because the AJAX Library invokes web services asynchronously, it needs to inform you when the call to the web service is complete. The two additional parameters are the names of the methods to call if the web service call completes successfully and the method to call if it fails. In this case, the function onComplete will be called if the web service call completes successfully, and the function onError will be called if there is a problem calling the web service.

In this example, you need to implement the callback functions like this:

```
function onComplete(result)
{
    alert("The car is worth s$" + result);
}

function onError(error)
{
    alert(error.get_message());
}
```

If the call to the web service completes successfully, then the result is passed back to the onComplete function, in this case, the calculated value of the car. If it fails, an error object is passed to the onError function. The message associated with the error can be obtained by calling the object's get_message method.

Figure 3-14 shows the application calculating the value of a 2005 Honda Pilot at $36,000, and the method onComplete displaying the results.

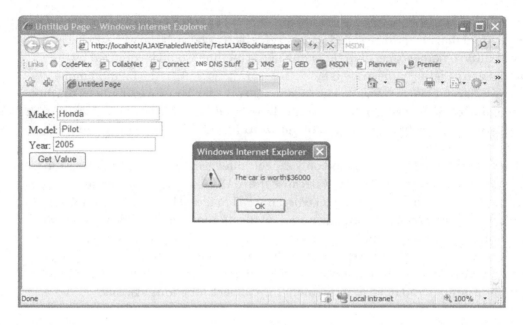

Figure 3-14. *The result of a call to the* `getCarValue` *web service*

Summary

In this chapter, you were introduced to the power that the Microsoft AJAX Library adds to JavaScript. You learned about the extensions implemented in the file *MicrosoftAjax.js* that add true object-oriented programming to JavaScript, with features such as inheritance, namespaces, interfaces, and classes. By walking through an example, you were able to see how these features work and how you can use them to make JavaScript easier to code, debug, and maintain. Additionally, you looked at the JavaScript features that automatically encapsulate asynchronous web service calls from your browser application. You saw how to implement and consume a web service as well as how to process the asynchronous results. Comparing the complexity of this call to the AJAX code in Chapter 1, you can see it is accomplishing almost the exact same task with less code and in an easier-to-read and easier-to-maintain manner.

From here, you can begin to see the value that ASP.NET AJAX brings to developing AJAX-style applications. The following chapter will provide details on the server-side portion of ASP.NET AJAX: the ASP.NET 2.0 AJAX Extensions.

CHAPTER 4

■ ■ ■

ASP.NET AJAX Client Libraries

In the first three chapters, you looked at the basics of ASP.NET AJAX and how you can use it to build web applications that provide slick, clean, high-performing UIs by restricting the need for full-page postbacks to the server and that use the intelligence of the browser on the client side. You also learned about the ASP.NET AJAX JavaScript extensions that bring about a great deal of object-oriented support to JavaScript, thereby allowing you to create classes, events, interfaces, and even the ability to implement inheritance in JavaScript. These additions bring JavaScript one step closer to the .NET programming model with which you're already familiar. In this chapter, you'll learn a bit more about the JavaScript extensions and the built-in types as well as explore the main components of the ASP.NET AJAX client library.

JavaScript Type Extensions

In the previous chapter, you saw the JavaScript extensions made available by the ASP.NET AJAX client library and how you can use them to build object-oriented script files for your web application. In this section, we'll revisit the JavaScript extensions and discuss some of the new types included in the base class libraries that to some extent resemble those found in the .NET Framework. Keep in mind, however, that JavaScript by nature is not a strongly typed language, and the classes discussed here are not natively supported types. You still need to have a `ScriptManager` control on your page to use any of these JavaScript type extensions.

Array and Boolean Extensions

Arrays are nothing new in JavaScript, but the added extensions in the ASP.NET AJAX libraries make them a whole lot more functional and similar to those available in the .NET Framework. Of course, these are not going to be exactly identical in signature and behavior to the `Array` object of the .NET Framework. Another important point to note is that the methods of the `Array` extension are provided as helper methods for an existing JavaScript `Array` object, and thus using them does not require instantiation in a similar manner to static methods. Therefore, you can start using the methods without having to instantiate the Array extension itself. Table 4-1 lists the methods of the Array extension.

Table 4-1. *Methods of the* Array *Extension*

Method Name	Description
add	Adds an element to the end of an array
addRange	Copies all elements of one array to the end of another array
clear	Deletes all elements of an array
clone	Creates a shallow copy of an array
contains	Boolean value indicating whether or not an element is in an array
dequeue	Deletes the first element of an array
enqueue	Another method for adding an element to the end of an array
forEach	Iterates through the elements of an array
indexOf	Returns the index of a specified element in an array (returns -1 if the element wasn't found in the array)
insert	Inserts a value at a specified location in an array
pars	Creates an Array object from a string variable
remove	Removes the first occurrence of an element in an array
removeAt	Removes an element at a specified location in an array

To better understand these methods and how they can be used, consider the following JavaScript snippet:

```
<script type="text/javascript" language=javascript>

    function ArraySample() {
        //Instantiate a JavaScript array object
        var myArray = [];
        myArray[0] = 'First';
        Array.add(myArray, 'Second');
        var newArray = ['Third','Fourth','Fifth'];

    //Add the newArray object to the myArray
     Array.addRange(myArray,newArray);

    //Remove the last item from the Array
    Array.removeAt(myArray, 4);
```

```
        DisplayArray(myArray);
    }
    function DisplayArray(arr) {
        var i;
        var strArray='';
        for (i in arr)
        {
            strArray+=(i+':'+arr[i]+', ');
        }
        alert (strArray);
    }
</script>
```

In this example, a classic JavaScript `Array` object is created and given a value (`First`) at the initial index. After that, the `add` and `addRange` methods of the `Array` extension are used to add additional values to the array. Then the last value of the array is removed using the `removeAt` method, and the underlying `Array` object is passed to the `DisplayArray` function to be displayed as shown in Figure 4-1. Once again, notice how the array object here, `myArray`, is passed in as a parameter to methods of the `Array` extension. It's important to realize that these additional methods listed in Table 4-1 are not new methods on the native JavaScript `Array` object itself.

Figure 4-1. *JavaScript output of the* Array *extension sample*

The `Boolean` extension provided in the ASP.NET AJAX client library is the simplest one with the least number of methods. It just provides one extra method, `parse`, which converts a string into a `Boolean` value. The native JavaScript `Boolean` type does not natively support string initialization. The following script simply declares a `Boolean` value set to `false` and displays the `Boolean` value if false.

```
boolVar = Boolean.parse("false");
if (!boolVar)
    alert ('False');
```

Note In Visual Studio 2008, there is great Intellisense support for all types in xyz.

Date Extensions

Months, days, or years are fairly easy to get access to via the native JavaScript Date object, but having globalization support for dates takes some work. The ASP.NET AJAX client library Date extension provides excellent support for globalization of dates by enabling a wide range of date formatting options based on the browser locale. Unlike the Array extension, the methods provided by the Date extension are instance methods, so you have to create a Date object before using them. Table 4-2 lists the four methods of this extension.

Table 4-2. *Methods of the* Date *Extension*

Method Name	Description
format	Formats a date by using the invariant (culture-independent) culture
localeFormat	Creates a date from a locale-specific string using the current culture
parseInvariant	Creates a date from a string using the invariant culture
parseLocale	Creates a date from a locale-specific string using the current culture

Note that there are two format methods here: format and localeFormat. The only difference is that the format method is culture invariant, meaning that regardless of the current culture, it always uses the same formatting for the date. If you wanted to display culture-sensitive dates (so that dates are displayed differently based on the country and/or language), you first have to set the EnableScriptGlobalization property of the ScriptManager control to true. This ensures that the current culture is serialized and sent to the browser for the ASP.NET AJAX client library to correctly process the desired date format based on the specified culture settings. Table 4-3 lists the various formatting options supported by the format methods of the Date extension.

Table 4-3. *List of the Supported Date Formats*

Format	Description
d	Short date pattern (e.g., 05/10/07)
D	Long date pattern (e.g., Thursday, 10 May 2007)
t	Short time pattern (e.g., 18:05)

Format	Description
T	Long time pattern (e.g., 18:05:12)
F	Full date pattern (e.g., Thursday, 10 May 2007 18:05:12)
M	Month and day pattern (e.g., May 10)
s	Sortable date and time pattern (e.g., 2007-05-10T18:05:12)
Y	Year and month pattern (e.g., 2007 May)

For instance, to display the present date, you can just instantiate a new Date object, and using the format method, pass in the intended format provider (as listed in Table 4-3).

```
function displayDate() {
    var today = new Date();
    alert (today.format('D'));
}
```

The formatted date as the result of the preceding script is shown in Figure 4-2.

Figure 4-2. *Displaying the current date in long format*

Error Extensions

JavaScript has an Error object and is often used in conjunction with try/catch blocks. However, this is a generic Error object used to encapsulate all types of errors and report them to the user. The ASP.NET AJAX client library Error extension provides support for some degree of typed exceptions on the client. It contains some of the commonly typed exceptions found in the .NET Framework. The Error extension allows developers to not only handle exceptions based on the type of the error generated but also manually throw errors of a certain type as needed.

The ASP.NET AJAX client library takes care of all necessary work required to properly serialize these typed errors into and from JSON. When using the Error extension to throw an exception, a new type of exception based on the underlying exception type in the Sys namespace (discussed in a later section in this chapter) is generated. You can even generate custom errors and make specific references pertaining to the original source of the error. Table 4-4 lists all ten of the supported static methods of the Error extension.

Table 4-4. *Methods of the* Error *Extension*

Method Name	Description
argument	Creates an Error object based on the Sys.ArgumentException exception.
argumentNull	Creates an Error object based on the Sys.ArgumentNullException exception.
argumentOutOfRange	Creates an Error object based on the Sys.ArgumentOutOfRangeException exception.
argumentType	Creates an Error object based on the Sys.ArgumentTypeException exception.
argumentUndefined	Creates an Error object based on the Sys.ArgumentUndefinedException exception.
create	Creates an Error object that can contain additional error information.
invalidOperation	Creates an Error object based on the Sys.InvalidOperationException exception.
notImplemented	Creates an Error object based on the Sys.NotImplementedException exception.
parameterCount	Creates an Error object based on the Sys.ParameterCountException exception.
popStackFrame	Adds extra information to the fileName and lineNumber properties of an Error instance regarding the source of the error. This is particularly useful when creating custom errors.

Suppose you are writing some validation logic for a function and want to generate a typed exception on the client for a missing parameter. You can use the Error.argumentNull method to generate an exception of that type by passing the name of the missing parameter and a description as shown here:

```
Error.argumentNull("x", "The x parameter was not provided.");
```

Also, suppose you had implemented the classic try/catch block in your JavaScript, and checking for a necessary condition turned out to be false. You can generate a custom typed exception for proper handling later. The create method is all that is needed to create a custom exception as shown in the following GenerateError function:

```
function GenerateError() {
    try
```

```
        {
            throw Error.create('A custom error was generated');
        }
    catch(e)
    {
        alert(e.message);
    }
}
```

Running the function displays the error message to the user as shown in Figure 4-3.

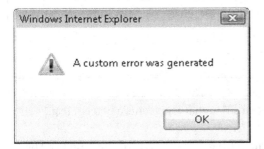

Figure 4-3. *Displaying a custom generated error*

Consequently, if you needed to have additional properties in the custom exception, you provide another object to the create method, which contains a list of key/value pairs to the create method such as those illustrated in the following script:

```
var errParms = {source: 'GenerateError', ErrorID: '999'};
Error.create('A custom error was generated', errParms);
```

This additional information in the errParms object can then be used in the catch clause for better error handling and logging.

Number Extension

The Number extension is similar to the Date extension in that it has a few static and instance methods for extending the underlying JavaScript type and providing support for parsing and output formatting. Just like dates, the formatting of numbers can vary based on the specified culture. This is especially true when displaying currencies that are stored as numbers. The Number extension has two methods for parsing and another two for formatting values as listed in Table 4-5.

Table 4-5. *Methods of the* Number *Extension*

Method Name	Description
format	Formats a number by the invariant culture
localeFormat	Formats a number by the current culture
parseInvariant	Parses a number value from a string
parseLocale	Parses a number from a locale-specific string

The two formatting methods of the Number extension support four format providers that can be used depending on a type of number (e.g., percentage, currency, etc.). These format providers are listed in Table 4-6.

Table 4-6. *List of the Supported Number Formats*

Format	Description
p	The number is converted to a string that represents a percent (e.g., -1,234.56 %).
d	The number is converted to a string of decimal digits (0-9), prefixed by a minus sign if the number is negative (e.g., -1234.56).
c	The number is converted to a string that represents a currency amount (e.g., $1,234.56).
n	The number is converted to a string of the form "-d,ddd,ddd.ddd..." (e.g., -1,234.56).

So as you can see the c format provider can be used to automatically format a number into currency and even localize as specified by the CultureInfo class on the server. The following script uses the parseInvariant method to parse out a number from a string value, and then using the localeFormat, the number is displayed as a currency value.

```
function DisplayCurrency() {
    var num = Number.parseInvariant("130.52");
    alert (num.localeFormat("c"));
}
```

And, because the current culture had been implicitly set to United States, the currency format is $ with cents displayed after the decimal place as shown in Figure 4-4.

Figure 4-4. *Displaying a currency value in US $*

Once again, just as with the `Date` extension, if you plan to use any culture-specific functionality, be sure to set the `EnableScriptGlobalization` property of the `ScriptManager` control to `true`.

Object Extension

The `Object` extension in the ASP.NET AJAX client library provides some level of reflection functionality to JavaScript types. This is a far cry from the rich feature set of reflection in the .NET Framework, but it is a potentially useful functionality in JavaScript. The `Object` extension contains methods to describe the type and the type name of an object. This extension contains only two static-like methods, `getType` and `getTypeName`, as shown in Table 4-7.

Table 4-7. *Methods of the* `Object` *Extension*

Method Name	Description
getType	Returns the type of a specified object
getTypeName	Returns the type name of an object

Type discovery can be particularly useful when you need to control the logic flow based on the type of a parameter or other variables. Consider the following script block:

```
<script language=javascript type="text/javascript">
    var num = new Number(4);
    var date = new Date('05/31/2007');
    function DisplayTypeInfo(obj) {
        document.writeln("Value: " + obj + "  | Type: "+
        Object.getType(obj)+ "  | Type Name: " +
                        Object.getTypeName(obj));
        document.writeln("<BR>");
```

```
    }
    DisplayTypeInfo(num);
    DisplayTypeInfo(date);
</script>
```

In this script, two variables of type Number and Date are instantiated and assigned initial values. After that, the DisplayTypeInfo function is called to display the type information for these two variables. The getType method is called here for the type of the variable followed by the getTypeName to get the name of the variable type. As you can see in Figure 4-5, the type contains more information than the type name.

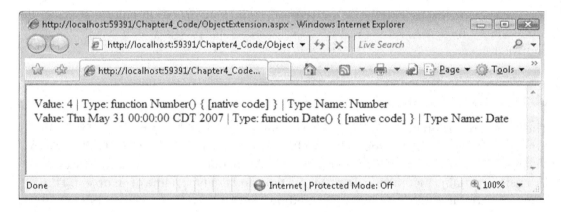

Figure 4-5. *Displaying type and type names of two variables*

String Extension

Last but not least, the JavaScript's native String object has been extended in the xyz to include a handful of useful additions to once again make it somewhat more similar to the String class in the .NET Framework. These additions can be very useful because string processing in one form or another is done quite often in most applications. Other than two formatting methods (similar to those found in the Date and Number extensions), the String extension includes a few trimming methods among others as shown in Table 4-8.

Table 4-8. *Methods of the* String *Extension*

Method Name	Description
endsWith	Returns a boolean value indicating whether or not the end of the String object matches the specified string
format	Formats a string by replacing placeholders with provided values

Method Name	Description
localeFormat	Formats a string by replacing placeholders with provided values with locale specificity
startsWith	Returns a boolean value indicating whether or not the start of the String object matches the specified string
trim	Removes leading and trailing spaces from a String object
trimEnd	Removes trailing spaces from a String object
trimStart	Removes leading white spaces from a String object

The following small script illustrates usage of some of the main methods of the String extension:

```
<script language=javascript type="text/javascript">
    var asp = " ASP";
    var dotnet =".NET ";
    var ajax = " Ajax ";
    alert (String.format("{0}{1} {2} String Extension!",
            asp.trimStart(),dotnet.trimEnd(),ajax.trim()));
</script>
```

In this script, all three available trimming methods were used to trim the extra space from the start, end, and overall part of the designated string. These string variables were then passed into the format method as arguments to be displayed (as shown in Figure 4-6) just like it would be with the .NET Framework's String class. One last point to note here is that the two formatting methods of the String extension are static methods, unlike the rest of the methods, which are instance based.

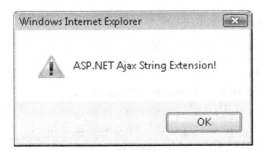

Figure 4-6. *Using methods of the String extension*

Note The ASP.NET AJAX client library also includes a `StringBuilder` class in the `Sys` namespace that is quite similar in terms of functionality to the `StringBuilder` class in the .NET Framework and is a great candidate to be used for extensive string manipulation on the client.

The `Sys` Namespace

The `Sys` namespace is the root namespace for xyz and basically is the running engine behind ASP.NET AJAX. The members of this namespace are classes responsible for the core AJAX functionality you have seen so far in the book. These classes do all the under the hood heavy lifting, handling issues such as data serialization, application life cycle, and asynchronous operation, to just name a few. Extensive coverage of all the classes and features of this namespace is well beyond the scope of this chapter, but you will learn about some of the key pieces of this important namespace.

Table 4-9 lists the main namespaces of the ASP.NET AJAX Client Library.

Table 4-9. *Namespaces of the ASP.NET AJAX Client Library*

Namespace	Description
`Sys`	Root namespace; also contains some base classes such as `Sys.CultureInfo`
`Sys.Net`	Provides networking and communication support such as facilities to access web services
`Sys.UI`	Contains a set of classes for comprehensive UI support, such as events and control properties
`Sys.Services`	Provides support for ASP.NET application services, such as Login/Authentication
`Sys.Serialization`	Provides support for data serialization/JSON
`Sys.WebForms`	Contains classes for asynchronous page loading, among others

The root `Sys` namespace includes classes and interfaces used throughout the ASP.NET AJAX Client Library by all other namespaces. One such interface is `IDisposable`, which much like its cousin interface in the .NET Framework, provides a consistent interface for proper deletion of objects in the ASP.NET AJAX Client Library. The root `Sys` namespace also includes the all-important `Sys.Application` class, which plays a major role in the page life cycle of an ASP.NET AJAX page. You can see the list of classes included in the root `Sys` namespace in Table 4-10.

Table 4-10. *Classes of the* Sys *Root Namespace*

Class Name	Description
Application	Provides objects and methods that expose client events and manage client components and their life cycles
ApplicationLoadEventArgs	Container object for arguments of the Application Load event
CancelEventArgs	Base class for events that can be canceled
Component	Base class for all ASP.NET AJAX objects, including the Control class and the Behavior class
CultureInfo	Culture information object that can be used to provide locale-specific functionality (can be used for globalization)
Debug code	Provides debugging and tracing functionality for client-side JavaScript
EventArgs	Base class used for storing event arguments
EventHandlerList	A collection of client events for a component containing event names and handlers as key/value pairs
PropertyChangedEventArgs	Contains event arguments associated with changed properties
StringBuilder	Provides facilities for better and more efficient string concatenation

As mentioned earlier, the classes of the Sys namespaces make up the underlying engine of ASP.NET AJAX. If you inspect the individual JavaScript files that are dynamically generated and loaded on the browser by the ScriptManager, you'll see references to the Sys namespace. With that said, let's start by talking about the page life cycle and the Sys.Application class.

Sys.Application

The Sys.Application class is an integral part of an ASP.NET AJAX page. After the initial load of resources, including script files and other rendered components, from the server onto the client, the Sys.Application class then manages the page life cycle. In fact, if you view the source of any ASP.NET AJAX page, you would find the following script near the bottom of the page:

```
<script type="text/javascript">
<!--
   Sys.Application.initialize();
// -->
</script>
```

The call to the initialize() method, as the name suggests, initializes an instance of the Application class by raising the load event, which then resides on the browser for the remainder of the application life cycle. Therefore, the role and function of the Application class is analogous to the role of the Page class in a typical ASP.NET page. For ASP.NET AJAX pages, the Sys.Application class picks up where the Page class left off on the server side. However, among other things, one big difference is that the client-side events of a page as included in the Sys.Application class are a lot fewer than those offered in the server-side Page class. In fact, there are only three events: init, load, and unload. Internally, the Sys.Application classes map events of JavaScript's window object to these three events. Table 4-11 lists these three events of the Sys.Application class.

Table 4-11. *Events of the* Sys.Application *Class*

Event Name	Description
init	Raised after scripts have been loaded and immediately before objects are created
load	Raised after scripts have been loaded and objects in the page have been created and initialized
unload	Raised right before all objects in the page are disposed of

Much like server-side ASP.NET, where Page_Load is the default event handler for the server-side Load event, the Sys.Application class also provides default event handlers for the client-side load and unload events. Consider the following script block:

```
function pageLoad()
{
    alert ('Loading Page...');
    //load components
}

function pageUnload()
{
    alert ('Page unloading...');
}
```

pageLoad is automatically executed as soon as the load event is triggered; the pageUnload method is executed when the unload event is triggered. Once again, you do not have to write any custom event handlers for these two methods. These two methods are automatically wired up to their corresponding events by the Sys.Application class.

Keep in mind that there can be many more than the aforementioned three events on a page because components in a page can expose their own sets of events. We'll discuss event handling in a later section in this chapter.

Other than events, the `Sys.Application` class also contains a number of methods for managing components in a page. For instance, you can use the `getComponents` method to get a list of all registered components on a page. You can also use the `findComponent` method to check the existence of a component in the page. This method takes in two parameters, the name of the component and the ID of the parent component (if any). In the following script, we check for the existence of a control called `CustomComponent` in a parent control with the ID of `Panel1`.

```
<script language=javascript type="text/javascript">
    if ((Sys.Application.findComponent('CustomComponent', Panel1)))
        alert ('CustomComponent was found on the page!');
</script>
```

Note You can use `$find` as a shortcut to `Sys.Application.findComponent`. This is one of many global shortcuts in the ASP.NET AJAX Client Library.

Table 4-12 contains a list of methods in the `Application.Sys` class.

Table 4-12. *Methods of the* `Sys.Application` *Class*

Method Name	Description
addComponent	Creates and initializes a component with the `Application` object
dispose	Releases all dependencies held by the objects in the page
findComponent	Finds and returns the specified component object
getComponents	Returns an array of all components that have been registered in the page using the `addComponent` method
initialize	Initializes the `Application` object
notifyScriptLoaded	Boolean value indicating whether all the scripts have been loaded
queueScriptReference	Used to queue script files that will be loaded in a sequential order
raiseLoad	Raises the `load` event
registerDisposableObject	Registers an object/component with the application and manages the object requiring disposal
removeComponent	Removes an object from the application or disposes the object if it is disposable
unregisterDisposableObject	Removes/unregisters a disposable object from the application

Sys.Component **and Client Component Model**

The Sys.Component class is another pivotal component of the ASP.NET AJAX Client Library. This is also the base class that is ultimately extended by all graphical or nongraphical client controls (Sys.UI.Control actually inherits from Sys.Component). Again, there is a good level of similarity in the model between this class and the System.ComponentModel.Component class of the .NET Framework, a recurring theme with many of the classes in the Sys namespace you have probably noticed by now.

Sys.Component uses three key interfaces and four properties. The interfaces include Sys.IDisposable, Sys.INotifyDisposing, and Sys.INotifyPropertyChange. Sys.IDisposable is just like its .NET Framework counterpart. An interface for implementing proper logic for disposing an object and the other two interfaces provide facilities for implementing events used to detect disposing and changes in property of the underlying control.

The four properties are events, id, isInitialized, and isUpdating. The events property returns an EventHandlerList object, which contains references to all event handlers that have subscribed to the events of the current component. And while the id property returns the ID field of the current object, isInitialized and isUpdated return boolean types depending on the self descriptive condition. Just like most properties of the classes in the ASP.NET AJAX Client Library, the properties of the Sys.Component class as well can be accessed with built-in get and set accessors as shown in the following script snippet:

```
if (myComponent.get_isInitialized())
    alert ('My component is initialized');
```

You can just as easily set a value to a property using the set accessor as done in the following script:

```
myComponent.set_id('UniqueComponentID');
```

Lastly, Table 4-13 lists the methods of the Sys.Component class.

Table 4-13. *Methods of the* Sys.Component *Class*

Method Name	Description
beginUpdate	A boolean value called by the create method to indicate that the process of setting properties of a component instance has begun
create	Creates and initializes a component
dispose	Removes the component from the application
endUpdate	Called by the create method to indicate that the process of setting properties of a component instance has finished
initialize	Initializes the component
raisePropertyChanged	Raises the propertyChanged event of the current Component object for a specified property
updated	Called by the endUpdate method of the current Component object

Sys.UI

The Sys.UI namespace provides much of the needed infrastructure for developing client visual controls. This includes numerous properties, events, and classes that can be extended. Sys.UI inherits some of its functionality from the Sys.Component namespace. Some of the members of this namespace are critical for anyone implementing custom client controls (Sys.UI.Control) or behaviors (Sys.UI.Behavior) but used less often for everyday AJAX development. Lastly, there are also classes for better control over DOM elements and events in the browser. Table 4-14 lists the classes of the Sys.UI namespace.

Table 4-14. *Classes of the* Sys.UI *Namespace*

Class Name	Description
Behavior	Base class for all ASP.NET AJAX client behaviors
Bounds	Object containing a number of properties for a specific position such as position, width, and height
Control	Base class for all ASP.NET AJAX client controls
DomElement	Main class for handling client-side controls in the browser DOM
DomEvent	Main class for handling client-side events in the browser, which includes the ability to dynamically attach and detach events from corresponding event handlers
Point	Object containing integer coordinates of a position

Sys.UI also includes three enumerations accounting for some key events of DOM elements. These enumerations are also used as properties in the Sys.UI.DomEvent class. These enumerations are listed in Table 4-15.

Table 4-15. *Enumerations of the* Sys.UI *Namespace*

Enumeration	Description
Key	Key codes. Values include nonalphanumeric keys (e.g., up, right, down, backspace, home, space, end, etc.).
MouseButton	Mouse button locations (leftButton, middleButton, rightButton).
VisibilityMode	Layout of a DOM element in the page when the element's visible property is set to false. Allowed values are hide and collapse.

Sys.UI.DomElement

The Sys.UI.DomElement and the Sys.UI.DomEvent, which we'll look at later, are both classes designed to provide better, more consistent, and browser-agnostic access and handling of DOM elements in the browser. With one programming interface, you can reliably work with all major browsers (IE, Firefox, Opera, Safari). Before looking at an example, take a look at the methods of the Sys.UI.DomElement class as shown in Table 4-16.

Table 4-16. *Methods of the* Sys.UI.DomElement *Class*

Method Name	Description
addCssClass	Adds a CSS class to a DOM element
containsCssClass	Returns a value indicating whether or not the DOM element contains the specified CSS class
getBounds	Returns the Bounds object for a specified DOM element
getElementById	Returns a DOM element by ID (the $get shortcut is mapped to this method)
getLocation	Returns the absolute position of a DOM element
removeCssClass	Removes a CSS class from a DOM element
setLocation	Sets the position of a DOM element
toggleCssClass	Toggles a CSS class in a DOM element

To better illustrate a few of the methods of the Sys.UI.DomElement class, consider the following markup:

```
<body>
    <form id="form1" runat="server">
        <asp:ScriptManager ID="ScriptManager1" runat="server">
        </asp:ScriptManager>
        <div id="MovePanel">
            <b>Move me to:</b> <br />
            X Coordinate
            <input type="text" id="txtX" />  <br />
            Y Coordinate
            <input type="text" id="txtY" /><br />
            <input id="Button1" type="button" value="Move"
              onclick="repositionPanel ()" />
        </div>
    </form>
</body>
```

Here, we have two text boxes and a button all in a `<div>` tag. The text boxes hold the new X and Y position for the entire panel to which it will be moved. When the user clicks the button, a function called `repositionPanel` is executed, and the panel is relocated using absolute positioning and set to the new coordinates. Figure 4-7 depicts the page when initially loaded.

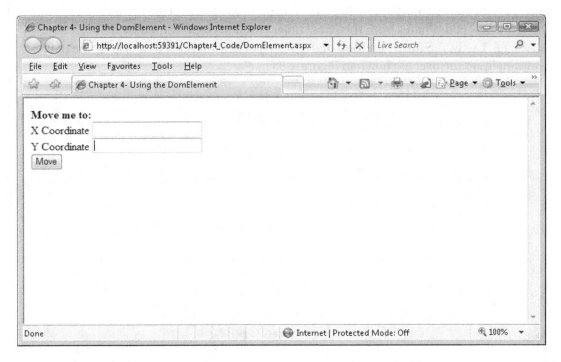

Figure 4-7. *Using* `DomElement` *sample page*

Let's now examine the script behind `repositionPanel` that is responsible for moving the panel to a new location on the page:

```
function repositionPanel()
{
    var panel = $get('MovePanel');
    var newX = Number.parseInvariant($get('txtX').value);
    var newY = Number.parseInvariant($get('txtY').value);
    Sys.UI.DomElement.setLocation(panel, newX,newY);

    //Now use getLocation to retrieve the new coordinates
    var newPos = Sys.UI.DomElement.getLocation(panel);
    alert(String.format("Moved to: {0}, {1}", newPos.x, newPos.y));
}
```

Notice how the $get shortcut is used to retrieve the control reference by a specified ID. This is definitely a lot shorter than having to write document.getElementById(…) as commonly done in raw JavaScript. After the X and Y coordinates are parsed out of the text boxes using the parseInvariant static method of the Number object, they are passed onto the setLocation method of the Sys.UI.DomElement for the panel to be moved to the new coordinates. setLocation takes in three parameters: the control name, the new X coordinate, and the new Y coordinate. After the relocation, the getLocation method is used to fetch the new coordinates from the panel object itself (as represented by the MovePanel <div> tag). Lastly, the format method of the String extension is used to display the new coordinates to the user as shown in Figure 4-8.

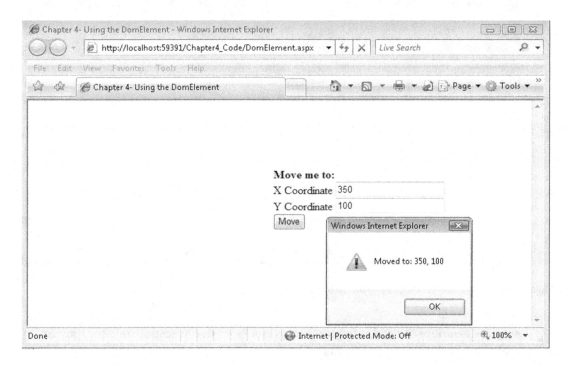

Figure 4-8. *The panel is relocated to the new coordinates with a message box showing the new positional values.*

Nothing is done here that could not be done by raw JavaScript alone. But using the ASP.NET AJAX Client Library is not only a lot cleaner with much less code, but it also provides a level of abstraction that guarantees expected behavior in all of the popular browsers (IE, Firefox, Opera, Safari).

Sys.UI.DomEvent

Sophisticated event handling has long been a major weakness of web applications in general when compared to the rich and stateful desktop applications. The ASP.NET AJAX Client Library takes a major step in closing the gap (to some extent) from a functional standpoint between the event modeling in .NET Framework and client-side ASP.NET. Sys.UI.DomEvent provides a browser-agnostic model packed with useful properties and events that can be easily used with DOM elements. This comes in particularly handy considering the fact that browsers at times differ in their API and handling of DOM events. Table 4-17 lists the methods of the Sys.UI.DomEvent class.

Table 4-17. *Methods of the* Sys.UI.DomEvent *Class*

Method Name	Description
addHandler	Adds a DOM event handler to the DOM element; also aliased by the $addHandler shortcut
addHandlers	Adds a list of DOM event handlers to the DOM element; also aliased by the $addHandlers shortcut.
clearHandlers	Removes all DOM event handlers from the DOM element that were added through the addHandler or the addHandlers methods; also aliased by the $clearHandlers shortcut
preventDefault	Prevents the default DOM event from executing
removeHandler	Removes a DOM event handler from the DOM element that exposes the event; also aliased by the $removeHandler shortcut
stopPropagation	Stops the propagation of an event to its parent elements

In the previous script sample, you saw how to move a panel around the screen with client-side only code using the methods of the Sys.UI.DomElement class. In that example, the function name was set to the onclick attribute of the button as is often done in classic JavaScript. We could just as easily use the addHandler method to wire up the click event of the button to the desired function.

The addHandler method has three required parameters: the target element, the name of the event, and the event handler. So in the case of the previous sample, we would have

```
Sys.UI.DomElement.addHandler(Button1, "click", repositionPanel);
```

or by using the $addHandler shortcut, we would have

```
$addHandler(Button1, "click", repositionPanel);
```

In such a case, another thing that would have to be different is the function signature of the click handler. It must now have support for the event object and the following signature:

```
function eventHandler (e) {…}
```

With that, we get all the added benefits of being able to extract potentially useful data out of the event object. Speaking of useful data, take a look at the fields of the Sys.UI.DomEvent class in Table 4-18.

Table 4-18. *Fields of the* Sys.UI.DomEvent *Class*

Parameter Name	Description
altKey	A boolean value indicating whether or not the event associated with the Alt key occurred
button	Returns a Sys.UI.MouseButton enumeration value indicating the actual button of the mouse that was clicked
charCode	Returns the character code of the key that initiated the event
clientX	Returns the x-coordinate (in pixels) of the mouse pointer when the event was triggered
clientY	Returns the y-coordinate (in pixels) of the mouse pointer when the event was triggered
ctrlKey	A boolean value indicating whether or not the event associated with the Ctrl key occurred
offsetX	Returns the x-coordinate (in pixels)of the mouse relative to the object that triggered the event
offsetY	Returns the y-coordinate (in pixels)of the mouse relative to the object that triggered the event
screenX	Returns the x-coordinate (in pixels)of the mouse relative to the center of the screen
screenY	Returns the y-coordinate (in pixels)of the mouse relative to the center of the screen
shiftKey	A boolean value indicating whether or not the event associated with the Shift key occurred
target	Returns the target object used by the triggered event
type	Returns the name of the triggered event

The `$addHandlers` shortcut (`Sys.UI.DomEvent.addHandlers`) can be used to wire up more than one event handler to a particular event; in which case, you can have multiple event handlers that will be executed when the target event has been triggered.

To dynamically remove an event handler from an event on a control, use the `Sys.UI.DomEvent.removeHandler` (or `$removeHandler`) with the identical signature as the `addHandler` method (the target control, the event name, and the event handler). To remove the `repositionPanel` method as the event handler of `Button1`, you would have the following script:

```
$removeHandler(Button1, "click", repositionPanel);
```

Also, if you wanted to clear all the associated event handlers with an event on a control, you could do so with the self-explanatory `Sys.UI.DomEvent.clearHandler` (or the `$clearHandler` shortcut).

Global Shortcuts

All these shortcuts have been either mentioned or explained by this point in the chapter. However, given their utility and importance, they're worth another look in one location. You will come across these not only in your development needs but also in countless places in ASP.NET AJAX controls and libraries. Table 4-19 lists all the global shortcuts in the ASP.NET AJAX Client Library.

Table 4-19. *Global Shortcuts in the ASP.NET AJAX Client Library*

Shortcut	Description
`$addHandler`	Shortcut to the `Sys.UI.DomEvent.addHandler` method
`$addHandlers`	Shortcut to the `Sys.UI.DomEvent.addHandlers` method
`$clearHandlers`	Shortcut to the `Sys.UI.DomEvent.clearHandlers` method
`$create`	Shortcut to the `Sys.Component.create` method
`$find`	Shortcut to the `Sys.Application.findComponent` method
`$get`	Shortcut to the `Sys.UI.DomElement.getElementById` method
`$removeHandler`	Shortcut to the `System.UI.DomEvent.removeHandler` method

Other Commonly Used Classes in the Sys Namespace

The following sections describe other often-used classes in the Sys namespace in greater detail.

Sys.Browser

One of the challenges of web development for more than a decade has been targeting and accounting for browser-specific behaviors. Typically, JavaScript is used to query the various user agent parameters (obtained from the HTTP headers) to identify the browser type and version. The Sys.Browser class makes the task of browser detection and targeting a lot simpler than the traditional approach with JavaScript. Consider the following line of script:

```
if (Sys.Browser.agent === Sys.Browser.Firefox)
    // Write browser-specific logic for Firefox
```

As you can see, it's extremely easy to identify the browser type here with much less code than it would take in raw JavaScript. There are four predefined browser types to account for the four most popular browsers on the market:

* Sys.Browser.InternetExplorer

* Sys.Browser.Firefox

* Sys.Browser.Opera

* Sys.Browser.Safari

Identifying the browser version can just as easily be done with the version property of the Sys.Browser class. Keep in mind that all methods of the Sys.Browser class are static like and do not require instantiation.

Sys.StringBuilder

String concatenation is a relatively common task in JavaScript especially when you need to dynamically inject HTML into a page via JavaScript. In such cases, plain old string concatenation can fast lead to very messy code. The Sys.StringBuilder class is somewhat similar to its .NET Framework counterpart (System.Text.StringBuilder) in that they both share similar method signatures for many of the methods. This class can also take in the initial string as its constructor. All methods are instance based and thus require an instance object to be executed. Table 4-20 lists the methods of the Sys.StringBuilder class.

Table 4-20. *Methods of the* Sys.StringBuilder *Class*

Method Name	Description
append	Appends a string to the end of the StringBuilder object
appendLine	Appends a new string with a line feed at the end of the StringBuilder instance
clear	Clears the contents of the StringBuilder object
isEmpty	Boolean value indicating whether or not the StringBuilder object has any content
toString	Returns a string from the contents of a StringBuilder instance

To see the Sys.StringBuilder class in action, take a look at the following function:

```
function stringBuilderSample()
{
    var sb = new Sys.StringBuilder("<html>");
    sb.appendLine('<head></head>');
    sb.appendLine('<body>');
    sb.appendLine('<div align=center>');
    sb.appendLine('Chapter 4 - ASP.NET Ajax Client Libraries');
    sb.append('</div>');
    sb.append('</body></html>');
    document.write(sb.toString());
}
```

In the preceding script snippet, a block of HTML is concatenated together to be sent to the browser. Here you see that an instance of the Sys.StringBuilder class is created with the initial string "<html>", and additional lines are added using the appendLine method. At the end, the entire content of the StringBuilder is thrown to the browser by using the toString method of the StringBuilder instance. You can see the result of the preceding script in Figure 4-9. This is a pattern you most certainly have already seen all too often with the System.Text.StringBuilder class in the .NET Framework.

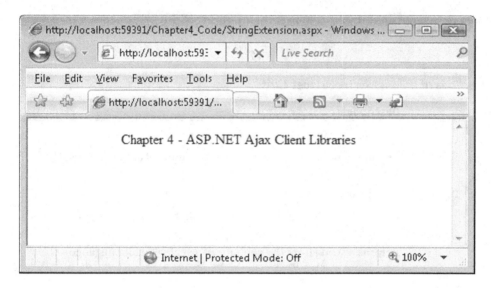

Figure 4-9. *Generating HTML dynamically via JavaScript using the* Sys.StringBuilder *class*

Summary

In this chapter, you learned about the JavaScript type extensions designed to enhance the native types and associated utilities in JavaScript. You also learned about some of the important classes in the Sys namespace of the ASP.NET AJAX Client Library and some of the rich functionality they bring to the table in an effort to bring some similarity to the .NET Framework in the world of client-side web development with JavaScript.

There is certainly a lot more to the ASP.NET AJAX Client Library that was not covered in this chapter, including a few entire namespaces (Sys.Webforms, Sys.NET, and Sys.Services). For a complete reference of the ASP.NET AJAX Client Library, feel free to view the online documentation at http://ajax.asp.net/docs. In the next chapter, we'll look into the rich and powerful server controls in ASP.NET AJAX and how easily they can be used to add quite capable AJAX functionality to your web applications.

■ ■ ■

CHAPTER 5

Introducing Server Controls in ASP.NET AJAX

The first three chapters of this book gave you an overview of ASP.NET AJAX and how you can use it to build web applications to restrict unnecessary full page postbacks and processing on your web pages, thus improving the performance and polish of your web applications. Chapters 3 and 4 introduced you to the client-side controls presented by ASP.NET AJAX and stepped you through many examples of how to use these controls in JavaScript and in a new XML-based script called ASP.NET AJAX Library.

You looked at some advanced aspects of the scripting framework, including actions, which are compound commands associated with an event or stimulus on a control; behaviors, which are automatic units of functionality that can be associated with a control, enabling things such as drag and drop; and data binding, which allows for controls to be wired up to each other or to themselves to pass data between them.

In this chapter, you will go to the other side of the action—the server—and begin exploring the various server-side controls available to you when building your AJAX applications. You have seen one of these controls, the ScriptManager control, already. In this chapter, you will look at ScriptManager in more detail among other ASP.NET AJAX server controls. In Chapter 6 you will learn more about how these controls work by navigating through an application that actually uses these controls.

Using ASP.NET AJAX Server Controls in Visual Studio 2005

Visual Studio 2005 and ASP.NET offer some great design tools that allow you to visually construct pages, which fits in neatly with the concepts that ASP.NET AJAX introduces. Developers can place controls on a page, and these controls generate the JavaScript that is necessary to implement the AJAX functionality. In the following sections, you'll look at how to use these controls within the integrated development environment (IDE).

In Chapter 3, you learned how to create a new AJAX-enabled ASP.NET site. Alternatively, you can just as easily create an AJAX-enabled ASP.NET web application if you have installed the Web Application Project add-on or Visual Studio 2005 SP1. Either way, upon creating the new project, you will notice the new added section to the Toolbox titled AJAX Extensions as shown in Figure 5-1.

Figure 5-1. *Your Toolbox tab containing AJAX server controls*

Now that you have the controls in your Toolbox, you can drag and drop them onto your web forms. The rest of this chapter discusses these controls and their object models, and in the next chapter, you'll start using these controls in hands-on examples. At the time of this writing, five server controls are included in the first release version of ASP.NET AJAX: Timer, ScriptManager, ScriptManagerProxy, UpdateProgress, and UpdatePanel. Currently, additional controls are packaged in the Futures CTP builds of ASP.NET AJAX, which should surface in future releases of ASP.NET AJAX.

Using ASP.NET AJAX server controls is the easiest and quickest path to implementing AJAX functionality in your ASP.NET application. They are also ideal for when a minimal amount of change in desired for existing ASP.NET applications that make extensive use of ASP.NET server controls.

■Note If you plan on using Visual Studio 2005 AJAX-enabled web applications (following the web application model and not the ASP.NET web site model), be sure to install ASP.NET AJAX after installing Visual Studio 2005 SP1.

Introducing the ScriptManager Control

The ScriptManager control is pivotal at the very heart of ASP.NET AJAX. This control, as its name suggests, manages the deployment of the various JavaScript libraries that implement the client-side runtime functionality of ASP.NET AJAX. This control is also heavily used by other sever controls to provide partial page rendering and script file management.

Using the ScriptManager

You've already used the ScriptManager control to create references on the client side with the ASP.NET AJAX Library. To add ScriptManager to your page, simply drag and drop it onto an ASP.NET page as shown in Figure 5-2.

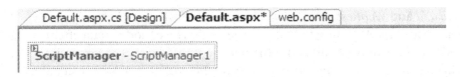

Figure 5-2. *The* ScriptManger *control*

Now, if you take a look at the code behind this page, you'll see that placing the ScriptManager control has caused the following script to be added to your page:

```
<asp:ScriptManager ID="ScriptManager1" runat="server" />
```

When you run the page and select View ~TRA Source in the browser, you'll see that the preceding one-line script generated the following scripts among other code in the page output:

```
<script src="/Ajax/WebResource.axd?d=HQhspev9RtnoVp5Ca4MubA2&amp;
t=633008366579531250" type="text/javascript">
</script>
<script src="/Ajax/ScriptResource.axd?d=rbfRw_fjV44N4zFu5uugvXCgOfpE5bOdbRFvvkMhZEO1
-ghFYTQ7i9aLWWp9hO2901tgv-pDZFxuTtMikT21d-q8lo-xXLBcAYv3xqOhiRM1&amp;t=
633051881703906250" type="text/javascript">
</script>
<script src="/Ajax3/ScriptResource.axd?d=rbfRw_fjV44N4zFu5uugvXCgOfpE5bOdbRFvvkMhZEO
1-ghFYTQ7i9aLWWp9hO2901tgv-pDZFxuTtMikT21d3JhQBwnJ44PsSIlv
SkVAgc1&amp;t=633051881703906250" type="text/javascript">
</script>
```

```
<script type="text/javascript">
//<![CDATA[
Sys.WebForms.PageRequestManager._initialize('ScriptManager1',
                                        document.getElementById('form1'));
Sys.WebForms.PageRequestManager.getInstance()._updateControls([], [], [], 90);
//]]>
</script>
```

■**Note** Because the client scripts are generated automatically, your results may vary somewhat from the preceding script block.

ScriptResource.axd and *WebResource.axd* are, in fact, ASP.NET HTTP handlers that emit client-side JavaScript for AJAX functionality in the page. The encoded data after the querystring holds metadata information about the pertinent resources. The last script block contains client-side scripts for any components on the page. If you look inside the *Web.config* file of your ASP.NET AJAX-enabled project, you'll notice the following block, which registers the aforementioned HTTP handlers for use in your project:

```
<httpHandlers>
    <add verb="*" path="*_AppService.axd" validate="false"
            type="System.Web.Script.Services.ScriptHandlerFactory,
            System.Web.Extensions, Version=1.0.61025.0, Culture=neutral,
            PublicKeyToken=31bf3856ad364e35"/>
    <add verb="GET,HEAD" path="ScriptResource.axd"
            type="System.Web.Handlers.ScriptResourceHandler, System.Web.Extensions,
            Version=1.0.61025.0, Culture=neutral, PublicKeyToken=31bf3856ad364e35"
        validate="false"/>
</httpHandlers>
```

Programming with the ScriptManager

As a core component of ASP.NET AJAX, the ScriptManager control has much functionality, including the capability to communicate with ASP.NET authentication services, to access web services, to render culture-specific information, to perform sophisticated script management, to do partial page rendering, and more. It inherits from the Control class (in the System.Web.UI namespace), and in addition to the members of that class, also has some of the following methods as shown in Table 5-1.

Table 5-1. ScriptManager *Control Methods*

Method Name	Function
GetCurrent	(Static) Gets the ScriptManager instance for a Page object.
RegisterAsyncPostBackControl	Registers a control for asynchronous postbacks.
RegisterDataItem	Sends custom data to a control during partial-page rendering.
RegisterDispose	Registers a script that can be used to properly dispose a control inside an UpdatePanel control. This script is executed when the UpdatePanel gets disposed.
RegisterExtenderControl	Registers an extender control with the existing ScriptManager instance.
RegisterPostBackControl	Registers a control for postback. This method can be used for existing controls inside an UpdatePanel that you require to do full postbacks.
RegisterScriptControl	Registers a script control with the existing ScriptManager instance.
SetFocus	Sets the browser focus to a specified control.

Table 5-2 lists the properties of the ScriptManager control excluding the properties inherited from the Control and Object classes.

Table 5-2. ScriptManager *Control Properties*

Property Name	Function
AllowCustomErrorsRedirect	Boolean value indicating whether or not to use the custom errors section of *Web.config* to handle errors in asynchronous postbacks
AsyncPostBackErrorMessage	The error message that is sent to the client when an unhandled server exception occurs during an asynchronous postback
AsyncPostBackSourceElementID	The unique ID of the control that caused the asynchronous postback
AsyncPostBackTimeout	Indicates the period of time, in seconds, before asynchronous postbacks time out if no response is received
AuthenticationService	Returns the AuthenticationServiceManager object that is associated with the current ScriptManager instance
EnablePageMethods	Boolean value indicating whether static page methods on an ASP.NET page can be called from client script
EnablePartialRendering	Boolean value that enables partial rendering of a page
EnableScriptGlobalization	Boolean value indicating whether the ScriptManager control renders script in the browser to support parsing and formatting culture-specific information

Continued

Table 5-2. *Continued*

Property Name	Function
EnableScriptLocalization	Boolean value indicating whether the ScriptManager control loads localized versions of script files
IsDebuggingEnabled	Boolean value indicating whether the debug versions of client script libraries will be rendered
IsInAsyncPostBack	Boolean value indicating whether the current postback is being executed in partial-rendering mode
LoadScriptsBeforeUI	Boolean value indicating whether scripts are loaded before or after markup for the page UI is loaded
ScriptMode	Determines whether to render debug or release versions of client script libraries
ScriptPath	The path to the location that is used to build the paths to ASP.NET AJAX Extensions as well as other script files
Scripts	Returns a ScriptReferenceCollection object that contains ScriptReference objects that are registered with the ScriptManager control declaratively or programmatically
Services	Returns a ServiceReferenceCollection object that contains a ServiceReference object for each web service that ASP.NET AJAX Extensions expose on the client
SupportsPartialRendering	Boolean value indicating whether the client supports partial-page rendering

Performing Partial Rendering

The EnablePartialRendering property of this control sets how your page will behave concerning updates. If this is false (the default), full-page refreshes occur on round-trips to the server. If this is true, then postbacks and full-page refreshes are suppressed and replaced with targeted and partial updates. Instead of the application performing a full postback, the application simulates full postbacks using the XMLHttpRequest object when this is set to true (as you would expect from an AJAX application).

On the server side, the page is processed in the normal way, responding to any controls that call _doPostBack(). Existing server-side postback events continue to fire, and event handlers continue to work as they always have. It is intended, by design, that AJAX-enabled applications change existing ASP.NET applications as little as possible.

The power of the ScriptManager control, when partial rendering is enabled, comes at render time. It determines, with the aid of the UpdatePanel control, which portions of the page have changed. The UpdatePanel, which you will see more of later in this chapter, defines regions in the page that get updated as a chunk. If, for example, you have a page containing a number of chat rooms and you want to update only a single chat room, you would surround that area of the page with an UpdatePanel control.

The ScriptManager control overrides the rendering of the page and instead sends HTML down to the XMLHttpRequest object for each of the UpdatePanel controls (which we will discuss later) on the page.

Specifying Additional Script Components Using the ScriptReference Tag

The ScriptManager control has a <Scripts> child tag that can specify additional scripts to download to the browser. This can contain one or more <asp:ScriptReference> tags that specify the path to the script. Upon registering a script file through this object, you will be able to call its methods on your page. The ScriptReference object has the capability to use scripts that are either stored as embedded resources in an assembly or as files on the web server.

To register an embedded script, you must first set the Name property of the ScriptReference tag to the name of the actual file that contains the script and then set the Assembly property to the name of the assembly containing the script. You can see an example of this in the following script snippet:

```
<asp:ScriptManager ID="ScriptManager1" runat="server">
   <Scripts>
      <asp:ScriptReference Assembly="MyAssembly" Name="MyAssembly.MyScript.js" />
   </Scripts>
</asp:ScriptManager>
```

More simply, to use a file-based script that resides on the web server, you can set the Path property of the ScriptReference tag to the location of the file as shown here:

```
<asp:ScriptManager ID="ScriptManager1" runat="server">
   <Scripts>
      <asp:ScriptReference Path="MyScript.js" />
   </Scripts>
</asp:ScriptManager>
```

When you run the page containing the preceding script and view the source of the browser output, you'll notice that a new script code block has been added:

```
<script src="MyScript.js" type="text/javascript"></script>
```

Before leaving the ScriptReference object, let's take a look at its properties as shown in Table 5-3.

Table 5-3. ScriptReference *Tag Properties*

Property Name	Function
Assembly	Actual name of the assembly that contains the client script file as an embedded resource
IgnoreScriptPath	Indicates whether the ScriptPath property is included in the URL when you register a client script file from a resource
Name	Name of the embedded resource that contains the client script file
NotifyScriptLoaded	Indicates whether the additional code should be added to the script file to notify the ScriptLoaded method of the Sys.Application class
Path	Specifies the path where the ScriptManager control can find the stand-alone script file to download
ResourceUICultures	Comma-delimited list of UI cultures that are supported by the Path property
ScriptMode	The mode of the target script (debug, release, etc.)

Specifying Services

In Chapter 2, you saw how a service can be directly consumed in a client application through a script-based proxy. You can use the ScriptManager control to reference this using the <Services> child tag. This tag should contain one or more <asp:ServiceReference> tags that specify the service you want to reference.

This tag has two attributes:

- Path: This specifies the path to the service. You briefly saw in Chapter 2 that JavaScript proxies to web services on ASP.NET AJAX web sites can be automatically generated by postfixing /js at the end of its URI. So, for example, the web service at *wstest.asmx* would return a JavaScript <asp:ServiceReference> proxy that could be used to call it at *wstest.asmx/js*. When using the tag to specify the service, most of the work would be done automatically for you on the client side with the help of the ScriptManager control. Here's an example:

```
<Services>
    <asp:ServiceReference Path="wstest.asmx"/>
</Services>
```

- InlineScript: This is a boolean value (true or false) that specifies whether the proxy generation script is included as an inline script block in the page itself or obtained by a separate request. The default is false. When running the page that has this property set to true and uses the <Services> tag of the ScriptManager control, you get the following additional code on the client:

```
<script src="wstest.asmx/js" type="text/javascript"></script>
```

Error Handling in the ScriptManager Control

The ScriptManager control provides an error-handling mechanism whereby you can specify an error message or implement more in-depth logic in the event of an error. This is particularly useful for the client experience because you can then help your users gracefully handle errors that occur within the contents of the ScriptManager.

The two easiest ways to implement error handling for the ScriptManager control are to use either the AsyncPostBackError event or set the AsyncPostBackErrorMessage property of the ScriptManager tag. Here's an example of using the AsyncPostBackErrorMessage property:

```
<asp:ScriptManager ID="ScriptManager1" runat="server" AsyncPostBackErrorMessage=
"An error has occured within the ScriptManger tag." />
```

For more sophisticated error handling, however, it's imperative to handle the AsyncPostBackError event. You can, for instance, capture the message of the exception and dynamically set it to the AsyncPostBackErrorMessage property among other desired logic to handle the error:

```
protected void ScriptManager1_AsyncPostBackError(object sender,
                              AsyncPostBackErrorEventArgs e)
{
    ScriptManager1.AsyncPostBackErrorMessage = e.Exception.Message;
    //Implement further error handling logic
}
```

This concludes the tour of the ScriptManager control. In the rest of this chapter, we'll look at the other server-side controls offered by the ASP.NET AJAX framework. In the next chapter, we'll revisit this control through several examples.

Introducing the ScriptManagerProxy Control

The ScriptManagerProxy control is available as an additional script manager for a page. It also allows for custom authentication services through its AuthenticationService property and profile services through the ProfileServiceManager property. Because only one ScriptManager control is allowed per ASP.NET page, if you use master and content pages, you cannot place additional ScriptManager controls on any of the content pages. The ScriptManagerProxy control enables you to place scripts and/or services in your content pages. Before delving deeper into this control, let's also look at the properties for the supported child tags of this control in Table 5-4.

Table 5-4. ScriptManagerProxy *Child Tags*

Property Name	Function
AuthenticationService	Returns the AuthenticationServiceManager object (for custom authentication service) that is associated with the current ScriptManagerProxy instance
ProfileService	Returns the ProfileServiceManager object that is associated with the current ScriptManagerProxy instance
Scripts	Returns a ScriptReferenceCollection object that contains a ScriptReference object for each script file that is registered with the ScriptManagerProxy control
Services	Returns a ServiceReferenceCollection object that contains a ServiceReference object for each service that is registered with the ScriptManagerProxy control

As mentioned earlier, the ScriptMangerProxy control is ideal for use in content pages where a ScriptManager has already been defined in the corresponding master page. To better illustrate this, consider the following master page, *MasterPage.aspx*:

```
<%@ Master Language="C#" AutoEventWireup="true" CodeBehind=
        "MasterPage.master.cs" Inherits="MasterPage" %>

<!DOCTYPE html PUBLIC "-//W3C//DTD XHTML 1.0 Transitional//EN"
"http://www.w3.org/TR/xhtml1/DTD/xhtml1-transitional.dtd">
<html xmlns="http://www.w3.org/1999/xhtml" >
<head runat="server">
```

```
        <title>Sample Master Page</title>
</head>
<body>
    <form id="form1" runat="server">
    <div>
            <asp:ScriptManager ID="ScriptManager1" runat="server" />
            This is the Master page <br />
            It contains this ScriptManager control: <br />
            <br />
            <asp:ContentPlaceHolder ID="ContentPlaceHolder1" runat="server">
            <br />
            </asp:ContentPlaceHolder>
    </div>
    </form>
</body>
</html>
```

And we also create a new content page based on this master page called
ContentPage.aspx with the following code:

```
<%@ Page Language="C#" MasterPageFile="~/MasterPage.Master" AutoEventWireup="true"
    CodeBehind="ContentPage.aspx.cs" Inherits="ContentPage" Title="Sample Page" %>
<asp:Content ID="Content1" ContentPlaceHolderID=➥
"ContentPlaceHolder1" runat="server">
</asp:Content>
```

If you run the *ContentPage.aspx* page and look at the output, as expected you will see
the same general output that is generated by the ScriptManager control from the master
page consisting of the three main script blocks (among others) pointing to the
WebResource.axd and *ScriptResource.axd* as shown here:

```
<script src="/Ajax/WebResource.axd?d=HQhspev9RtnoVp5Ca4MubA2&amp;➥
t=633008366579531250" type="text/javascript"></script>
<script src="/Ajax/ScriptResource.axd?d=rbfRw_fjV44N4zFu5uugvXCgOfpE5bOdbRFvvkMhZEO1
-ghFYTQ7i9aLWWp9hO2901tgv-pDZFxuTtMikT21d-q8lo-xXLBcAYv3xqOhiRM1
&amp;t=633051881703906250" type="text/javascript">
</script>
<script
src="/Ajax/ScriptResource.axd?d=rbfRw_fjV44N4zFu5uugvXCgOfpE5bOdbRFvvkMhZEO1➥
-ghFYTQ7i9aLWWp9hO2901tgv-pDZFxuTtMikT21d3JhQBwnJ44PsSIlvSkVAgc1➥
 &amp;t=633051881703906250" type="text/javascript"></script>
```

But suppose you need additional AJAX functionality in your content page. For example, you might want to take advantage of one of many great controls available in the ASP.NET AJAX Control Toolkit (covered extensively in Chapters 7 and 8). These controls require additional scripts that may not have been included in the master page. That is precisely where the ScriptManagerProxy control comes in.

Without getting into discussions about the ASP.NET AJAX Control Toolkit, we'll add one of its controls, the DragPanelExtender, to the content page with the help of the ScriptManagerProxy control. To do this, drag and drop a ScriptManagerProxy control, followed by a Label control, and a DragPanelExtender (from the AJAX Control Toolkit) onto the page. Set the text property of the Label control to some text such as "You can drag and drop this label." At this point, your page should look similar to Figure 5-3 with the following code:

```
<%@ Page Language="C#" MasterPageFile="~/MasterPage.Master" AutoEventWireup="true" ➥
        CodeBehind="ContentPage.aspx.cs" Inherits="Ajax.ContentPage" ➥
        Title="DragPanelExtender Demo" %>

<%@ Register Assembly="AjaxControlToolkit" Namespace="AjaxControlToolkit" ➥
TagPrefix="cc1" %>
<asp:Content ID="Content1" ContentPlaceHolderID="ContentPlaceHolder1" ➥
runat="server">
<asp:ScriptManagerProxy ID="ScriptManagerProxy1" runat="server">
</asp:ScriptManagerProxy>
<cc1:DragPanelExtender ID="DragPanelExtender1" runat="server" EnableViewState=➥
"False" TargetControlID="Label1">
</cc1:DragPanelExtender>
 
<asp:Label ID="Label1" runat="server" Text="You can drag and drop this label.">
</asp:Label>
</asp:Content>
```

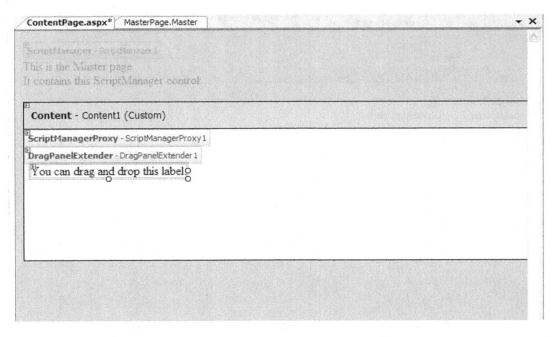

Figure 5-3. *Adding a* ScriptManagerProxy *control to a content page*

The last step before running the page is to set the TargetControlID property of the
DragPanelExtender to the name of the Label control (i.e., Label1). When you run the page,
you can drag and drop the actual label throughout the page as shown in Figure 5-4.

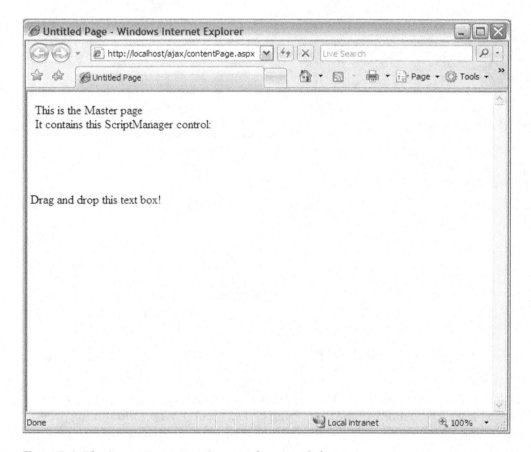

Figure 5-4. *Placing an* UpdatePanel *control on a web form*

Now, if you view the browser output, you'll notice that six additional script blocks have been added to page output:

```
<script src="/Ajax3/ScriptResource.axd?d=IV7jia2nXbc7sCg1SWf3RbWQWNeQtdO8PGyfXw5p➡
BCt7QucJL9oE4uI487xHlPYvLbUfoMzAxODl7veKacOLUw2&amp;t=633083898300000000" ➡
type="text/javascript">
</script>
<script src="/Ajax3/ScriptResource.axd?d=IV7jia2nXbc7sCg1SWf3RbWQWNeQtdO8PGyfXw5pBC➡
t6I1vaIgM5kgWHpAx-XLCYADQCoaENHDXR_fmnXYiB5Q2&amp;t=633083898300000000"➡
type="text/javascript">
</script>
<script src="/Ajax3/ScriptResource.axd?d=IV7jia2nXbc7sCg1SWf3RbWQWNeQtdO8PGyfXw5p➡
BCuGnLpMX4aibann483UFkP4UcDhmgCv77Gz2BPJzbOsGQ2&amp;t=633083898300000000"➡
type="text/javascript">
</script>
```

```
<script src="/Ajax3/ScriptResource.axd?d=IV7jia2nXbc7sCg1SWf3RbWQWNeQtdO8PGyfXw5p➡
BCtjSYyc7zoec8BYAEgCq7Xfw8Q1uMQbSmJ5pFsFPdNdi53i7U-TPJGeX-iRo2uSjUM1&amp➡
;t=633083898300000000" type="text/javascript">
</script>
<script src="/Ajax3/ScriptResource.axd?d=IV7jia2nXbc7sCg1SWf3RbWQWNeQtdO8PGyfXw5p➡
BCsJ5ep-dAHOns9-VxfadeqV_ZfemVlTAoDxNenJwjPNYSz3EWAPxxWj3tXQmN4a7DI1&amp➡
;t=633083898300000000" type="text/javascript">
</script>
<script src="/Ajax3/ScriptResource.axd?d=IV7jia2nXbc7sCg1SWf3RbWQWNeQtdO8PGyfXw5p➡
BCtKZKNEWlh6Oo9nJAvWsOew_AfDKm3BP43z3sXqwMBrtQT-xZwKhUvOddRO4WY6Is41&amp➡
;t=633083898300000000" type="text/javascript">
</script>
```

These additional script blocks contain the extra scripting logic required for the functionality by members of the AJAX Control Toolkit that were dynamically inserted into the page by the `ScriptManagerProxy` control. Without `ScriptManagerProxy`, you couldn't have the required scripts handled automatically for you because this was all in the content page.

Introducing the `UpdatePanel` Control

In typical ASP.NET 2.0 applications, if you do a postback on the web page, the entire page will be rerendered. This causes a "blink" or a "flash" in the client or browser. On the server, the postback is detected, which triggers the page life cycle. This ends up raising the specific postback event handler code for the control that caused the postback, and this calls upon the page's event handler.

When you use `UpdatePanel` controls along with a `ScriptManager` control, you eliminate the need for a full-page refresh. The `UpdatePanel` control is similar to a `ContentPanel` control in that it marks out a region on the web page that will automatically be updated when the postback occurs (but without the aforementioned postback behavior on the client). It instead communicates through the `XMLHttpRequest` channel—in true AJAX style. The page on the server still handles the postback as expected and executes, raising event handlers, and so on, but the final rendering of the page means that only the regions specified in the `UpdatePanel` control's regions are created. Also, unlike the `ScriptManager`, you can actually have multiple `UpdatePanel` controls on the same page and even have nested `UpdatePanel` controls within one another.

Using the `UpdatePanel` Control

To use an `UpdatePanel` control, you simply drag and drop it onto the design surface of your web form (see Figure 5-5).

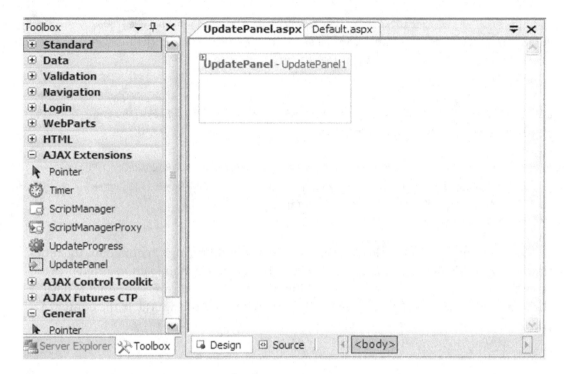

Figure 5-5. *Placing an* UpdatePanel *control on a web form*

However, as you know, the UpdatePanel control cannot function without a
ScriptManager control on the page. Additionally, the ScriptManager control must be
located before any UpdatePanel controls on your page. In other words, as you read your
source code from top to bottom, the ScriptManager reference should appear before the
UpdatePanel ones. Using the Tasks Assistant will ensure that it is placed correctly. If your
ScriptManager control is not present or is incorrectly placed, you'll get an error when you
try to open the page in a browser (see Figure 5-6).

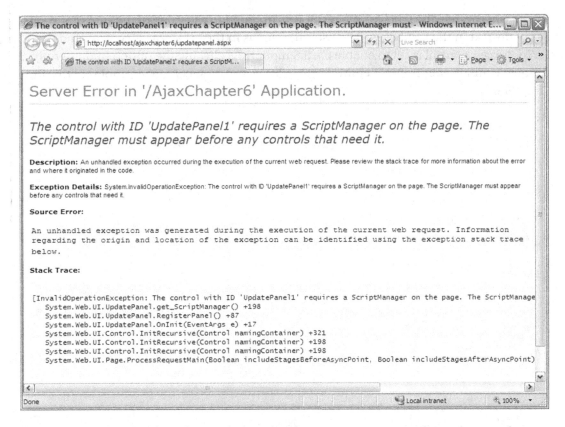

Figure 5-6. *Error page when the* UpdatePanel *and* ScriptManager *controls aren't properly configured*

The UpdatePanel control contains a designer surface where you can place HTML. This markup is the only one updated upon a postback if the ScriptManager control is enabled for partial updates. Consider Figure 5-7, where several text boxes and a button appear on the screen. This application has two text boxes, two labels, and a button *outside* the UpdatePanel control, and it has a label *inside* the UpdatePanel designer. The label on the inside is called lblResult. The code behind the button reads as follows:

```
int x = Convert.ToInt16(txt1.Text);
int y = Convert.ToInt16(txt2.Text);
int z = x+y;
lblResult.Text = z.ToString();
```

As you can see, the label for the result gets updated to the value of the sum of the values of the text in the text boxes. Because lblResult is in the UpdatePanel control, and the ScriptManager control is set to enable partial rendering, clicking the button updates only the text within the UpdatePanel control. You will see and dissect more examples of this in Chapter 6.

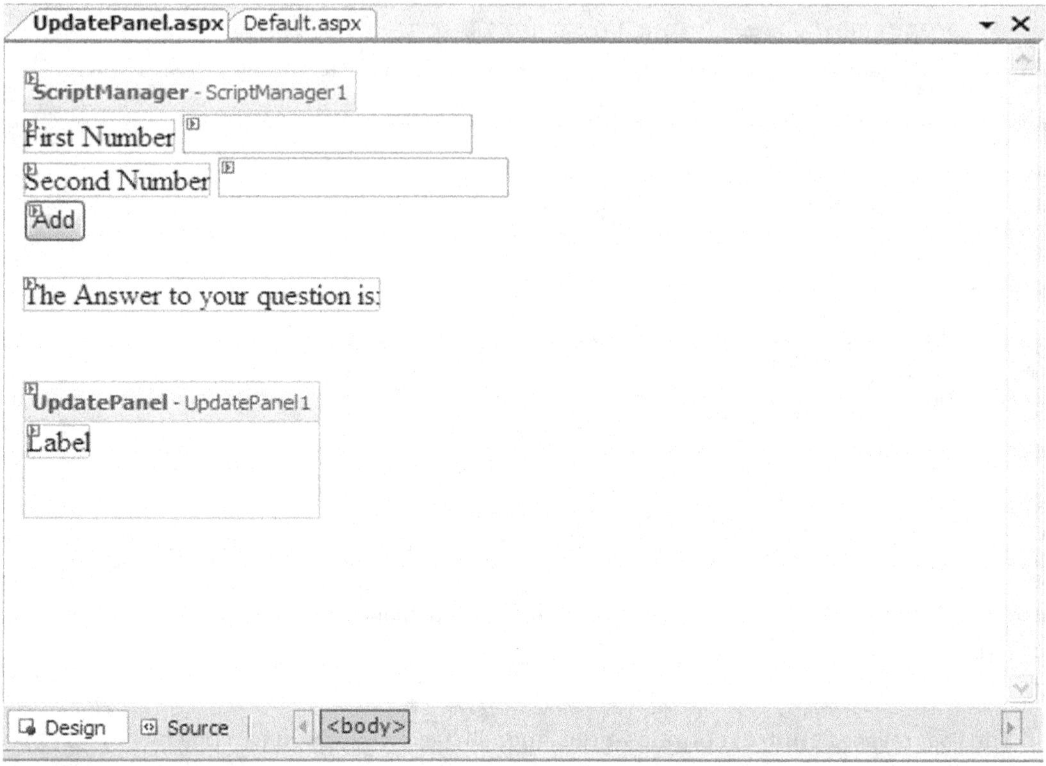

UpdatePanel.aspx | Default.aspx   ▼ ✕

ScriptManager - ScriptManager 1

First Number

Second Number

Add

The Answer to your question is:

UpdatePanel - UpdatePanel 1
Label

☐ Design   ⊡ Source   ◄ <body>   ►

Figure 5-7. *Simple application that uses the* UpdatePanel *control*

Programming with UpdatePanel

The markup for the UpdatePanel control in the previous example is as follows:

```
<asp:UpdatePanel ID="UpdatePanel1" runat="server">
  <ContentTemplate>
     <asp:Label ID="lblResult" runat="server" Text="Label"></asp:Label>
  </ContentTemplate>
  </asp:UpdatePanel>
```

The `<asp:UpdatePanel>` tag supports two child tags: the `<ContentTemplate>` tag and the `<Triggers>` tag. Before moving on to discuss these tags, note the properties of the `UpdatePanel` control excluding those inherited from the `Control` class as listed in Table 5-5.

Table 5-5. `UpdatePanel` *Control Properties*

Property Name	Method
ChildrenAsTriggers	Boolean value indicating whether postbacks from immediate child controls of an UpdatePanel control update the panel's content.
ContentTemplateContainer	Returns a control object that you can then use later to add child controls to.
Controls	Returns ControlCollection object that contains the child controls for the UpdatePanel control.
IsInPartialRendering	Indicates whether the UpdatePanel control is being updated because of an asynchronous postback.
RenderMode	Indicates whether an UpdatePanel control's content is enclosed in an HTML <div> or <span> element.
RequiresUpdate	Indicates whether the content of the UpdatePanel control will be updated.
UpdateMode	Indicates when an UpdatePanel control's content is updated. The default is "always."

Using the `ContentTemplate` Tag

The `<ContentTemplate>` tag defines the HTML or ASP.NET that will get updated by the `UpdatePanel` control. You can use the designer to generate this HTML. If, for example, you drag and drop a `Calendar` control onto the `UpdatePanel` control's content template area (see Figure 5-8), it will be defined within the `<ContentTemplate>` tag area.

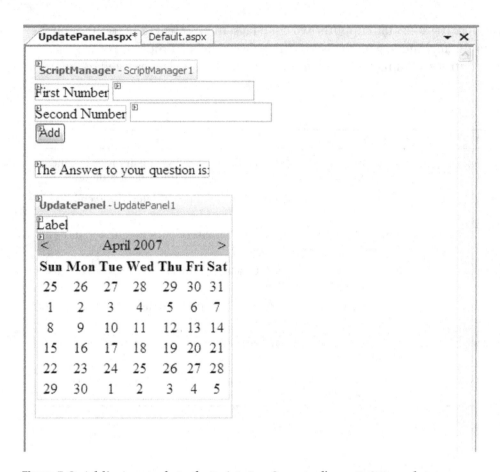

Figure 5-8. *Adding controls to the* UpdatePanel *control's content template*

You can see the markup that is produced by adding the calendar as follows:

```
<asp:UpdatePanel ID="UpdatePanel1" runat="server">
<ContentTemplate>
    <asp:Label ID="lblResult" runat="server" Text="Label"></asp:Label>
    <asp:Calendar ID="Calendar1" runat="server"></asp:Calendar>
</ContentTemplate>
</asp:UpdatePanel>
```

Using Triggers

The other child tag for the UpdatePanel control is <Triggers>. This allows you to define triggers for the update. As seen in the previous table, the UpdatePanel control has a property calledUpdateMode. If you set this to Conditional (the default is Always), then updates to the rendering of the markup will occur only when a trigger is hit. The Triggers tag contains the collection of trigger definitions. In Visual Studio 2005, there is a designer-based Trigger Collections Editor (accessed by clicking on the Triggers Collection property in the property box for the UpdatePanel) that can be used to view and edit triggers within an UpdatePanel as shown in Figure 5-9.

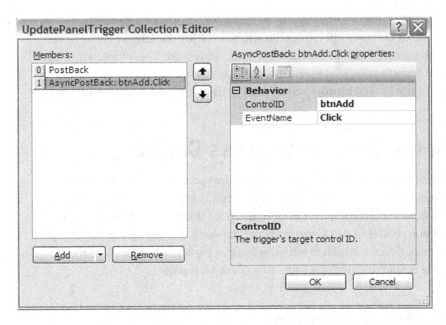

Figure 5-9. *UpdatePanelTrigger Collections Editor in Visual Studio 200*

There are two types of triggers supported within the <Triggers> tag: AsyncPostBackTrigger and PostBackTrigger. You can actually use these triggers for controls that are not within the UpdatePanel. The two tags differ only in the fact that AsyncPostBackTrigger, as the name suggests, can handle asynchronous postback when the trigger is raised. It also has an additional property called EventName, which allows you to specify the event name of the target control responsible for initiating the update.

You define an AsyncPostBackTrigger trigger with an associated control (specified by ControlID) and an event name (specified by the EventName). If the event is raised on that control, then the trigger fires, and the UpdatePanel control is rendered. You specify a PostBackTrigger with the <asp:PostBackTrigger> tag and an AsyncPostBackTrigger with the <asp:AsyncPostBackTrigger> tag. Here's a quick sample based on the last example we used:

```
<asp:Button ID="btnAdd" runat="server" Text="Add" OnClick="btnAdd_Click" />
<br />
        <asp:UpdatePanel ID="UpdatePanel1" runat="server" UpdateMode=Conditional >
        <ContentTemplate>
            <asp:Label ID="lblResult" runat="server" Text="Label"></asp:Label>
            <asp:Calendar ID="Calendar1" runat="server"></asp:Calendar>
        </ContentTemplate>
        <Triggers>
            <asp:AsyncPostBackTrigger ControlID="btnAdd" EventName="Click" />
        </Triggers>
        </asp:UpdatePanel>
```

Here the `AsyncPostBackTrigger` specifies that the source for the trigger is the button called `btnAdd`, and the event on which to trigger is the `Click` event. Therefore, when the button is clicked, the `AsyncPostBackTrigger` fires, and the partial update occurs. Notice that the declaration of the `btnAdd` button was actually outside the `UpdatePanel` block.

Introducing the UpdateProgress Control

Another server control that ASP.NET AJAX provides is the `UpdateProgress` control. This indicates the progress of an asynchronous operation that is taking place. Typically, the browser's status bar serves as an indicator of activity. With the partial-rendering and asynchronous postback model in AJAX applications, viewing the status bar of the browser is no longer applicable, which is why the `UpdateProgress` control is ideal and more user friendly for displaying activity indicators on a web page.

Using the UpdateProgress Control

You can have a single `UpdateProgress` control on your page for multiple `UpdatePanels` or have multiple `UpdateProgress` controls with different UIs for the `UpdatePanels` if you want to have different progress indicators for different sections of the page. By default, if you don't set the `AssociatedUpdatePanelID` property of the `UpdateProgress` control, it will be triggered by events in all `UpdatePanels` on the page (assuming there is more than one). To use an `UpdateProgress` control, you drag and drop it onto your page to create an `<asp:UpdateProgress>` tag on your page:

```
<asp:UpdateProgress ID="UpdateProgress1" runat="server" />
```

The actual markup to display when the call is taking place is then defined using the `<ProgressTemplate>` tag.

When your application executes calls to the server, the HTML defined in the `<Pro-gressTemplate>` tag is then displayed. This is where you could have an animating GIF or some other custom message to inform the user about the status of the execution.

Programming with the `UpdateProgress` Control

Before showing an example using the `UpdateProgress` control, view its properties in Table 5-6.

Table 5-6. *Properties of the* `UpdateProgress` *Control*

Property Name	Function
`AssociatedUpdatePanelID`	ID of the `UpdatePanel` control that the `UpdateProgress` control displays the status for.
`DisplayAfter`	The value in milliseconds before the `UpdateProgress` control is displayed.
`DynamicLayout`	A value that determines whether the progress template is rendered dynamically. If set to `false`, it will take up the required space at all times even if the progress content is not displayed.

In many large web applications today, long running data operations are not uncommon. In such cases, it's helpful to use the `UpdateProgress` control to notify the user about the running status of the application. For the sake of simplicity, let's create a page that simulates a long running process by pausing the running thread for a few seconds.

To build this page, drop new `ScriptManager`, `UpdatePanel`, and `UpdateProgress` controls on a new `WebForm` page. After that, create a new `Button` control in the `UpdatePanel`. In the source view of the *.aspx* page, create a new `<ProgressTemplate>` tag within the `UpdateProgress` tag with the following markup:

```
<ProgressTemplate>
          Calculating...
 </ProgressTemplate>
```

Your page should now look similar to Figure 5-10.

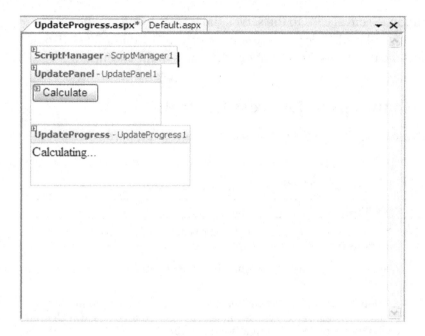

Figure 5-10. *Using the* UpdateProgress *control*

Now, we can simulate a long running process when the button is clicked by pausing the existing thread for four seconds in the event handler of the button:

```
protected void Button1_Click(object sender, EventArgs e)
{
    System.Threading.Thread.Sleep(4000);
}
```

When you run the page and click the Calculate button, you'll see that the string, "Calculating…" appears for four seconds and then disappears as shown in Figure 5-11.

Figure 5-11. UpdateProgress *control demo*

If you now view the browser output, you'll notice a new <div> tag along with extra JavaScript that has been emitted by the UpdateProgress control:

```
<div id="UpdateProgress1" style="display:none;">
                 Calculating...
  <div>
```

The new scripts that have been injected into the page dynamically toggle the style property of the div without you having to do any additional coding.

Introducing the Timer Control

Probably the simplest of the ASP.NET AJAX server controls is the Timer control. Similar in many ways to the Timer control that has existed for some time for Winforms, the Timer control provides a simple-to-use timer functionality that can be configured to perform operations repeatedly based on the time elapsed. Therefore, you can run certain operations at a regular interval in a synchronous or asynchronous manner without having to do a manual page refresh. This can come in handy in many scenarios for web applications.

Imagine, for instance, that your page contains critical and dynamic information such as stock quotes or flight arrival information that needs to be updated on a regular basis. You can use the Timer control on your page to trigger updates to an UpdatePanel control, all without having to do any full-page refreshes.

Using the Timer Control

To use a Timer control, you of course need a ScriptManager control on the page. You can add a Timer control to a page by dragging and dropping it onto the control surface. A good use for timers is to update the contents of an UpdatePanel control when the timer ticks.

To see the Timer control in action, you can add an UpdatePanel control to a blank page along with a ScriptManager control. After you've done this, you can drag and drop a Timer control onto the page. Also, place a Label control in the UpdatePanel. You can see what this looks like in the designer in Figure 5-12.

Figure 5-12. *Using a* Timer *control in the designer*

Lastly, double-click the Timer control so that it will generate the event handler stub for the OnTick event of the Timer control. The markup in your page now has the <asp:Timer> tag already defined. Here's an example of a timer that has been customized with a 4,000-millisecond interval (4 seconds), with the name Timer1, and the event handler Timer1_Tick:

```
<asp:Timer ID="Timer1" runat="server"  Interval="4000" OnTick="Timer1_Tick">
</asp:Timer>
```

Now, within the Timer1_Tick method in the code-behind class, you can perform an operation each time the timer fires, such as updating the time. An AsyncPostBackTrigger trigger is used within an UpdatePanel to trigger an update on the Timer's Tick event. You can see this in the following markup:

```
<div>
    <asp:ScriptManager ID="ScriptManager1" runat="server">
    </asp:ScriptManager>

</div>
    <asp:Timer ID="Timer1" runat="server"  Interval="4000" OnTick="Timer1_Tick">
    </asp:Timer>
    <asp:UpdatePanel ID="UpdatePanel1" runat="server">
        <Triggers>
        <asp:AsyncPostBackTrigger ControlID="Timer1" EventName="Tick" />
        </Triggers>
        <ContentTemplate>
            <asp:Label ID="Label1" runat="server" Text=""></asp:Label>
        </ContentTemplate>
    </asp:UpdatePanel>
```

If you run the page, you'll notice that the Label control updates every four seconds with the new time without doing a full page refresh (see Figure 5-13).

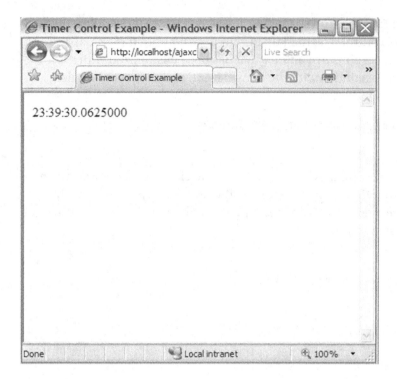

Figure 5-13. Timer *control demo*

Summary

This chapter introduced you to the server controls that are available to ASP.NET AJAX programmers. It walked you through using the ScriptManager control, which is at the heart of ASP.NET AJAX. This control takes care of managing the ASP.NET AJAX runtime as well as associated scripts. Additionally, you looked at the UpdatePanel control, which is at the heart of how ASP.NET AJAX enables AJAX functionality in existing ASP.NET pages using partial-page updates.

This chapter gave you a high-level overview of the main ASP.NET AJAX server controls and how they work. There is another group of ASP.NET AJAX server controls called the extender controls that ship in the ASP.NET AJAX Control Toolkit. Although we didn't discuss these controls here, they will be covered thoroughly in Chapters 7 and 8. In the next chapter, you will look at some applications and samples that use this functionality, dissecting them to understand how you can program similar applications of your own in ASP.NET AJAX.

■ ■ ■

Using Server Controls in ASP.NET AJAX

This chapter follows on from Chapter 5, which introduced you to the ASP.NET AJAX server controls and showed you how to use them. In this chapter, you'll look at two small ASP.NET AJAX applications and dissect them to see how they work. In the process, you'll glean a lot of new information about how to use the ASP.NET AJAX server controls to build powerful AJAX-style applications and how to extend your existing applications with asynchrony.

One of the applications that will be discussed happens to be also one of the first small apps built to showcase some of the features of ASP.NET AJAX. This application, called Scott's ToDo List, is a great example of a simple data-driven AJAX-enabled ASP.NET web application. But before that, let's combine the controls discussed in the previous chapter to create a practical solution to a common scenario.

Using the `UpdatePanel`, `UpdateProgress`, and `Timer` Controls

For this first example, consider the following scenario: You have a data-driven web page that needs to continuously alert the user with fast changing data, for instance, a page that displays the major financial indices in the U.S. capital markets: Dow Jones Industrial Average (DJIA), NASDAQ, and S&P500. One approach is to place a <META> tag in your page with refresh values that then force the page to refresh itself in regular intervals based on the provided value. But if you wanted to make the page behave more like a desktop application and update the data without page refresh, AJAX is definitely the recommended path.

By now, you have seen the basics of the `ScriptManager`, `UpdatePanel`, `UpdateProgress`, and the `Timer` server controls in ASP.NET AJAX and have a good understanding of their functionality. So, with that in mind, let's build a quick application that does exactly what was talked about earlier: displays the three main indices of the American capital markets and continues to update the page with (simulated) real-time data without any page refresh.

To accomplish this, create a new ASP.NET AJAX-enabled web site. Because the ScriptManager control has already been placed on the page, drop new UpdatePanel, UpdateProgress, and Timer controls onto the page called *MarketData.aspx* as shown in Figure 6-1.

Figure 6-1. *New page with ASP.NET AJAX server controls*

After that, you just need an HTML table and a few label controls for the user interface. Let's take a look at the actual markup for this page:

```
<%@ Page Language="C#" AutoEventWireup="true" CodeFile="MarketData.aspx.cs" ➥
Inherits="MarketData" %>
<!DOCTYPE html PUBLIC "-//W3C//DTD XHTML 1.0 Transitional//EN" ➥
"http://www.w3.org/TR/xhtml1/DTD/xhtml1-transitional.dtd">
<html xmlns="http://www.w3.org/1999/xhtml" >
<head runat="server">
    <title>Market Summary</title>
</head>
<body>
    <form id="form1" runat="server">
    <div>
        <asp:ScriptManager ID="ScriptManager1" runat="server">
        </asp:ScriptManager>
    </div>
        <u>Market Summary:</u>
    <br /><br />
        <asp:UpdatePanel ID="UpdatePanel1" runat="server">
            <Triggers>
                <asp:AsyncPostBackTrigger ControlID="Timer1" EventName="Tick" />
```

```
        </Triggers>
        <ContentTemplate>
        <table border="1">
        <tr>
            <td><asp:Label ID="Label1" runat="server" Text="DJIA"></asp:Label>
          </td>
            <td align=right><asp:Label ID="lblDowJones" runat="server"
            Text="12000"></asp:Label></td>
        </tr>
         <tr>
            <td><asp:Label ID="Label2" runat="server" Text="NASDAQ"></asp:Label>
          </td>
            <td align=right><asp:Label ID="lblNasdaq" runat="server"
            Text="2500"></asp:Label></td>
        </tr>
         <tr>
            <td><asp:Label ID="Label3" runat="server" Text="S&P 500">
            </asp:Label></td>
            <td align=right><asp:Label ID="lblSnp" runat="server" Text="1400">
            </asp:Label></td>
        </tr>
         </table>
        </ContentTemplate>
      </asp:UpdatePanel>
      <asp:UpdateProgress ID="UpdateProgress1" runat="server">
          <ProgressTemplate>Updating...</ProgressTemplate>
      </asp:UpdateProgress>
      <asp:Timer ID="Timer1" runat="server" Interval="2000" OnTick="Timer1_Tick" />

    </form>
</body>
</html>
```

By now, you are probably familiar with most of this code. Basically, we are using an
<asp:AsyncPostBackTrigger> trigger in the main UpdatePanel control and associating it with
the Tick event of the Timer control. To better show the updates taking place, you use an
UpdateProgress control with the text "Updating…" in its <ProgressTemplate> tag. In the
Timer control, you set the interval to 2 seconds (2000 milliseconds) and point the OnTick
event to the Timer1_Tick event handler in the code behind, which will be responsible for
writing the logic to fetch and display the new values for the three indices.

Obviously, the point of this application is to showcase a good scenario for using
ASP.NET AJAX server controls and not to build a practical market data reporting
application. As such, the initial values for the three indices have been hard-coded in the
tags themselves. The initial value for the DJIA is set to 12000, the NASDAQ is set to 2500,

and the S&P is set to 1400. There will also be some simple logic to update the display values of those indices with some fictitious data as shown in the following code block in the code-behind class:

```
protected void Timer1_Tick(object sender, EventArgs e)
    {
        System.Threading.Thread.Sleep(1000);
        lblDowJones.Text = ((int.Parse(lblDowJones.Text)) + 1).ToString();
        lblNasdaq.Text = ((float.Parse(lblNasdaq.Text)) + 0.5).ToString();
        lblSnp.Text = ((float.Parse(lblSnp.Text)) + 0.25).ToString();
    }
```

First, you initiate a one-second delay by pausing the current thread, and then you increment the values of each label control by holding the value for the market indices and assigning them back to the corresponding labels. As you can see, the value for DJIA is incremented by one point, the NASDAQ index is incremented by a half point, and the S&P 500 index is incremented by a quarter point. This update effectively takes place every three seconds because the Timer1_Tick event is called every two seconds followed by a one-second delay in the method.

Figure 6-2 shows *MarketData.aspx* in the browser during an update.

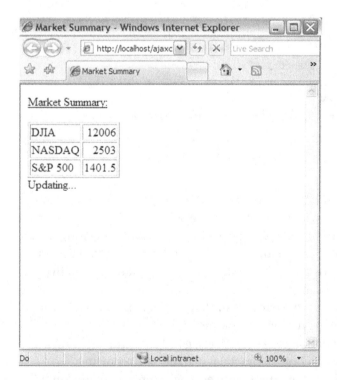

Figure 6-2. *MarketData.aspx updates the values for the indices every three seconds.*

As you can see, the index values in the page change every two seconds (with a one-second pause between updates and one second after the update without any refresh at all). If you were to refresh the page, you would notice all three values being reset to their initial values that were set in the page designer. Now view the source in the browser, and notice the generated client code:

```
<!DOCTYPE html PUBLIC "-//W3C//DTD XHTML 1.0 Transitional//EN" ➥
"http://www.w3.org/TR/xhtml1/DTD/xhtml1-transitional.dtd">

<html xmlns="http://www.w3.org/1999/xhtml" >
<head><title>
            Market Summary
</title></head>
<body>
    <form name="form1" method="post" action="marketdata.aspx" id="form1">
<div>
<input type="hidden" name="__EVENTTARGET" id="__EVENTTARGET" value="" />
<input type="hidden" name="__EVENTARGUMENT" id="__EVENTARGUMENT" value="" />
<input type="hidden" name="__VIEWSTATE" id="__VIEWSTATE"
value="/wEPDwULLTEONDcxODQxOTNkZBVyy3kZPCaHntKg63oJ/pIvM3rf" />
</div>
<script type="text/javascript">
<!--
var theForm = document.forms['form1'];
if (!theForm) {
    theForm = document.form1;
}
function __doPostBack(eventTarget, eventArgument) {
    if (!theForm.onsubmit || (theForm.onsubmit() != false)) {
        theForm.__EVENTTARGET.value = eventTarget;
        theForm.__EVENTARGUMENT.value = eventArgument;
        theForm.submit();
    }
}
// -->
</script>

<script src="/AjaxChapter7/WebResource.axd?d=2k35oXVI5C1fsATKa8kOpQ2&
amp;t=633008366579531250" type="text/javascript"></script>
<script src="/AjaxChapter7/ScriptResource.axd?d=zmjix_FO7KXpA6mO2uaB_q52a3TPiFz24p4h
x51TaC3HYCrvlQk4ongK5kg1IR8XFf7DTDlMUGM-Uucre6H3Yy1K_8vru25LXaz6lsl_pOU1&amp;t=
633051881703906250" type="text/javascript"></script>
```

```
<script src="/AjaxChapter7/ScriptResource.axd?d=zmjix_F07KXpA6m02uaB_
q52a3TPiFz24p4hx51TaC3HYCrvlQk4ongK5kg1IR8XFf7DTDlMUGM-Uucre6H3Y1DyFBKNihsy-
OGXMoZEYtg1&amp;t=633051881703906250" type="text/javascript"></script>
<script src="/AjaxChapter7/ScriptResource.axd?d=zmjix_F07KXpA6m02uaB_
q52a3TPiFz24p4hx51TaC3HYCrvlQk4ongK5kg1IR8XFf7DTDlMUGM-Uucre6H3Y9OmwbS8Igy_KW_
7MLdflso1&amp;t=633051881703906250" type="text/javascript"></script>
    <div>
        <script type="text/javascript">
//<![CDATA[
Sys.WebForms.PageRequestManager._initialize('ScriptManager1',
                                    document.getElementById('form1'));
Sys.WebForms.PageRequestManager.getInstance()._updateControls(['tUpdatePanel1'],
                                            ['Timer1'], [], 90);
//]]>
</script>
    </div>
        <u>Market Summary:</u>
    <br /><br />
        <div id="UpdatePanel1">

            <table border="1">
            <tr>
                <td><span id="Label1">DJIA</span></td>
                <td align=right><span id="lblDowJones">12000</span></td>
            </tr>
             <tr>
                <td><span id="Label2">NASDAQ</span></td>
                <td align=right><span id="lblNasdaq">2500</span></td>
            </tr>
             <tr>
                <td><span id="Label3">S&P 500</span></td>
                <td align=right><span id="lblSnp">1400</span></td>
            </tr>
             </table>
</div>
        <div id="UpdateProgress1" style="display:none;">
                Updating...
</div>
        <span id="Timer1" style="visibility:hidden;display:none;"></span>
<script type="text/javascript">
<!--
Sys.Application.initialize();
```

```
Sys.Application.add_init(function() {
    $create(Sys.UI._UpdateProgress, {"associatedUpdatePanelId":null,"displayAfter"
    :500,"dynamicLayout":true}, null, null, $get("UpdateProgress1"));
});
Sys.Application.add_init(function() {
    $create(Sys.UI._Timer, {"enabled":true,"interval":2000,"uniqueID":"Timer1"},
    null, null, $get("Timer1"));
});
// -->
</script>
</form>
</body>
</html>
```

The ASP.NET AJAX server controls emit JavaScript functions that copy and build a new innerHTML property of the <span> or <div> tags that contain the value getting updated. They are also responsible for generating a request on XMLHttpRequest and a callback for when the client request is complete. The callback then builds HTML code to put on the innerHTML property of the named <span> or <div> tags.

This is basically how the UpdatePanel works under the hood. It uses Sys.WebForms.PageRequestManager to set up an asynchronous callback. These scripts are all automatically generated by the ScriptManager. Near the end of the source in the last lines of script in the page, you can also see the parameters of the Timer control being passed via JavaScript with the interval set to two seconds and the ID of the control being Timer1. Delving deeper into the generated script details piece by piece would fast take us beyond the scope of this chapter. If you are interested in having a more in-depth understanding of the inner workings of these script blocks on the page, you can view them by using either an HTTP sniffer, the JSView plug-in for FireFox (https://addons.mozilla.org/en-US/firefox/addon/2076), or other third-party tools designed to capture the browser output.

Using a Task List Manager

One of the first reference applications publicly available for ASP.NET AJAX was Scott Guthrie's task list manager, ToDo List. This application is a simple yet powerful demonstration of the power of the ASP.NET 2.0 Framework and how easy it is to extend it for AJAX-style functionality using ASP.NET AJAX.

This application is a simple task manager using SQL Server 2005 Express edition as a container for its data. You can download and run it on your local machine with the complete source available online. Feel free to customize this app in any way you want by adding or modifying new items as long as you accommodate these changes in the provided database. The entire application really consists of a single *.aspx* page and a *.master* page. Figure 6-3 shows the main screen for this application.

Note You can download Scott's ToDo List application in addition to video tutorials about this and other ASP.NET AJAX topics on http://ajax.asp.net.

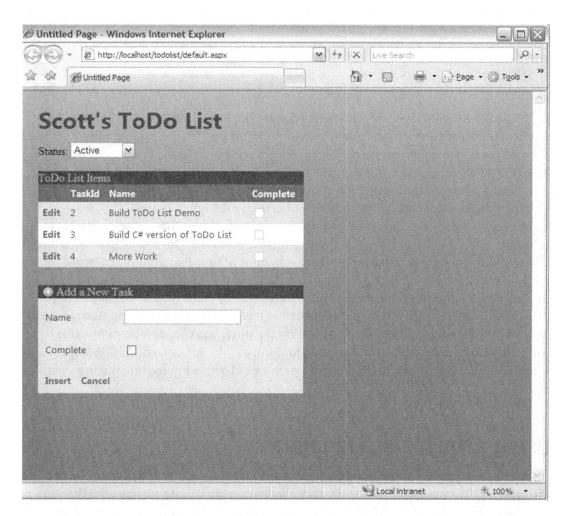

Figure 6-3. *The task list manager application*

The main screen for this application shows a sortable list of tasks that you can add to, edit, or mark complete. The drop-down button on the top switches the view between Active and Completed status of the tasks. If you have already installed this application, you can open the folder as an existing site in Visual Studio 2005. Let's start by taking a look at the *MasterPage.master* page in the designer as shown in Figure 6-4.

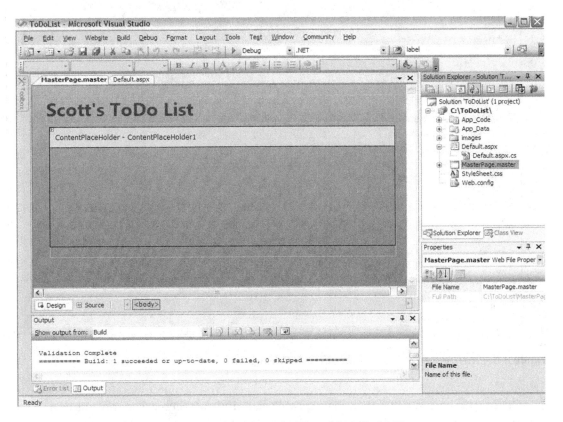

Figure 6-4. *The task list manager master page in Visual Studio 2005*

This page basically consists of a ContentPlaceHolder control in addition to the style sheet. The main part of the application, as mentioned earlier, resides in the *Default.aspx* page. Figure 6-5 shows this page in the designer.

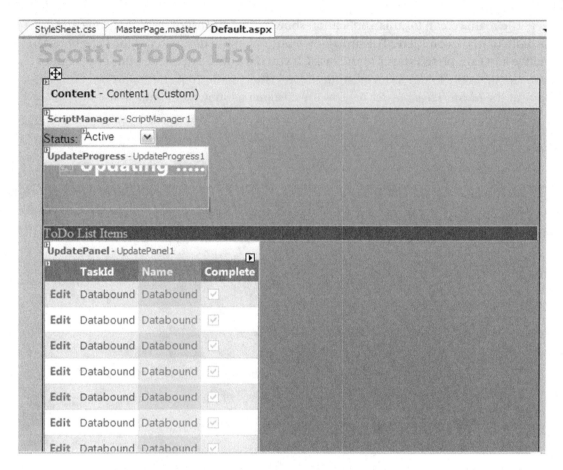

Figure 6-5. *Editing the task list in the ASP.NET designer*

Once again, you see ScriptManager, UpdatePanel, and UpdateProgress controls as a recurring theme. Let's start by looking at the markup for the UpdateProgress control in this page:

```
<asp:UpdateProgress ID="UpdateProgress1" runat="server">
    <ProgressTemplate>
        <div class="progress">
        <img src="images/indicator.gif" />
        Updating .....
        </div>
    </ProgressTemplate>
</asp:UpdateProgress>
```

You won't find anything out of the ordinary here. Just a simple `<asp:UpdateProgress>` tag with an animating GIF image and the text "Updating…" to notify the user about the status in case there is a delay with data access during an operation such as update or insert.

This page also contains two UpdatePanel controls. The first one is for the list of tasks, whereas the second one allows the user to insert a new task. The top UpdatePanel control contains an ASP.NET GridView control. Because it's in an UpdatePanel control, and partial rendering is enabled, postbacks caused by actions on this panel should incur only partial refreshes, which improves the user experience. Let's take a look at the markup for this UpdatePanel control containing the GridView and other controls:

```
<asp:UpdatePanel ID="UpdatePanel1" runat="server">
    <ContentTemplate>
    <asp:GridView ID="GridView1" runat="server" AllowPaging="True"
                                  AllowSorting="True"
                                  AutoGenerateColumns="False"
                                  DataKeyNames="TaskId"
                                  DataSourceID="ObjectDataSource1"
                                  CssClass="gridview"
                                  AlternatingRowStyle-CssClass="even"
                                  GridLines="None">
       <Columns>
         <asp:CommandField ShowEditButton="True" />
         <asp:BoundField DataField="TaskId" HeaderText="TaskId" InsertVisible=
         "False" ReadOnly="True"  SortExpression="TaskId" />
         <asp:BoundField DataField="Name" HeaderText="Name" SortExpression=
                                    "Name" />
         <asp:CheckBoxField DataField="Complete" HeaderText="Complete"
                                    SortExpression="Complete" />
       </Columns>
     </asp:GridView>
    </ContentTemplate>
    <Triggers>
    <asp:AsyncPostBackTrigger ControlID="DropDownList1" EventName=
                                    "SelectedIndexChanged" />
    </Triggers>
</asp:UpdatePanel>
```

The `<ContentTemplate>` tag holds the main grid containing the content that is going to be partially updated. The GridView control is bound to ObjectDataSource1, which in turn is bound to the Items dataset. Columns are set up as before with bindings to fields within the dataset and with inline editing capability that allow these fields to be changed. Because the grid is bound, changes to the underlying dataset trigger a refresh to the grid and as such an update of the content via an event that fires when the bound data changes. Really, the only trace of ASP.NET AJAX visible here is the `<asp:UpdatePanel>` element.

The `GridView` control also has some properties defined for aesthetics, such as the `AlternatingRowStyle-CssClass` property, and defines its content using the `<Columns>` tag. Also, you automatically get sorting and paging capability by setting the `AllowPaging` and `AllowSorting` properties of the `GridView` control to `true`.

The `<asp:CommandField>` tag defines actions such as Edit and Delete, whereas the `<asp:BoundField>` tag defines data fields that are bound to a data source. Lastly, the `<asp:CheckBoxField>` tag, as the name implies, defines the check box for the completed tasks. Before leaving the `<Columns>` tag, let's make a very quick and easy addition to this to be able to delete tasks. You can do so by simply adding the `ShowDeleteButton` property to the `<asp:CommandField>` tag as shown in the following line:

```
<asp:CommandField ShowEditButton="True"  ShowDeleteButton="true"/>
```

Without any additional code, this single property adds the ability to easily delete tasks from the grid as you'll see a bit later.

After the `<ContentTemplate>` tag, you'll notice an `<asp:AsyncPostBackTrigger>`, which is used to associate the `SelectedIndexChanged` event of the main `DropDownList` with the `UpdatePanel` as shown here:

```
<asp:AsyncPostBackTrigger ControlID="DropDownList1" EventName=➡
"SelectedIndexChanged"/>
```

The second `UpdatePanel` in the page is for inserting a new task and contains a `DetailsView` control as opposed to a `GridView` inside the `<ContentTemplate>` tag.

```
<asp:UpdatePanel ID="UpdatePanel2" runat="server" UpdateMode="Conditional">
    <ContentTemplate>
        <asp:DetailsView ID="DetailsView1" runat="server"
```

```
                    AutoGenerateRows="False"
                    DataKeyNames="TaskId"
                    DataSourceID="ObjectDataSource1"
                    DefaultMode="Insert"
                    CssClass="detailsview"
                    GridLines="None">
        <Fields>
            <asp:BoundField DataField="TaskId" HeaderText="TaskId" InsertVisible=
                "False" ReadOnly="True"
               SortExpression="TaskId" />
            <asp:BoundField DataField="Name" HeaderText="Name" SortExpression="Name"
            />
            <asp:CheckBoxField DataField="Complete" HeaderText="Complete"
             SortExpression="Complete" />
            <asp:CommandField ShowInsertButton="True" />
        </Fields>
        </asp:DetailsView>
    </ContentTemplate>
    </asp:UpdatePanel>
```

If you noticed, the UpdateMode property of this UpdatePanel control is set to Conditional, meaning that it relies on external source to instigate an actual updated rendering such as a <Triggers> tag, which was defined in the previous UpdatePanel control. Note that these are two distinct mechanisms via which UpdatePanel implements updates. Other than that, it's very similar to the previous UpdatePanel control in structure, and the <asp:CommandField> tag only has the ShowInsertButton property defined because the user can only insert a task in this pane.

The other major portion of the markup for this page defines the ObjectDataSource control, which handles the data for this page. But before getting into discussions about the data side of this application, let's try to use the app and see it in action. Figure 6-6 shows the main page after the Completed status was selected in the drop-down control at the top of the page.

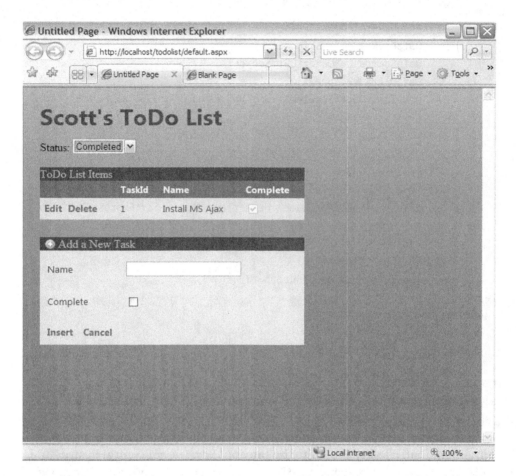

Figure 6-6. *Viewing completed tasks*

Toggling the status between Completed and Active changes the data of the GridView almost instantaneously without any page refresh. Now, let's add a new task called "Become an AJAX expert" and click Insert on the lower UpdatePanel of the page. You'll see the task being immediately added to the Active list as shown in Figure 6-7.

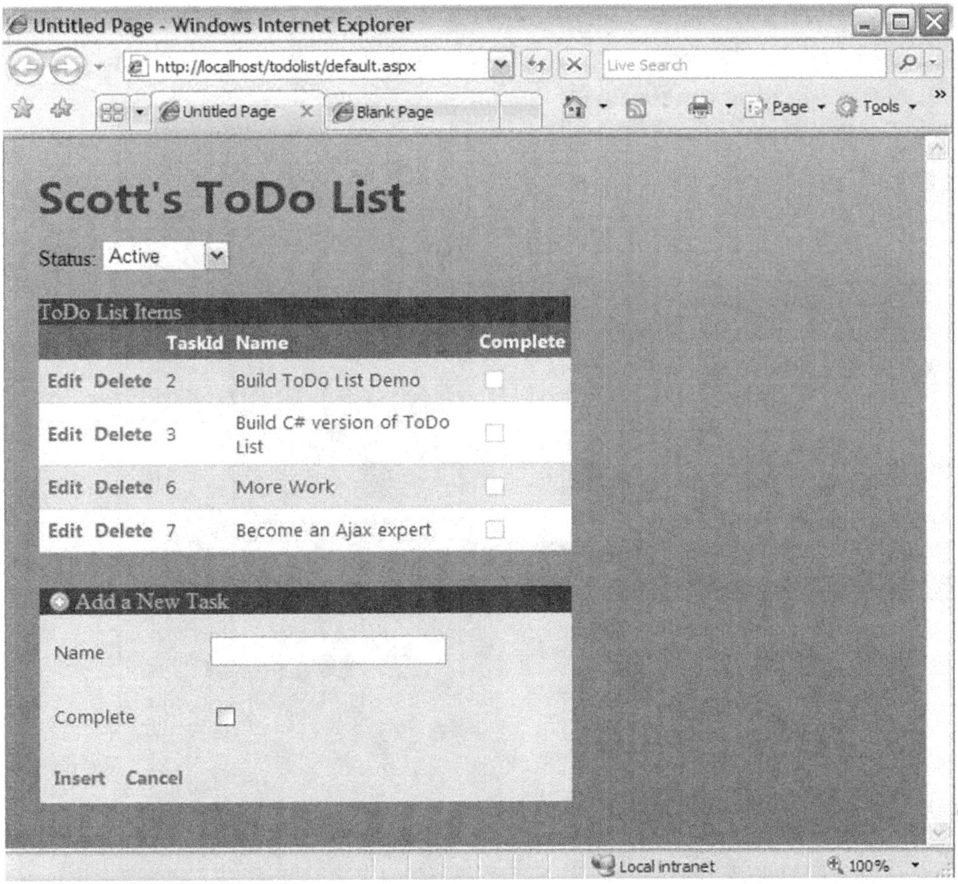

Figure 6-7. *Newly added task in the Active list*

As you can see, the task was added to the active list with the TaskId of 7. The TaskId is an identity field in the table that is simply incremented with each new addition. Now, if you were to mark the task completed by clicking the Edit link and then checking the Complete check box followed by the Update link, you would see the contents of the UpdateProgress control while the update is taking place. Figure 6-8 shows the update in progress.

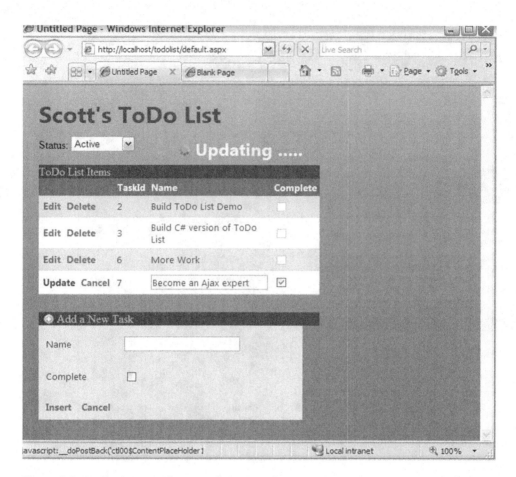

Figure 6-8. *Updating a task to mark it complete*

Upon updating the status change, you can switch to the *Completed* view by toggling the main drop-down box, and you'll see the recently created task marked as completed as shown in Figure 6-9. Also, you can now delete a task by simply clicking the Delete link.

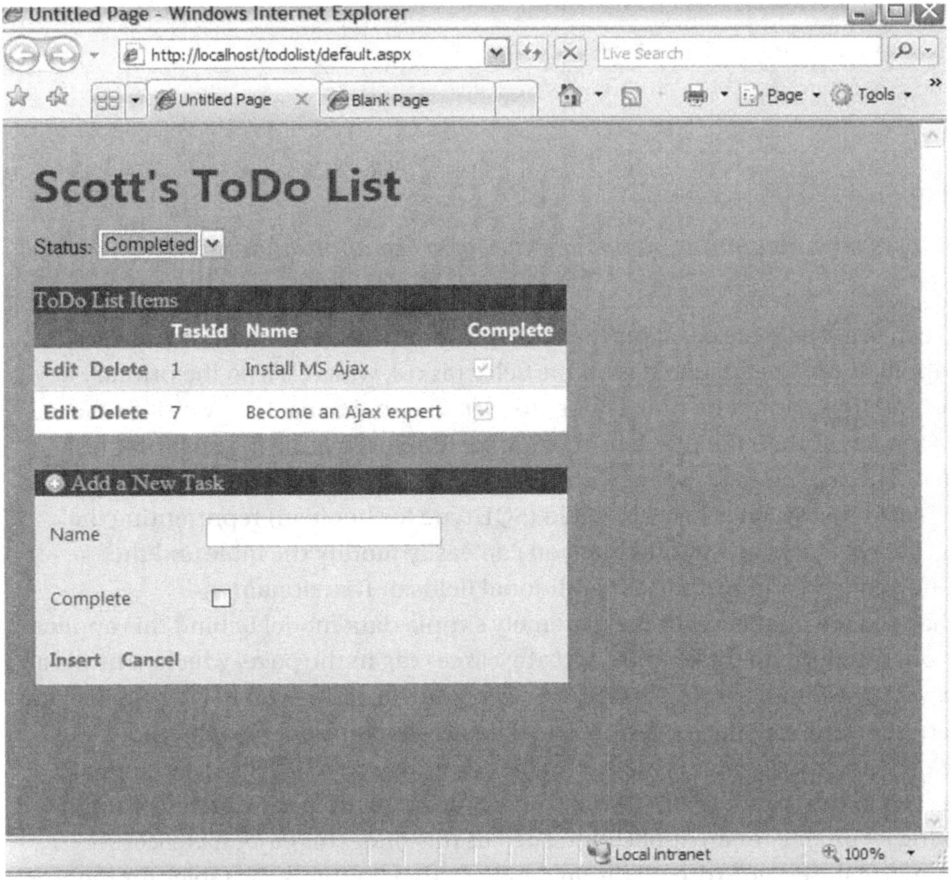

Figure 6-9. *The updated task is now in Completed status.*

Let's now turn our attention back to the code and look at the data side of this app. As mentioned earlier, a SQL 2005 Express data file is the data container for Scott's ToDo List application and resides in the *App_Data* folder of the site. You may have to manually add the ASP.NET user of your machine to this database before being able to access it. This database has only one table called Tasks with three fields as shown in Figure 6.10.

Tasks

	Column Name	Data Type	Allow Nulls
🔑	TaskId	int	☐
	Name	varchar(100)	☑
	Complete	bit	☑
			☐

Figure 6-10. *Tasks table containing all data for the ToDo List application*

As you can see, this table contains the bare minimum columns required to run a ToDo List application. The first field is an `int` field, `TaskId`, which is also the primary key of this table and thus cannot be null. It is set to `Identity` so that each new task gets a unique ID (one larger than the previous ID) that increments by one for each new task that is added. The second field is `Name` with `varchar(100)` as its type. The third and the final field is `Complete`, which is just a `bit` field (SQL type for boolean) representing the check box. Once again, keep in mind that you can easily modify the table and the corresponding code to add support for additional fields or functionality.

Now that you are familiar with the extremely simple data model behind this application, turn your attention to the `<asp:ObjectDataSource>` tag in the page, which controls all interaction with the database. An `ObjectDataSource` control allows you to create a declarative link between your web page controls and data access components that query and update data. The control contains methods that describe how to select, insert, update, and delete rows in the database. It's flexible and can work with many different components, making it suitable for an application such as this one. This `ObjectDataSource` control ties to a SQL Server Express Edition database that contains the tables for the tasks and items lists. Note that most of the code for this tag can usually be auto generated by Visual Studio because there are great design-time tools for configuring the `ObjectDataSource` control (see Figure 6.11). You can view that tool by right-clicking the `ObjectDataSource` control and selecting the Configure Data Source option.

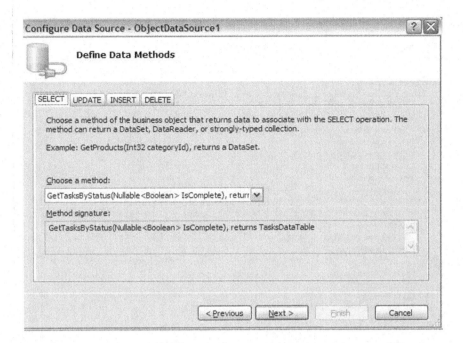

Figure 6-11. *Design-time tool for configuring the* ObjectDataSource *control*

This tool includes support for defining SELECT, INSERT, UPDATE, and DELETE operations on the selected data source. Each tab enables you to specify which method in the underlying Data Access Component (DAC) class to invoke to perform a data-access operation. For example, the SELECT tab here is linked to the GetTasksByStatus method in the DAC class. This particular method receives a boolean parameter to indicate whether you want to find the completed tasks or the active tasks. The ObjectDataSource control invokes this method automatically when it needs to get task data from the database; you'll see how it supplies the parameter (i.e., the IsComplete boolean parameter in this example) shortly.

You have probably also noticed that there is an *.xsd* file in the *App_Code* folder of this site. This also can be (and often is) generated with the help of the aforementioned design-time tool of the ObjectDataSource control. The actual SQL code for the various operations, such as SELECT and UPDATE, reside here. Part of this code is shown in Figure 6-12.

```
App_Code/TaskDataSet.xsd   App_Code/TaskDataSet.xsd                                    ▼ ✕
              <Tables>
                <TableAdapter BaseClass="System.ComponentModel.Component" DataAccessorMod
                  <MainSource>
                    <DbSource ConnectionRef="DatabaseConnectionString (Web.config)" DbObj
                      <DeleteCommand>
                        <DbCommand CommandType="Text" ModifiedByUser="False">
                          <CommandText>DELETE FROM [Tasks] WHERE (([TaskId] = @Original_T
                          <Parameters>
                            <Parameter AllowDbNull="False" AutogeneratedName="" DataSourc
                            </Parameter>
                          </Parameters>
                        </DbCommand>
                      </DeleteCommand>
                      <InsertCommand>
                        <DbCommand CommandType="Text" ModifiedByUser="False">
                          <CommandText>INSERT INTO [Tasks] ([Name], [Complete]) VALUES (@
                          <Parameters>
                            <Parameter AllowDbNull="True" AutogeneratedName="" DataSource
                            </Parameter>
                            <Parameter AllowDbNull="True" AutogeneratedName="" DataSource
                            </Parameter>
                          </Parameters>
                        </DbCommand>
                      </InsertCommand>
                      <SelectCommand>
                        <DbCommand CommandType="Text" ModifiedByUser="True">
                          <CommandText>SELECT      TaskId, Name, Complete
  FROM          Tasks
  WHERE         (Complete = @IsComplete)</CommandText>
                          <Parameters>
                            <Parameter AllowDbNull="True" AutogeneratedName="IsComplete"
```

Figure 6-12. *TaskDataSet.xsd containing the SQL code for the main operations*

Once again, you can enter most of the query information and/or other configuration data using a graphical interface by viewing the *TaskDataSet.xsd* file in design mode as shown in Figure 6-13.

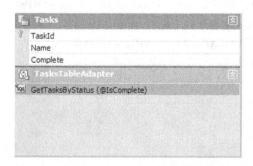

Figure 6-13. *TaskDataSet.xsd in design mode*

Whether done manually or by using this tool, the end result for the `ObjectDataSource` control is the script code generated in the *.aspx* page as you can see in the following code snippet:

```
<asp:ObjectDataSource ID="ObjectDataSource1" runat="server" DeleteMethod=
"Delete"  InsertMethod="Insert" OldValuesParameterFormatString="original_{0}"
    SelectMethod="GetTasksByStatus"
    TypeName="TaskDataSetTableAdapters.TasksTableAdapter" UpdateMethod="Update"
    OnUpdating="ObjectDataSource1_Updating">
    <DeleteParameters>
        <asp:Parameter Name="Original_TaskId" Type="Int32" />
    </DeleteParameters>
    <UpdateParameters>
        <asp:Parameter Name="Name" Type="String" />
        <asp:Parameter Name="Complete" Type="Boolean" />
        <asp:Parameter Name="Original_TaskId" Type="Int32" />
    </UpdateParameters>
    <SelectParameters>
        <asp:ControlParameter ControlID="DropDownList1" Name="IsComplete"
         PropertyName="SelectedValue" Type="Boolean" />
    </SelectParameters>
    <InsertParameters>
        <asp:Parameter Name="Name" Type="String" />
        <asp:Parameter Name="Complete" Type="Boolean" />
    </InsertParameters>
</asp:ObjectDataSource>
```

The parameters are clearly defined by their intended operations (e.g., `InsertParameters`, `UpdateParameters`, etc.). The SQL operation method name attributes are equally well defined with names such as `SelectMethod` and `UpdateMethod`. The `ObjectDataSource` is a great control for small web applications but may not always be so ideal for larger and more sophisticated apps that need logical and physical separation of the data tier that has complex data objects and a data access layer.

Summary

The ToDo List application is an excellent example of an ASP.NET application and how it can be enhanced with AJAX functionality using ASP.NET AJAX server controls. The server control set you saw in the previous chapter has been carefully designed and implemented to allow you to enhance existing applications as easily as possible and in a manner that involves touching your existing code as little as possible.

Additionally, for new applications, it involves reusing your existing skills in ASP.NET and lowers the learning curve drastically.

CHAPTER 7

■ ■ ■

Using the ASP.NET AJAX Control Toolkit (Part 1)

By now, you are quite familiar with the ASP.NET AJAX server controls and have seen many examples of their use. The first release version of ASP.NET AJAX also shipped with a set of controls packed under the ASP.NET AJAX Toolkit moniker. These are open source control extensions that have been created by Microsoft as well as the broader community. This package is readily available at http://ajax.asp.net along with documentation and instructional videos. You can also obtain the latest source code at CodePlex (http://codeplex.com), Microsoft's open source project depository. Either way, you have the option to download just the binaries or the full source code.

You will find the ASP.NET AJAX Control Toolkit extremely useful because it contains some very rich UI functionality ideal for AJAX-enabled Web 2.0 sites. And the best part is that these controls are just as easy as other server controls to use. You don't have to write any custom JavaScript to add effects to your page. The controls in this toolkit are also often referred to as *control extenders* because they rely on existing ASP.NET server controls and augment them with built-in client-side JavaScript code to provide impressive effects.

You can also easily create your own custom extensions because this toolkit also comes with Visual Studio templates to assist you. At the time of this writing, there are about 40 controls (there will most likely be even more controls due to community contributions by the time you read this), which we will cover in this and the next chapter. As you work through this chapter and the next, you'll learn more about the structure of these control extenders and how they complement the existing ASP.NET server controls. You will also see by example, going through most of the controls this toolkit offers and finding out how to use them in your applications. The examples in this chapter only cover the basics of this toolkit and, in some cases (such as the animation control), there is much functionality that is beyond the scope of this chapter.

Installing the ASP.NET AJAX Control Toolkit

The ASP.NET AJAX Control Toolkit is not a stand-alone entity and requires ASP.NET AJAX to be installed because it heavily relies on certain controls, such as ScriptManager, and libraries for its infrastructure. Also, at the time of this writing, unlike the ASP.NET AJAX installable *.Msi* package, the toolkit is simply shipped as a ZIP file containing the source code and therefore requires a little work before it's ready to use.

You can download the ASP.NET AJAX Toolkit at `http://ajax.asp.net/downloads`. After unzipping the files to a folder such as *AjaxToolKit*, you can add the controls to your Visual Studio 2005 toolbox. First create a new tab in the toolbox, and name it something similar to ASP.NET AJAX Control Toolkit. After that, right-click the new tab, and select Choose Items from the context menu. At that point, simply browse to the designated folder to which you had extracted the compressed files, and you'll find a DLL named *AjaxControlToolkit.dll* in a subfolder of the *Bin* folder. Selecting this file populates the controls in the new tab created in your toolbox as shown in Figure 7-1. You are now ready to use these controls in your ASP.NET AJAX-enabled web application.

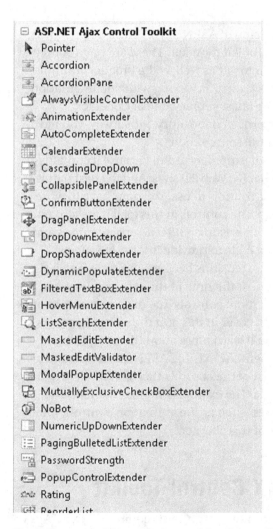

Figure 7-1. *ASP.NET AJAX Control Toolkit toolbox in Visual Studio 2005*

Alternatively, you can open and build the TemplateVSI project, which creates a new project template to Visual Studio 2005 for creating ASP.NET AJAX Control Toolkit web sites. Now let's talk about the individual controls in this toolkit and see how they can be used.

The `Accordion` and `AccordionPane` Controls

You have most certainly seen this UI element in one form or shape before. Outlook 97 was one of the first big applications to use this type of information organization in a UI. Basically, this control includes multiple panes where only one pane at a time is displayed with the rest of the panes visible in a collapsed manner showing only the headers (as the `Accordion` name suggests). The `Accordion` control, much like many others in the AJAX Control Toolkit, derives from the `WebControl` class. It is used in conjunction with `AccordionPane` controls, which represent the actual panes. These `AccordionPane` controls are held within the `<Pane>` tag of the `Accordion` control. You'll explore the `Accordion` control in more depth through an example but first some of its properties are listed in Table 7-1.

Table 7-1. *A Few of the* `Accordion` *Control Properties*

Property Name	Description
AutoSize	Controls the growth and collapse of the panes. There are three enumerations: `None`, `Limit`, and `Fill`. `None` allows the control to grow unrestricted, whereas `Limit` confines the maximum size of the accordion by the `Height` property. `Fill` always keeps the size of the overall accordion constant.
ContentCssClass	CSS class applied to the content.
DataMember	Field name of the data source (databinding).
DataSource	Data source used for binding (databinding).
DataSourceID	The ID of the data source control.
FramesPerSecond	Frames per second used for animation during the transition between panes.
FadeTransitions	Boolean value indicating whether or not to apply the fade effect during transition.
HeaderCssClass	CSS class applied to the header.
RequireOpenedPane	Boolean value indicating whether or not a pane is always open.
SelectedIndex	The initial pane that is visible in the accordion.
SuppressHeaderPostbacks	Blocks events from the controls in the header of the accordion.
TransitionDuration	The duration of the transition animation for when one pane is closing with another one opening (in milliseconds).

To see this control in action, you will create a simple page with an Accordion control that has three sections each containing four lines of text. First, you drag and drop an Accordion control on a new AJAX-enabled *.aspx* page. As always, remember to have already added the ScriptManager control to the page when working with any of the control extenders in the AJAX Control Toolkit if the created web application project or web site was not AJAX enabled. Set the FramesPerSecond property to 30 and the TransitionDuration to 100 ms. Within the Accordion control, first create a <Panes> tag followed by three <AccordionPane> tags with the corresponding text within the <Panes> tag as shown in the following code snippet:

```
<cc1:Accordion ID="Accordion1" runat="server"➥
    FadeTransitions="true" FramesPerSecond="30"
    TransitionDuration="100" AutoSize="None">
<Panes>
  <cc1:AccordionPane ID="AccordionPane1" runat="server">
  <Header>➥
    <div style="background-color:Black; color:White;
        font-weight:bold;"> Section 1</div>
  </Header>
  <Content>
    Item 1 <br>
    Item 2 <br>
    Item 3 <br>
    Item 4 <br>
  </Content>
  </cc1:AccordionPane>
  <cc1:AccordionPane ID="AccordionPane2" runat="server">
   ...
  </cc1:AccordionPane>
  <cc1:AccordionPane ID="AccordionPane3" runat="server">
   ...
  </cc1:AccordionPane>
 </Panes>
</cc1:Accordion>
```

As you can see, the AccordionPane tags are within the <Panes> tag of the Accordion control. The <Panes> tag is a container for one or more <AccordionPane> tags. When you run this page in the browser, you'll see the collapsible panels (see Figure 7-2). Additional styling code has been added to signify the three sections, which is why the three sections have different shades.

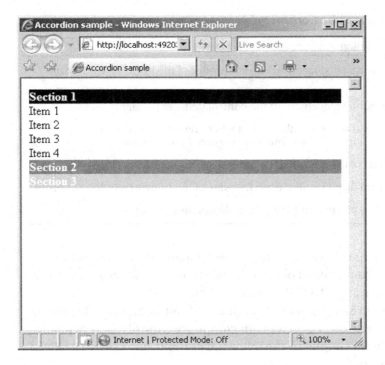

Figure 7-2. *The* Accordion *control with three headers*

If you view the browser output from this page, you'll notice that a collection of <div> tags with a lot of JavaScript is used to simulate the accordion effects on the client browser. This JavaScript was dynamically emitted by the Accordion control in conjunction with support from the ScriptManager.

AlwaysVisibleControlExtender **Control**

This self-descriptive control needs little introduction as its name more or less sums up its functionality. You can use this extender to pin down a control, or a composite control containing other controls, to a part of the page. AlwaysVisibleControlExtender then makes sure that the target control remains visible irrespective of window resizing or scrolls up and down. It also has properties to allow for specific displacement in the page as shown in Table 7-2.

Table 7-2. AlwaysVisibleControlExtender *Control Properties*

Property Name	Description
HorizontalOffset	Horizontal displacement from the edge of the browser window (in pixels)
HorizontalSide	Horizontal placement of the control (left, center, right)
ScrollEffectDuration	Duration of the scrolling effect when the target control is being repositioned to the same relative place in the screen
TargetControlID	The ID of the control to be pinned down and always visible
VerticalOffset	Vertical displacement from the edge of the browser window (in pixels)
VerticalSide	Vertical placement of the control (top, middle, bottom)

You have surely seen this type of control before in web pages. Often, the control is used as a quick customer feedback control or for an advertisement of some sort. It's usually best to use absolute positioning (DHTML) for control(s) used with this extender, otherwise, the AlwaysVisibleControlExtender may at times exhibit unexpected behavior. As mentioned earlier, you can use this extender with composite controls such as panels containing other controls, but for simplicity, the following example just uses an ASP.NET Label control as the target control:

```
<cc1:AlwaysVisibleControlExtender ID="AlwaysVisibleControlExtender1"➥
    runat="server"  TargetControlID="Label1" HorizontalOffset="2"➥
    ScrollEffectDuration="1" HorizontalSide="Right" VerticalSide="Top" >
</cc1:AlwaysVisibleControlExtender>
<asp:Label ID="Label1" runat="server" BackColor="#0000C0" Font-Bold="True"➥
    Font-Size="Larger" ForeColor="White" Height="28px" Text="ASP.NET ➥
    AJAX" Width="127px">
</asp:Label>
```

The preceding code snippet uses the AlwaysVisibleControlExtender to pin down a Label control to the top right of the screen. When scrolling down to see if there are pages of content below it, you would notice that this Label control is static in its top-right corner of the page position as shown in Figure 7-3.

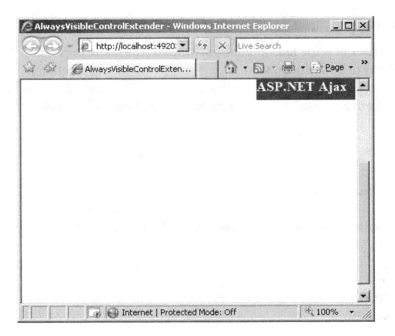

Figure 7-3. *Using the* AlwaysVisibleControlExtender *to pin down a label on the top-right part of the page*

The AnimationExtender Control

The Animation control is by far the most capable and feature-packed control in the ASP.NET Control Toolkit. It provides excellent support for a wide range of animation features in an AJAX-enabled ASP.NET page. This powerful control, which can also be considered a framework given its depth, enables rich animation in a declarative/XML fashion. Coverage of this control in its entirety is well outside the scope of this chapter, so we'll cover only a few animation types.

The AnimationExtender control attaches on to some of the key events of the target control within the page, such as Onclick, OnMouseOver, and so on. The target control is specified with the TargetControlID property. The AnimationExtender control also provides the means to manage the target control and/or other controls involved in animation via *actions*. Actions allow you to include/exclude certain controls from the animation, and restrict their behavior and visibility, among other things. To better understand the Animation control, let's now explore three of the many supported animation types: fade animation, length animation, and discrete animation.

Using Fade Animation

The first animation that we'll look at is the fade animation, which as the name implies, allows you to add fading effects to a control on your page. Two types of fading animation are supported: FadeIn and FadeOut. To illustrate fade animation, let's look at a small example that shows a control fading in and out. The target control is a Label control with blue text and yellow background.

```
<asp:Label ID="Label1" runat="server" BackColor="Yellow" Font-Size="X-
Large"
    ForeColor="Blue" Height="68px" Text="Fading In & Out" Width="165px">
</asp:Label>
<cc1:AnimationExtender ID="AnimationExtender1"  TargetControlID="Label1"➥
        runat="server">
            <Animations>
                <OnMouseOver>
                  <FadeOut Duration="1.5" Fps="30"  />
                </OnMouseOver>
                 <OnMouseOut>
                  <FadeIn Duration="1.5" Fps="30"  />
                </OnMouseOut>
            </Animations>
</cc1:AnimationExtender>
```

After running this page, you will see that when you hover the mouse over the Label control, it begins to fade as shown in Figure 7-4.

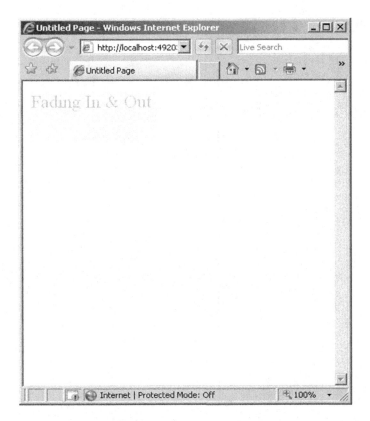

Figure 7-4. *Hovering over the* Label *control makes it start to fade out.*

Subsequently, when the mouse cursor is moved away from the Label (target control) control, it starts fading right back in (see Figure 7-5).

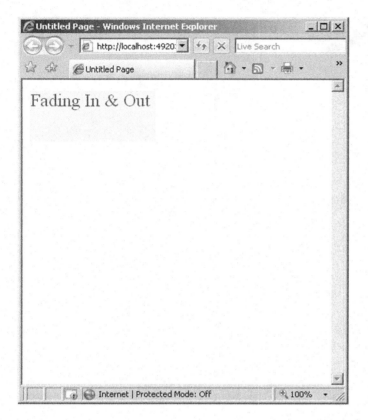

Figure 7-5. *Moving the mouse away from the target control makes it fade back in.*

In the code segment, the `<OnMouseOver>` event was defined along with the `<FadeOut>` tag. After that, the exact opposite was done with the `<OnMouseOut>` event over `<FadeIn>` tag. In both cases, the `Fps` (frames per second used for the animation) property was set to `30` and the `Duration` (duration of the animation) property set to `1.5` seconds.

Using Length Animation

The length animation changes the state of a property between a start value and an end value that you can specify. You can typically use this to animate the setting of the width or height of a control that uses them. Before you see a short example, look at the properties of the `<Length>` tag used in length animation as listed in Table 7-3.

Table 7-3. *Properties of the* <Length> *Tag*

Property Name	Description
AnimationTarget	The target control for the animation. This is the control that will be affected as the result of the animation.
Duration	Duration (in seconds) that it should take to play the animation.
EndValue	The end value of a specified range used for animation.
Fps	Frames per second used for the animation. Higher FPS values can yield smoother animation but are potentially slower.
Property	The property that will be the target for the animation (e.g., Height).
PropertyKey	Property key of the target control.
StartValue	Starting value of a specified range used for animation.
Unit	Actual unit of the property such as % or px (px by default).

Once again, to understand this animation type better, examine the following small code segment:

```
<asp:Image ID="Image1" runat="server" ImageUrl="sample.jpg" />
<cc1:AnimationExtender ID="AnimationExtender1" TargetControlID="Image1"➥
    runat="server">
    <Animations>
        <OnClick>
        <Sequence>
            <Length AnimationTarget="Image1" fps="30" property="style"
                propertyKey="width" startValue="800" endValue="200"
                duration="15"  unit="px" />
        </Sequence>
        </OnClick>
    </Animations>
</cc1:AnimationExtender>
```

Here you have an <asp:Image> control with an image being the target control of the animation. The actual animation is defined where a sequence is described within the <OnClick> event of the image control. The length animation itself is defined in a single line with the <Length> tag and its corresponding properties. This <Length> tag resides inside a <Sequence> tag, which basically defines an animation sequence segment. Start by setting the AnimationTarget property to the target control, Image1. The default unit on the length animation property is "px", so the animation will change the width property to a number of pixels.

You define this number by specifying startValue and endValue. In this case, set startValue to 800, and set endValue to 200. Because you want these values to apply to the width of the image, set the Property to "style" and the PropertyKey property to "width". Finally, set the duration to 15. This means the values 800px–200px will be sent to the width property of the image over a duration of 15 seconds. Changing the duration to a smaller value will mean that the image will grow to its final size more quickly, and changing it to a larger value will mean that it grows more slowly.

Additionally, the animation is smart enough to know that if startValue is greater than endValue, the animation will play backward, reducing the text from startValue to endValue, and in a case like this, the image will shrink in size over the specified duration.

You can see the length animation in action in Figure 7-6, Figure 7-7, and Figure 7-8. Figure 7-6 shows the application before the animation begins, Figure 7-7 shows the animation as it is in progress and the image is growing, and Figure 7-8 shows the completed animation.

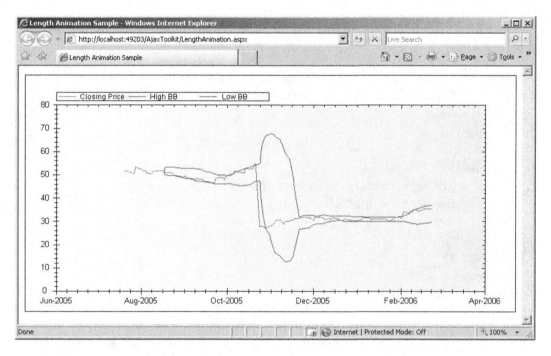

Figure 7-6. *Beginning the animation*

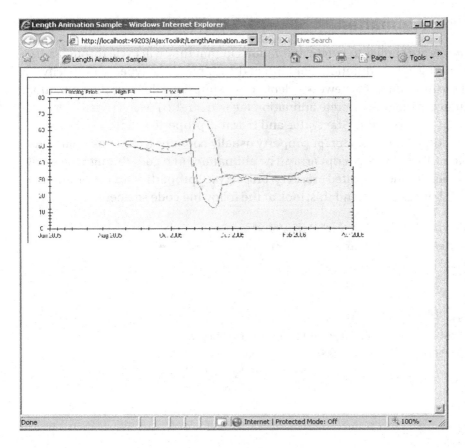

Figure 7-7. *The animation as it progresses*

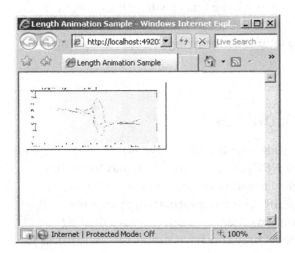

Figure 7-8. *The completed animation*

Using Discrete Animation

Discrete animations are similar to length animations in that they will cycle through a range of values during a fixed duration. For both of these animation types, you specify the values, and the Animation framework calculates the interim values for the animation. The main difference is that the discrete animation tag (<Discrete>) uses a parameter called ValuesScript as opposed to StartValue and EndValue properties that the <Length> tag uses for animation. The ValuesScript property usually contains a comma-separated list of values that resemble a JavaScript array. The animation then goes through these values and applies them to the indicated property/propertyKey properties for the duration of the animation. To better understand this, look at the following code segment:

```
<asp:Image ID="Image1" runat="server" ImageUrl="sample.jpg" />
<cc1:AnimationExtender ID="AnimationExtender1" runat="server"➡
      TargetControlID="Image1">
  <Animations>
   <OnClick>
      <Sequence>
          <Discrete fps="30" Duration="10" Property="style"
           PropertyKey="width"ValuesScript="['700', '600', '500',
                                              '400', '300']"/>
      </Sequence>
   </OnClick>
  </Animations>
</cc1:AnimationExtender>
```

In this case, five numbers will be the different width values for the image during the animation, but it can be any width value within the visible screen size. The end result will be very much like the previous example, but instead, the image will shrink in set time intervals (2 seconds in this case because there are five items in the animation with a total duration of 10 seconds) as opposed to the continuous shrinking you saw using length animation.

AutoCompleteExtender Control

The AutoCompleteExtender control is used to suggest text as a user types into a text box and therefore needs to be associated with an ASP.NET TextBox control. You may think that most browsers already have the AutoComplete feature turned on because you often see your name, phone number, and other frequently entered information appear with Auto-Complete as you type in the same information in other sites. But there is a distinct difference. The kind of AutoComplete that most browsers have support for only works for certain fields where it recognizes the field type and suggests text based on your previous entries.

The AutoCompleteExtender control allows you to define a web service as the data provider for suggestions. It can query this web service and serve the data back to the client in true AJAX form without the user noticing any postbacks. The properties of this control are listed in Table 7-4.

Table 7-4. *Attribute Properties of the* AutoCompleteExtender *Control*

Property Name	Description
CompletionInterval	Elapsed time between suggestions (in milliseconds)
CompletionSetCount	Number of suggestions to get from the web service
EnableCaching	Boolean value indicating whether or not client caching is enabled
MinimumPrefixLength	Minimum number of characters before suggestions are made
ServiceMethod	Name of the web method used to retrieve the suggestions
ServicePath	Path of the web service used to retrieve a list of suggestions
TargetControlID	Target TextBox control for which suggestions will be made

To see this control in action, you would need to create a web service in addition to the ASP.NET page in which the AutoCompleteExtender will reside. But first, let's start with the page itself. Create an ASP.NET TextBox control on the page, followed by the ScriptManager and the AutoCompleteExtender control. After that, specify the parameters as shown here:

```
<asp:TextBox ID="TextBox1" runat="server"></asp:TextBox>
<cc1:AutoCompleteExtender ID="AutoCompleteExtender1"
      ServicePath="AutoComplete.asmx" MinimumPrefixLength="3"
      ServiceMethod="GetSuggestedStrings" TargetControlID="TextBox1"
      CompletionInterval="10" CompletionSetCount="3"
      EnableCaching="true" runat="server">
</cc1:AutoCompleteExtender>
```

The code basically set the AutoCompleteExtender control up to suggest three pieces of text as long as at least three characters have been entered into the text box. The code also specified the ServicePath and set the ServiceMethod property to GetSuggestedStrings, so the control now expects this web method as its data source for the suggestions. The expected web service method must match the following signature:

```
public string[] GetSuggestedStrings(string prefixText, int count)
```

The name of the method of course can be different from what is listed here, but the parameters and return types much match that exactly, or the AutoCompleteExtender will not work properly. With that in mind, create a new .*asmx* page and use the following code to create the main web method:

```
[WebMethod]
    public string[] GetSuggestedStrings(string prefixText, int count)
    {
        //Default to 3 if the count is zero
        if (count == 0)
            count = 3;
        List<string> stringList = new List<string>(count);
        for (int i = 0; i < count; i++)
        {
            stringList.Add(prefixText + i.ToString());
        }
        return stringList.ToArray();
    }
```

This simple web method returns at least three suggested strings that, for the purposes of this sample, are simply the prefix with the index number of the list array. In most practical cases, you want to use more complex logic for suggestions of value, but you must be careful about performing very long and resource-intensive operations here. If you are planning to make database calls with intricate queries, make sure you have done ample testing to ensure its feasibility because the suggestions are useless if they take a long time to return. When you run this page in the browser, you can see the suggested terms three at a time as you type in the text box (see Figure 7-9).

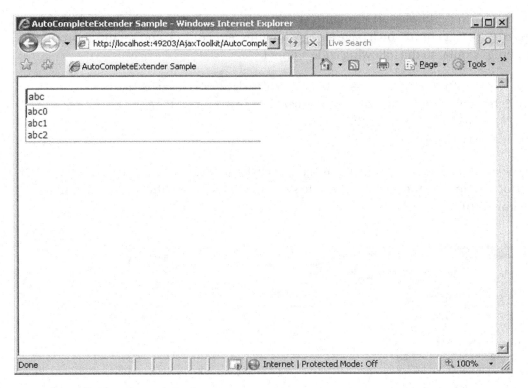

Figure 7-9. TextBox *in a page suggesting terms*

CalendarExtender **Control**

ASP.NET already provides a great and capable Calendar control. However, it requires post-backs for many of its operations. The CalendarExtender control in the ASP.NET AJAX Toolkit enables better overall user experience with its enhanced visual capabilities and postback-free performance. This control is used in conjunction with a TextBox control and has four properties as listed in Table 7-5.

Table 7-5. *Attribute Properties of the* CalendarExtender *Control*

Property Name	Description
CssClass	The CSS class used for the CalendarExtender control
Format	Format string for the date generated
PopupButtonID	The ID of the Button control used to show the CalendarExtender control (optional)
TargetControlID	ID of the corresponding Textbox to be used

This is a very simple and straightforward control to use. Simply drag and drop the CalendarExtender control on a page along with a TextBox control, and set the appropriate properties similar to the following code snippet:

```
<asp:TextBox ID="TextBox1" runat="server" Width="173px"></asp:TextBox>
<cc1:CalendarExtender ID="CalendarExtender1"  TargetControlID=
    "TextBox1" runat="server">
</cc1:CalendarExtender>
```

When you run this page, you only have to click the text box to see the Calendar control pop up with the result of the date selection entered into the text box as shown in Figure 7-10.

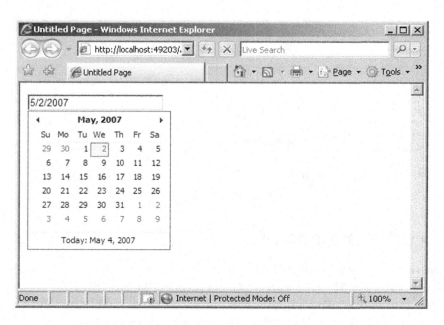

Figure 7-10. *ASP.NET AJAX* Calendar *control*

Notice the great transition from month to month when you click on the arrows of the Calendar control. Of course, you can further enhance the appearance of the control by using CSS and assigning it to the CssClass property of the Calendar control. Also, if you click on the month (on top of the control), the calendar switches to the year view (see Figure 7-11).

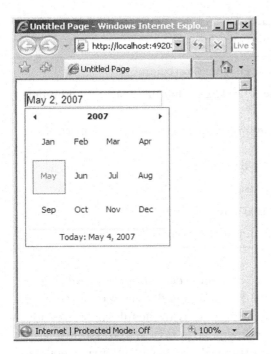

Figure 7-11. *ASP.NET AJAX* Calendar *control (Year view)*

Lastly, if you wanted to have a little button next to the text box as the agent to open the calendar, all you have to do is set the PopupButtonID property of this control to the ID of the button.

CascadingDropDown **Control**

The CascadingDropDown control is ideal for situations when you need to have multiple drop-downs on a web page with the value(s) of each drop-down control being dependent on the selection from the previous one. In fact, you've probably seen many sites taking advantage of this pattern. For instance, when you visit your printer or other computer accessories' manufacturer site in search of the appropriate driver(s), you are often presented with a list of drop-down controls in order to find the right model.

CascadingDropDown, much like the AutoCompleteExtender control, relies on web services to provide the necessary data. This allows for much flexibility in retrieving the data. You could, for instance, fetch the data from a database, serialized file, XML file, or some third-party source. Before jumping right into an example, Table 7-6 shows the properties of the CascadingDropDown control.

Table 7-6. *Properties of the* CascadingDropDown *Control*

Property Name	Description
Category	Category name of the CascadingDropDown control
LoadingText	Status text shown on the control itself while the data for the drop-down is being fetched
ParentControlID	The ID of the other drop-down control whose selection impacts this control
PromptText	Text shown if the drop-down is empty
ServiceMethod	Name of the web method used to retrieve the data
ServicePath	Path of the web service used to retrieve the data
TargetControlID	ID of the target corresponding DropDown control

You may have also seen cascading drop-downs on many car shopping/searching sites, in which you start with the manufacturer of the car and end up with the exact model of the car. We'll look one such example, which comes with the full-source version of the ASP.NET AJAX Control Toolkit available for download at http://ajax.asp.net.

After you load the solution into Visual Studio, under the SampleWebSite project, locate the *CascadingDropDown* folder with an *.aspx* and *.asmx* page. Set *CascadingDrop-Down.aspx* as the start page, and then run the application (Ctrl+F5). You are presented with three drop-down controls asking you to enter the make, model, and color of a car. With each selection, the values of the subsequent drop-down control change, and the complete specs of the car are displayed (see Figure 7-12).

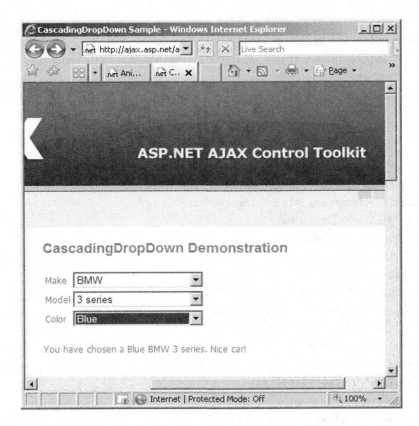

Figure 7-12. *Selecting a car using* CascadingDropDown *controls*

Let's examine the markup for this page:

```
<div class="demoheading">CascadingDropDown Demonstration</div>
    <table>
        <tr>
            <td>Make</td>
            <td><asp:DropDownList ID="DropDownList1" runat="server"
                    Width="170" />
            </td>
        </tr>
        <tr>
            <td>Model</td>
            <td><asp:DropDownList ID="DropDownList2" runat="server"
                    Width="170" />
            </td>
        </tr>
        <tr>
```

```
            <td>Color</td>
            <td><asp:DropDownList ID="DropDownList3" runat="server"
                Width="170" AutoPostBack="true" OnSelectedIndexChanged="DropDownList3
                SelectedIndexChanged" />
            </td>
        </tr>
      </table>
      <br />

<ajaxToolkit:CascadingDropDown ID="CascadingDropDown1" runat="server"
            TargetControlID="DropDownList1" Category="Make"
            PromptText="Please select a make"
            LoadingText="[Loading makes...]"
            ServicePath="CarsService.asmx"
            ServiceMethod="GetDropDownContents" />
<ajaxToolkit:CascadingDropDown ID="CascadingDropDown2" runat="server"
            TargetControlID="DropDownList2" Category="Model"
            PromptText="Please select a model"
            LoadingText="[Loading models...]"
            ServiceMethod="GetDropDownContentsPageMethod"
            ParentControlID="DropDownList1" />
<ajaxToolkit:CascadingDropDown ID="CascadingDropDown3" runat="server"
            TargetControlID="DropDownList3" Category="Color"
            PromptText="Please select a color" LoadingText="[Loading
            colors...]" ServicePath="CarsService.asmx"
            ServiceMethod="GetDropDownContents" ParentControlID="DropDownList2" />
    ...
</div>
```

The three ASP.NET drop-down controls at the beginning of this code segment make up the three selection points, which are followed by the three CascadingDropDown controls. Each of these extender controls specifies the corresponding drop-down (by using the TargetControlID property) as well as the ServicePath ServiceMethod properties, which will be used as a data source. And that's it! Beyond that, there is a little more code on the web form itself that displays text to the users in the appropriate event handlers. The rest of the work is done in a web service as listed here:

```
[WebMethod]
    public AjaxControlToolkit.CascadingDropDownNameValue[]
        GetDropDownContents(string knownCategoryValues, string category)
```

```
    {

StringDictionary knownCategoryValuesDictionary = AjaxControlToolkit.
CascadingDropDown.ParseKnownCategoryValuesString(knownCategoryValues);

 return AjaxControlToolkit.CascadingDropDown.
        QuerySimpleCascadingDropDownDocument(Document, Hierarchy,
        knownCategoryValuesDictionary, category);
    }
```

The main part of this web service is the GetDropDownContents web method shown in
the preceding code segment. This method first gets a dictionary object of known cate-
gory/value pairs and queries the data document for results. This data document is
nothing more than an XmlDocument object loaded with data from an XML file. In fact, if
you look in the *App_Data* folder in the solution, you'll see an XML file called
CarService.xml, which holds the data for the drop-down controls. Figure 7-13 shows the
contents of *CarService.xml*.

Figure 7-13. *CarService.xml*

CollapsiblePanelExtender **Control**

The CollapsiblePanelExtender control allows you to easily make visually appealing collapsing and expanding effects on panels used in your web page with minimal code. This extender is quite simple yet very flexible and is particularly useful in scenarios where you have large amounts of text, some of which does not need to be initially presented to the users. Also with many useful properties, its collapse/expansion behavior can be well customized. This includes the ability to have the panel auto expand or auto collapse depending on the mouse hovering. Table 7-7 lists some of the properties of the CollapsiblePanelExtender control.

Table 7-7. *Properties of the* CollapsiblePanelExtender *Control*

Property Name	Description
AutoCollapse	Boolean value indicating whether or not to collapse the panel when the mouse moves away from it
AutoExpand	Boolean value indicating whether or not to expand the panel when the mouse hovers over it
Collapsed	The initial state of the panel
CollapseControlID	ID of the control responsible for collapsing the panel
CollapsedImage	Path to the image file used by ImageControlID (when collapsed)
CollapsedSize	Collapsed size of the target control in pixels
CollapsedText	Displayed text when the panel is collapsed
ExpandControlID	ID of the control responsible for expanding the panel
ExpandDirection	Direction of expansion of the panel (horizontal/vertical)
ExpandedImage	Displayed image when the panel is expanded
ExpandedSize	Expanded size of the target control in pixels
ExpandedText	Displayed text when the panel is expanded
ImageControlID	ID of the image control serving as status indicator for the state of the panel (collapsed/expanded)
ScrollContents	Boolean value indicating whether or not to make the panel scrollable
TargetControlID	ID of the target panel control
TextLabelID	ID of the Label control containing the status text of the panel

Let's turn our attention again to the SampleWebSite project that ships the full source version of the ASP.NET AJAX Control Toolkit where the CollapsiblePanel is used extensively in nearly all pages. Specifically, in Solution Explorer, expand the CollapsiblePanel folder, and take a look at the *CollapsiblePanel.aspx* page where the focus is this extender.

For the purposes of this demo, let's focus only on the first panel on top of the page as shown in Figure 7-14.

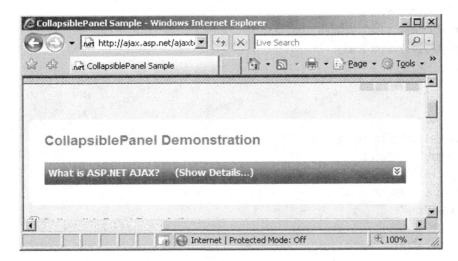

Figure 7-14. *Example of* CollapsiblePanel *(in collapsed mode)*

This portion of the page consists of two panels with a CollapsiblePanelExtender, and it displays some basic information about ASP.NET AJAX. There is a little image on the right side of the panel that collapses or expands the panel when clicked. Here's the .*aspx* markup for this portion of the page:

```
<asp:Panel ID="Panel2" runat="server" CssClass="collapsePanelHeader" Height="30px">
    <div style="padding:5px; cursor: pointer; vertical-align: middle;">
    <div style="float: left;">What is ASP.NET AJAX?</div>
    <div style="float: left; margin-left: 20px;">
      <asp:Label ID="Label1" runat="server">(Show
          Details...) ➡
      </asp:Label>
    </div>
    <div style="float: right; vertical-align: middle;">
        <asp:ImageButton ID="Image1" runat="server"
ImageUrl="~/images/expand_blue.jpg" AlternateText="
(Show Details...) " />
    </div>
    </div>
</asp:Panel>
<asp:Panel ID="Panel1" runat="server" CssClass="collapsePanel" Height="0">
<br />
```

```
<p>
    <asp:ImageButton ID="Image2" runat="server"

  ImageUrl="~/images/AJAX.gif"
  AlternateText="ASP.NET AJAX" ImageAlign="right" />
    <%= GetContentFillerText() %>
</p>
</asp:Panel>
    </div>

    <ajaxToolkit:CollapsiblePanelExtender ID="cpeDemo" runat="Server"
        TargetControlID="Panel1"
        ExpandControlID="Panel2"
        CollapseControlID="Panel2"
        Collapsed="True"
        TextLabelID="Label1"
        ExpandedText="(Hide Details...)"
        CollapsedText="(Show Details...)"
        ImageControlID="Image1"
        ExpandedImage="~/images/collapse_blue.jpg"
        CollapsedImage="~/images/expand_blue.jpg"
        SuppressPostBack="true" />
```

The first panel (Panel2) is essentially the header where the image to expand/collapse the panel is located. The majority of the actual content is in the second panel. In this case, the content is being generated by a method called GetContentFillerText. So notice that while the TargetContronID property of the CollapsiblePanelExtender is set to Panel1, the ExpandControlID and CollapseControlID properties are both set to Panel2, which is essentially the header panel. The small icon on the right portion of the header changes depending on the state of the panel as specified by the ExpandedImage and CollapsedImage properties. Figure 7-15 shows this panel in expanded mode.

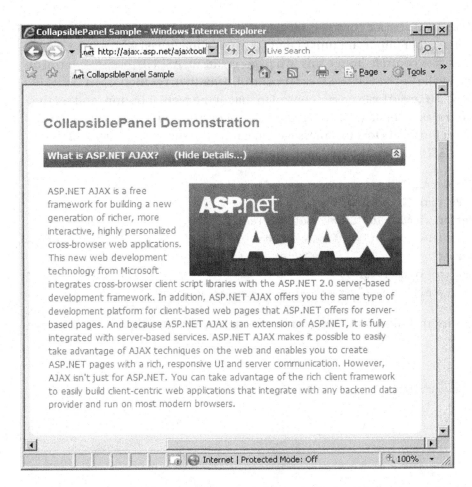

Figure 7-15. *Example of* CollapsiblePanel *(in expanded mode)*

ConfirmButtonExtender Control

The ConfirmButtonExtender control, as the name suggests, captures the Click event of a button and displays a confirmation dialog box. If the user clicks OK after that, the button will function as implemented; otherwise, the Click event will simply be ignored. This control is so simple that it only has two properties: TargetControlID and ConfirmText. As you probably have guessed already, TargetControlID contains the ID of the target button, and ConfirmText holds the text message that will be displayed in the dialog box requiring user confirmation.

The `ConfirmButtonExtender` control is ideal in situations where the user is about to submit an order or other important unit of data. It works equally well with ASP.NET `Button` and `LinkButton` controls. To see this in a page, create an ASP.NET `button` control on a page followed by the `ConfirmButtonExtender` control. After that, set the `TargetControlID` property of your `ConfirmButtonExtender` control to that of the regular button, and set the text for the `ConfirmText` property. Lastly, create a `Label` control, and in the event handler for the button, set the label's text to a message indicating the successful receipt of the `Click` event. Your ASPX markup should look similar to the following code snippet:

```
<asp:Button ID="Button1" runat="server" Text="Submit"➡
    OnClick="Button1_Click" />
<cc1:ConfirmButtonExtender ID="ConfirmButtonExtender1"
    TargetControlID="Button1" ConfirmText="Are you sure ?"
    runat="server">
</cc1:ConfirmButtonExtender><br />
 <asp:Label ID="Label1" runat="server" Width="360px"></asp:Label>
```

When you click this submit button, you will be presented with a dialog box as shown in Figure 7-16.

Figure 7-16. *Dialog box of the* `ConfirmButtonExtender` *control*

If you cancel the dialog box, the initial `Click` event of the Submit button will be discarded. However, if you click OK, the `Click` event is accepted, and the `click-event` method is invoked. The `click-event` method displays a confirmation message in the `Label` control as shown in Figure 7-17.

Figure 7-17. *Submit button accepted*

DragPanelExtender **Control**

The DragPanelExtender control is without a doubt one of the coolest controls in the
ASP.NET AJAX Control Toolkit; it allows the user to drag around a panel on a web page.
As you can imagine, manually implementing this type of functionality with client-side
JavaScript is a grand endeavor.

In addition to that, this control has only two properties and is extremely easy to use.
Other than the TargetControlID property, which you know all too well by now, the
DragPanelExtender control has another property called DragHandleID. This property specifies the subpanel with which the user can drag the overall panel. In the SampleWebSite
project that you saw earlier, there is also an excellent example for the DragPanelExtender
control found in *DragPanel.aspx*. Before looking at the code, run the page, and drag the
panel around to see how nicely it works (see Figure 7-18).

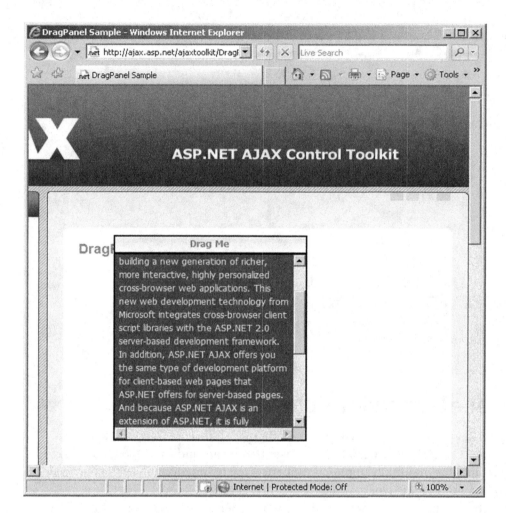

Figure 7-18. DragPanel *control in action*

When you view the ASPX markup for this page, you'll see a few nested Panel controls and the DragPanel control:

```
<asp:Panel ID="Panel6" runat="server" Width="250px" ➥
    style="z-index: 20;">
  <asp:Panel ID="Panel7" runat="server" Width="100%" Height="20px"
  BorderStyle="Solid" BorderWidth="2px" BorderColor="black">
    <div class="dragMe">Drag Me</div>
  </asp:Panel>
  <asp:Panel ID="Panel8" runat="server" Width="100%" Height="250px"
    Style="overflow: scroll;" BackColor="#0B3D73"
    ForeColor="whitesmoke" BorderWidth="2px" BorderColor="black"
```

```
      BorderStyle="Solid" >
  <div>
    <p>This panel will reset its position on a postback or
       page refresh.
    </p>
    <hr />
    <p><%= GetContentFillerText() %></p>
  </div>
  </asp:Panel>
</asp:Panel>
</div>
<div style="clear: both;"></div>

<ajaxToolkit:DragPanelExtender ID="DragPanelExtender1" runat="server"➥
TargetControlID="Panel6" DragHandleID="Panel7" />
```

The key thing to note is that Panel6 was set as the TargetControlID because it is the topmost panel and contains all the content, whereas Panel7 is being assigned to the DragHandleID because it makes up the top part of the panel and the ideal point for the user to drag.

DropDownExtender Control

The DropDownExtender control is another extender that can be used with a number of ASP.NET controls for enhanced visual rendering of a drop-down control. Despite its name, the DropDownExtender is not only limited to ASP.NET DropDownList controls and can, in fact, be used with many other controls such as a TextBox control or even a Label control. And much like the previous control, it has an additional property called DropDownControlID, which is the ID of the control containing the actual content for Drop-Down. Take a look at the sample that comes with the ASP.NET AJAX Control Toolkit and focus your attention on the *DropDown.aspx* page as shown in Figure 7-19.

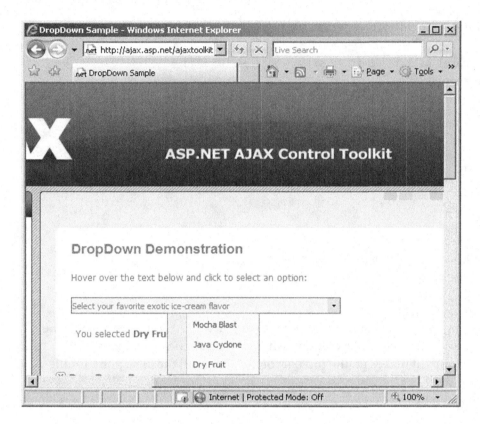

Figure 7-19. *Example of the* DropDown *extender control*

Viewing the code reveals a few LinkButton controls as options for the drop-down:

```
<asp:Label ID="TextLabel" runat="server" Text=" Select your favorite➥
    exotic ice-cream flavor" Style="display: block; width: 300px; ➥
    padding:2px; padding-right: 50px;font-family: Tahoma; font-size: ➥
    11px;" />
<asp:Panel ID="DropPanel" runat="server" CssClass="ContextMenuPanel"➥
    Style="display :none; visibility: hidden;">
  <asp:LinkButton runat="server" ID="Option1" Text=" Mocha Blast "➥

    CssClass="ContextMenuItem" OnClick="OnSelect" />
  <asp:LinkButton runat="server" ID="Option2" Text=" Java Cyclone "➥
    CssClass="ContextMenuItem" OnClick="OnSelect" />
  <asp:LinkButton runat="server" ID="Option3" Text=" Dry Fruit➥
    CssClass="ContextMenuItem" OnClick="OnSelect" />
</asp:Panel>
<ajaxToolkit:DropDownExtender runat="server" ID="DDE"
```

```
TargetControlID="TextLabel"
DropDownControlID="DropPanel" />
```

So, in this case, the drop-down list items are `LinkButton` controls held within a `Panel` control and not an ASP.NET `DropDownExtender` control—a perfect example of the flexibility of this extender control.

Summary

The ASP.NET AJAX Control Toolkit is a fantastic add-on to the UI control arsenal of any ASP.NET developer. It contains a number of very useful and attractive controls that can leverage the existing ASP.NET server controls and are relatively easy to implement. This toolkit is available with many samples as well as the full source code allowing developers to customize it even further.

In the next chapter, we'll continue to tour through the various other controls in the ASP.NET AJAX Control Toolkit.

■ ■ ■

CHAPTER 8

Using the ASP.NET AJAX Control Toolkit (Part 2)

In the previous chapter, you were introduced to some of the controls in the ASP.NET AJAX Control Toolkit. As mentioned before, this package is readily available on `http://ajax.asp.net` along with documentation and instructional videos. You can also obtain the latest source code on CodePlex.com, Microsoft's open source project depository. In this chapter, we will continue going over some of the remaining controls in the toolkit and how they can be applied in ASP.NET web applications.

DropShadow **and** RoundedCorners **Extenders**

The `DropShadow` and `RoundedCorners` extenders are similar in that they both offer visual enhancements to panels and other controls, particularly curved corners. First, let's examine the `DropShadow` extender.

DropShadow Extender

The `DropShadow` extender enables you to enhance the appearance of panels by adding curved corners and background shadow to the panel control. Typically, this is done by using images for the curved corners and CSS styling, among other things, for the shadow effect. The `DropShadow` extender allows you to easily add such effects to any panel with a number of parameters to tweak the appearance of these effects (see Table 8-1).

Table 8-1. DropShadow *Extender Properties*

Property Name	Description
BehaviorID	ID of the client-side Behavior (used for custom DOM behaviors) to be applied to the target panel
Opacity	Opacity of the DropShadow extender (ranges from 0 to 1 on a percentage point basis)
Radius	Radius of the curved corners of the panel bar (in pixels)
Rounded	Boolean value indicating whether or not to round the corners of the panel
TargetControlID	ID of the target control to which the DropShadow extender will be applied
TrackPosition	Boolean value indicating whether or not the drop shadow will track the position of the target panel control
Width	Width of the background shadow of the panel (in pixels)

To see a working example of the DropShadow extender, let's take a look at the example for the DropShadow extender provided in the documentation for the ASP.NET AJAX Control Toolkit shown in Figure 8-1.

Figure 8-1. *An example of the* DropShadow *extender applied to a panel*

Basically, you just need to set the TargetControlID property of the DropShadow extender to the ID of the panel control to which you want to add shadow and curved corners. After that, you can set the appropriate properties to get the desired visual appearance such as those used in this example. In the following code snippet, the panel is given 75% opacity with the radius of 6 pixels for the rounded corners and a width of 5 pixels for the background shadow.

```
<ajaxToolkit:DropShadowExtender ID="DropShadowExtender1" runat="server"
        BehaviorID="DropShadowBehavior1"
        TargetControlID="Panel1"
        Width="5"
        Rounded="true"
        Radius="6"
        Opacity=".75"
        TrackPosition="true" />
```

RoundedCorners Extender

As mentioned earlier, this is very similar to the DropShadow extender and has many of the same properties. However, the RoundedCorners extender is most ideal when you simply want to add rounded corners to your panel or another control. This extender provides a property, Corners, with which you can specify the corners of the target control you want rounded. This is convenient in cases where you want one half of your panel to merge into anther control and only want one side with rounded edges. The Corners property supports the following self-descriptive values: None, TopLeft, TopRight, BottomLeft, BottomRight, Top, Right, Bottom, Left, and All. You can apply this extender to your control with just three properties as shown here:

```
<ajaxToolkit:RoundedCornersExtender ID="RoundedCornersExtender1" runat="server"
        TargetControlID="Panel1"
        Radius="6"
        Corners="All" />
```

Also, much like the DropShadow extender, the Radius property is provided, and thus the radius of the rounded corners is adjustable. Figure 8-2 shows a great example of the RoundedCorners extender as included in the ASP.NET AJAX Toolkit samples.

Figure 8-2. RoundedCorners *extender applied to a panel with all corners rounded*

DynamicPopulate **Extender**

The DynamicPopulate extender can asynchronously populate an ASP.NET control (e.g.,
TextBox, Panel) with HTML content generated by a method either in the same page or an
external web service. Although using this extender can save much time and effort in
some cases, it's not ideal in all situations, such as when the back-end functionality is
abstracted away via various access layers. However, if you are using a web service directly
in your page and/or have some business logic in the same page, the DynamicPopulate
extender can be a good alternative to writing custom code to manually populate a control with data. Table 8-2 lists the properties of this extender.

Table 8-2. DynamicPopulate *Extender Properties*

Property Name	Description
CacheDynamicResults	Boolean value indicating whether or not values fetched from a web service should be cached for subsequent use. This is set to False by default.
ClearContentsDuringUpdate	Boolean value indicating whether or not the present content of the target control should be cleared during the update.
ContextKey	A key value used to pass context information to the data-providing method.
CustomScript	Name of custom script to be used instead of a web service method for fetching data.
PopulateTriggerControlID	ID of the control that will trigger the update on the target control (where the data will be displayed).
ServiceMethod	Name of the web method used to retrieve the data.
ServicePath	Path of the web service used to retrieve the data.
TargetControlID	Target control of the DynamicPopulate extender.
UpdatingCssClass	CSS class applied to the target control while its inner content is being updated.

The following code segment displays the current date onto a Panel control. It gets the date from a web service method called GetHtml as set in the ServiceMethod property:

```
<ajaxToolkit:DynamicPopulateExtender ID="dp" runat="server"
        TargetControlID="Panel1"
        ClearContentsDuringUpdate="true"
        PopulateTriggerControlID="Label1"
        ServiceMethod="GetHtml"
        UpdatingCssClass="dynamicPopulate_Updating" />
```

The GetHtml method is provided as a web service in the same page, *DynamicPopulate.aspx,* for the purposes of this example. Based on the contextKey parameter (which is passed to it via the various radio buttons for date formatting), this method returns the date with appropriate formatting after a 250ms delay. The following is the actual code of the GetHtml web method:

```
[System.Web.Services.WebMethod]
[System.Web.Script.Services.ScriptMethod]
    public static string GetHtml(string contextKey)
    {
```

```
    // A little pause to mimic a latent call
    System.Threading.Thread.Sleep(250);

    string value = (contextKey == "U") ?
        DateTime.UtcNow.ToString() :
        String.Format("{0:" + contextKey + "}", DateTime.Now);
    return String.Format("<span style='font-family:courier➥
                new;font-weight:bold;'>{0}</span>", value);
}
```

The contextKey variable contains the value of the selected radio button in this case and is used to determine the selected formatting for the date. You can see the *DynamicPopulate.aspx* page in Figure 8-3.

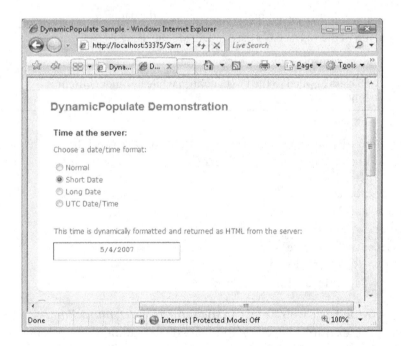

Figure 8-3. DynamicPopulate *extender displaying the date fetched from a web service*

One last point to notice about this example is that during the update of the panel bar, the circular animating GIF image informs the user of the update status of this control. This is accomplished by setting the UpdateCssClass property of the DynamicPopulate extender in which you can have animating GIFs along with any other desired CSS code to have the proper decoration for the target control during the update.

FilteredTextBox **Extender**

A common function of a client web application is data entry through forms. The typical workflow for forms is that the user enters information, and a special type of input tag called a submit button triggers an HTTP postback of the information to a server. The server then processes the submitted information and returns a response. If the data is invalid, the server returns a message indicating this, and the page developer writes a script that emphasizes this to the user. This transaction involves at least one round-trip to the server. You can also perform basic validation in JavaScript prior to form submission; this can be very effective and certainly faster for the user. However, performing validation using JavaScript can be a complex task, which ASP.NET AJAX control extenders lend themselves naturally to.

The FilteredTextBox extender is very useful in that it forces inline validation on a target control. You can apply a custom validator or one of the provided ones to a TextBox control and prevent the user from entering invalid input. This guarantees that invalid data cannot be passed on from the text box (excluding HTTP data injection or other advanced malicious attempts). The main properties of the FilteredTextBox extender are listed in Table 8-3.

Table 8-3. FilteredTextBox *Extender Properties*

Property Name	Description
FilterMode	If the selected FilterType property is Custom, FilterMode can be either InvalidChars or ValidChars.
FilterType	Type of filter to be applied to the target TextBox (can be more than one value separated by a comma). Potential values are Numbers, LowercaseLetters, UppercaseLetters, and Custom.
InvalidChars	When FilterType is set to Custom, and FilterMode is set to InvalidChars, this property can contain a list of all invalid characters.
TargetControlID	ID of the target TextBox control.
ValidChars	When FilterType is set to Custom, and FilterMode is set to ValidChars, this property can contain a list of all valid characters.

For instance, if you want an input box that only accepts digits, you can use this extender with the FilterType property set to Numbers to prevent the user from entering any other nonnumeric characters as shown in the following code snippet and in Figure 8-4.

```
You can only type numbers here:  <asp:TextBox ID="TextBox1" runat="server" />
    <ajaxToolkit:FilteredTextBoxExtender
        ID="FilteredTextBoxExtender1"
        runat="server"
        TargetControlID="TextBox1"
        FilterType="Numbers" />
```

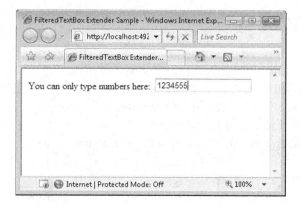

Figure 8-4. `FilteredTextBox` *extender displaying the date fetched from a web service*

FilterType has four types that can be used in conjunction with one another: Numbers, LowercaseLetters, UppercaseLetters, and Custom. If you choose Custom, then you must provide a list of characters to the ValidChars or InvalidChars property depending on the need. If you have a combination of values for FilterType, (e.g., Numbers, Custom), the FilterTextBox extender applies the more stringent inclusion or exclusion of character as specified on top of allowing only digits.

HoverMenu **Extender**

Hover menus can be a powerful UI tool in any application, and until recently, it took a good amount of effort to implement them in most web applications. The HoverMenu extender allows you to add a hover menu to any ASP.NET web control in your page. When the user hovers over the target control, another control (as specified in the properties) pops up along with any defined CSS styles applied. Table 8-4 lists the properties of the HoverMenu extender.

Table 8-4. HoverMenu *Extender Properties*

Property Name	Description
HoverCssClass	CSS class to be applied when the pop-up menu is displayed.
OffsetX/OffsetY	Offset values (in pixels) for the pop-up control when the mouse hovers over the target control from the top-left corner.
PopDelay	Amount of time elapsed (ms) until the pop-up control disappears after the initial hover.
PopupControlID	ID of the pop-up control that will be displayed when the mouse hovers over the target control.

Property Name	Description
PopupPosition	Position of the pop-up control relative to the target control (Left, Right, Center, Top, Bottom).
TargetControlID	ID of the target control over which the pop-up control will display when the mouse hovers over it.

Once again, the provided sample in the ASP.NET AJAX Toolkit, which can also be found online at http://ajax.asp.net, does a great job of illustrating the potential use of this extender. In this example, a hover menu, which is composed of a panel with two links, is used with a GridView control. When the user hovers over the items in the grid, a pop-up menu appears to the left of the item with two links: Edit and Delete. If Delete is clicked, the target row is deleted, and the user can choose to edit the data inline as specified in the EditTemplate of the GridView control. You can see this sample in Figure 8-5.

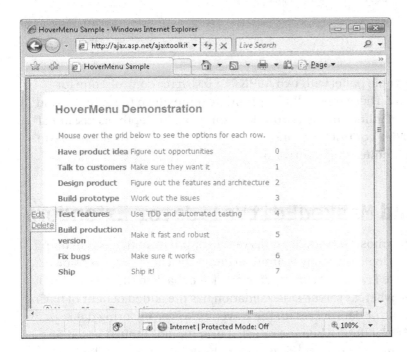

Figure 8-5. HoverMenu *extender used on a* GridView *control*

```
<ajaxToolkit:HoverMenuExtender ID="hme2" runat="server"
                               HoverCssClass="popupHover"
                               PopupControlID="PopupMenu"
                               PopupPosition="Left"
                               TargetControlID="Panel9"
                               PopDelay="25" />
```

In the preceding code segment, we have an instance of the HoverMenu extender with its PopupControlID property set to PopupMenu, which is the ID of the panel control containing the menu items displayed when a user hovers over an item in the GridView control. PopupPosition is set to Left, so a menu will appear to the left of the GridView row. With that in mind, take a look at the code for the PopupMenu panel.

```
<asp:Panel CssClass="popupMenu" ID="PopupMenu" runat="server">
   <div style="border:1px outset white;padding:2px;"➡
   <div>
     <asp:LinkButton ID="LinkButton1" runat="server" CommandName="Edit"➡
       Text="Edit" />➡
   </div>
   <div>
     <asp:LinkButton ID="LinkButton2" runat="server"➡
         CommandName="Delete" Text="Delete" />
   </div>
   </div>
</asp:Panel>
```

This is essentially a simple panel with two ASP.NET LinkButton controls, one for Delete and another for Edit. These trigger the appropriate template in the GridView and provide the functionality of inline editing or row deletion. More in-depth discussion of the templates in the GridView control is beyond the scope of this section but feel free to view the code because it is quite straightforward.

MaskedEdit **and** MaskedEditValidator **Extenders**

As mentioned earlier, often most web applications require input from the user in one form or another. Validation logic is usually written on either the client or server side or quite often both. Client-side JavaScript can provide quick feedback to the user without a round-trip to the server, whereas server-side validation has the added benefit of having access to business logic and/or data access on the server. However, ensuring data integrity and validation is best done when the range of user input is limited based on expected data. Much like the FilteredTextBox extender, the MaskedEdit extender is designed to enforce validation on user input by using a "mask" and thus restricting the range of possible values entered into a TextBox control. The MaskedEdit is a little more sophisticated than the FilteredTextBox extender in that it offers visual guidance to the user to enter the correct data and supports more complex rules through the use of MaskedEditValidator controls. Table 8-5 lists the properties of this extender.

Table 8-5. *Main Properties of the* MaskedEdit *Extender*

Property Name	Description
AcceptAMPM	Boolean value indicating whether or not to display AM/PM for time values.
AcceptNegative	Whether or not negative values are allowed in the target TextBox. Possible values are None, Left, and Right.
AutoComplete	Boolean value indicating whether or not to enable autocomplete for the target TextBox.
AutoCompleteValue	Default character set to use when autocomplete is enabled.
Century	Default century used when the date mask has only two digits for the year.
ClearMaskOnLostFocus	Boolean value indicating whether or not to clear the input mask when the target TextBox loses focus.
ClearTextOnInvalid	Boolean value indicating whether or not to clear the existing text in the target TextBox if the input has proven to be invalid.
ClipboardEnabled	Boolean value indicating whether or not to allow access to the clipboard for input into the target TextBox.
DisplayMoney	Whether or not the currency symbol is displayed in the target TextBox. Possible values are None, Left, and Right.
ErrorTooltipCssClass	CSS class applied to the tool tip error message.
ErrorTooltipEnabled	Boolean value indicating whether or not to display an error tool tip when the user hovers over an invalid entry in the target TextBox.
Filtered	Valid characters for mask type "C" (case-sensitive).
InputDirection	Input direction for the target TextBox. Possible values are LeftToRight and RightToLeft.
Mask	Actual mask to be applied (e.g., 00/00/0000).
MaskType	Type of the specified mask (None, Number, Date, DateTime, Time).
MessageValidatorTip	Message displayed in target TextBox when its value is being changed.
PromptChararacter	Prompt character used for unspecified mask characters.
UserDateFormat	Custom date format string for the target TextBox.
UserTimeFormat	Custom time format string for the target TextBox.
OnFocusCssClass	CSS class applied to the target TextBox when it receives focus.
OnFocusCssNegative	CSS class applied to the target TextBox when it receives focus with a negative value.
OnBlurCssNegative	CSS class applied to the target TextBox when it loses focus with a negative value.
OnInvalidCssClass	CSS class applied to the target TextBox when it contains an invalid entry.
CultureName	Name of the culture applied to the input mask.

The two important properties to note here are Mask and MaskType. MaskType simply specifies the type of the target validation mask, which can be None, Number, Date, DateTime, and Time. The Mask property contains the actual mask itself, which can be a combination of characters, digits, and/or separators, including wildcard characters. Suppose we take the TextBox from the earlier example and now ask the user to enter a nine-digit social security number (United States only) following the standard format DDD-DD-DDDD as shown in the following code snippet:

```
Please enter your SSN number:  <asp:TextBox ID="TextBox1" runat="server" />
        <ajaxToolkit:MaskedEditExtender ID="MaskedEditExtender1" runat="server"
                            TargetControlID="TextBox1"
                            MaskType= "Number"
                            Mask="999-99-9999"
                            ClearTextOnInvalid=true />
```

With that small code segment, the text box now has an input mask guiding the user through entering the data. The user can only type in nine numbers and nothing else. All other characters are completely ignored. The mask also helps the user by applying the appropriate formatting to the entered data. You can see this Figure 8-6.

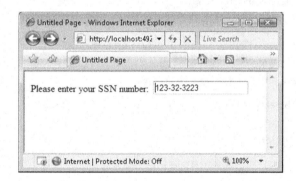

Figure 8-6. MaskedEdit *extender used for entering proper social security numbers*

You may have noticed that although the MaskedEdit control offers an excellent mechanism for restricting user input to the intended values, it lacks a way to further control the input data as well as a good notification mechanism for informing the user about missing or invalid data in the TextBox.

This is precisely where the MaskedEditValidator control comes in handy. This control was specifically designed to work alongside the MaskedEdit extender. The MaskedEditValidator control can be used to further validate the user input and display a custom message back to the user. The properties for this control are listed in Table 8-6.

Table 8-6. *Properties of the* MaskedEditValidator *Control*

Property Name	Description
AcceptAMPM	Boolean value indicating whether or not AM/PM is an acceptable entry in time fields.
ClientValidationFunction	Client-side JavaScript stated for client-side JavaScript validation.
ControlExtender	ID of the MaskedEditExtender extender attached to the TextBox.
ControlToValidate	ID of the target TextBox control to validate.
EmptyValueMessage	Error message displayed when the target TextBox is empty and has focus.
InitialValue	Initial value of the target TextBox control.
InvalidValueMessage	Error message displayed when the target TextBox has an invalid value and has focus.
IsValidEmpty	Boolean value indicating whether or not it is valid for the target TextBox to be empty.
MaximumValue	Maximum allowed input value.
MaximumValueMessage	Error message displayed when the value of target TextBox has exceeded the maximum allowed value and the TextBox still has focus.
MinimumValue	Minimum allowed input value.
MinimumValueMessage	Error message displayed when the value of target TextBox is less than the minimum allowed value and the TextBox still has focus.
TooltipMessage	Tool tip message displayed when the target TextBox is empty.
ValidationExpression	Regular expression used to validate the input. (This offers the greatest level of control and flexibility with the input.)

As you can see in the preceding table, the MaskedEditValidator control has a number of useful properties to allow you to enforce better data integrity and user experience for input controls in your form. You can even assign a regular expression to this extender for validation by using the ValidatonExpression property.

ModalPopup **Extender**

Modal pop-ups are commonly seen in desktop applications. This UI construct is often used in cases where user input (such as login or configuration information) is imperative for access to the main application. The other option, of course, is to have a regular HTML pop-up that is not modal; however, that defeats the whole purpose of the pop-up in that the user can easily bypass it en route to the target page. Due to the limitations of web technologies early on and the difficulty associated with creating modal pop-ups in recent years, few web applications implemented them. In many cases, users were directed to other pages, and upon successful entry of the required data, were then redirected back to the original page. Again, a perfect example of this scenario is a login page.

The ModalPopup extender is ideal when there is a need in web pages to display a pop-up in a modal fashion. The modal pop-up is triggered by an event on the target control, after which it blocks all user access to the underlying page until the user makes a selection in the modal pop-up. The pop-up itself is typically a Panel control, although it could be other controls as well. This control can be positioned anywhere on the page as stated by its X and Y properties. Table 8-7 lists the main properties of this extender.

Table 8-7. ModalPopup *Extender Properties*

Property Name	Description
BackgroundCssClass	CSS class to be applied to the background when the modal pop-up is displayed.
DropShadow	Boolean value indicating whether or not to display a drop shadow for the modal pop-up.
CancelControlID	ID of the Cancel button for the modal pop-up.
OkControlID	ID of the OK button for the modal pop-up.
OnCancelScript	Client JavaScript script to load when the modal pop-up is dismissed with the Cancel button.
OnOkScript	Client JavaScript script to load when the modal pop-up is dismissed with the OK button.
PopupControlID	ID of the control to display as a modal pop-up (often a Panel control).
PopupDragHandleControlID	ID of the control used as the drag handle for the modal pop-up.
TargetControlID	ID of the control that instigates the modal pop-up.
X	The initial X coordinate of the modal pop-up.
Y	The initial Y coordinate of the modal pop-up.

For a great example of the ModalPopup extender, turn to the sample web site provided with the ASP.NET AJAX Toolkit and view the file *ModalPopup.aspx*. When you click the Click here to change the paragraph style link, a modal pop-up menu appears offering a range of paragraph styling options to the user via several radio buttons. After the selection, the user can then click on the OK or Cancel button to gain back control of the page. You can see this in Figure 8-7.

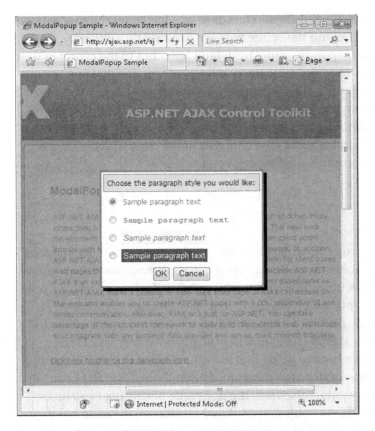

Figure 8-7. ModalPopup *extender used to block access to the main page*

Take a look at the following code segment, which was used to define the ModalPopup in this page:

```
<ajaxToolkit:ModalPopupExtender ID="ModalPopupExtender" runat="server"
        TargetControlID="LinkButton1"
        PopupControlID="Panel1"
        BackgroundCssClass="modalBackground"
        OkControlID="OkButton"
        OnOkScript="onOk()"
        CancelControlID="CancelButton"
        DropShadow="true"
        PopupDragHandleControlID="Panel3" />
```

As specified in the properties, the link button (LinkButton1) instigates the modal pop-up with Panel1 being the control behind the actual pop-up. Because no X and Y parameters have been defined, the pop-up panel by default launches in the center of the screen. Also the Panel3 control is used to define the header of the main panel as a section where the user can drag and drop the panel anywhere throughout the page. To best take advantage of this extender, CSS styling is highly recommended to provide the panel with proper UI decorations. The *ModalPopup.aspx* page also showcases an example where a modal pop-up is generated dynamically from the contents of the page with the help of some additional server-side and client-side JavaScript code.

NoBot Extender

In an effort to prevent crawlers, automated scripts, and/or other programs (also referred to as BOTS) from creating false accounts or getting access to sensitive information, many web sites started using CAPTCHA (Completely Automated Public Turing test to tell Computers and Humans Apart) controls, which are credited to the Carnegie Mellon University. CAPTCHAs are simply distorted images of encoded text that are displayed alongside a text box that the user is challenged to enter the encoded text into. Once again, this is done to ensure that a human being is at the other end of the terminal using the web application and not some automated program. Although the CAPTCHA controls can offer somewhat better security, they also have the downside of causing extra inconvenience for the users. Not only do they require additional input from the user, but they could be at times cumbersome to read. They are also not 100% bullet proof as more advanced crawlers use OCR technology to decipher the encoded text in them.

NoBot attempts to provide the same functionality as CAPTCHA controls without requiring the user to read and enter cryptic text. It's essentially invisible and works by setting a number of parameters designed to protect against the bots. One such measure is to request the browser to perform a simple JavaScript task, which can help ensure there is a browser at the other end. Figure 8-8 shows a sample page with login information using the NoBot extender without asking the user for any additional information.

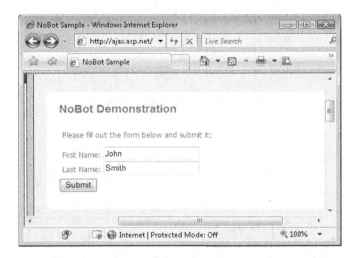

Figure 8-8. NoBot *control used invisibly in a login page*

The NoBot extender can also limit the number of requests per IP address as well as a delay between the request and postbacks. These are all attributes of a human user accessing the web application through a browser. Table 8-8 lists the main properties of the NoBot control.

Table 8-8. NoBot *Control Properties*

Property Name	Description
CutoffMaximumInstances	Maximum number of postbacks allowed by a single IP address within the allowed timeframe
CutoffWindowSeconds	Cutoff window (in seconds) for previous postbacks from an IP address
OnGenerateChallengeAndResponse	An event used to implement custom challenge/response logic
ResponseMinimumDelaySeconds	Minimum number of seconds required for a postback

To use the NoBot extender in your page, you can start with a couple of TextBox controls for user input signifying a typical form and an instance of the NoBot extender. In the following code segment, a method name is assigned to the OnGenerateChallengeAndResponse property.

```
<ajaxToolkit:NoBot ID="NoBot1" runat="server" OnGenerateChallengeAndResponse= ➥
"CustomChallengeResponse" />
```

Let's briefly look at the CustomChallengeResponse method in the page's code behind:

```
protected void CustomChallengeResponse(object sender, NoBotEventArgs e)
{
    Panel p = new Panel();
    p.ID = "NoBotSamplePanel";
    Random rand = new Random();
    p.Width = rand.Next(300);
    p.Height = rand.Next(200);
    p.Style.Add(HtmlTextWriterStyle.Visibility, "hidden");
    p.Style.Add(HtmlTextWriterStyle.Position, "absolute");
    ((NoBot) sender).Controls.Add(p);
    e.ChallengeScript = string.Format("var e = document.getElementById('{0}');
    e.offsetWidth * e.offsetHeight;", p.ClientID);
    e.RequiredResponse = (p.Width.Value * p.Height.Value).ToString();
}
```

This method is trying to access and set properties accessible only in the browser DOM in an effort to verify the validity of the user and the absence of bots. One key object here is NoBotEventArgs, which contains the event arguments of the underlying object. BOTS/automated agents are usually incapable of processing JavaScript and also obviously do not have the browser DOM that browsers have, therefore failing the brief but often effective test code of the CustomChallengeResponse method.

One last note to mention about the NoBot extender is that it must be tested thoroughly before deployed. It may not be consistent in all environments and may falsely identify legitimate users as bots. When developing the Challenge/Response mechanism or tweaking the other parameters, be sure to test your application for the legitimacy of the NoBot extender results.

NumericUpDown **Extender**

The NumericUpDown extender can easily be associated with any TextBox control and allow the user to increment or decrement numeric values as well as custom-defined values defined at design time, such as the days in a week or months in a year. By default, this extender assumes +/- 1 for incrementing or decrementing values, but you can define a set of values for the NumericUpDown extender to enumerate through by using the RefValues property. Table 8-9 lists the main properties of this extender.

Table 8-9. NumericUpDown *Extender Properties*

Property Name	Description
Minimum	Smallest value allowed in the target TextBox
Maximum	Largest value allowed in the target TextBox
RefValues	List of semicolon-delimited values used as a data source for the NumericUpDown extender
ServiceDownMethod	Web method used to retrieve the next value when the Down button is clicked
ServiceUpMethod	Web method used to retrieve the next value when the Up button is clicked
ServiceDownPath	Path of the web service used to retrieve the next value when the Down button is clicked
ServiceUpPath	Path of the web service used to retrieve the next value when the Up button is clicked
Step	Numeric steps used for incrementing/decrementing values (default is 1)
Tag	Custom parameter to be passed to the web service for the data
TargetButtonDownID	ID of the down Button control
TargetButtonUpID	ID of the up Button control
TargetControlID	ID of the target TextBox control
Width	Width of the target TextBox combined with the Up/Down buttons

The ASP.NET AJAX Control Toolkit reference application mentioned before has four great examples showcasing the various types of increment/decrement values that can be implemented with this extender. The first one is very simple because it just increments/decrements a number between 1 and 7:

```
<ajaxToolkit:NumericUpDownExtender ID="NumericUpDownExtender1" runat="server"
                TargetControlID="TextBox1"
                Width="120"
                RefValues=""
                ServiceDownMethod=""
                ServiceUpMethod=""
                TargetButtonDownID=""
                TargetButtonUpID=""
                Minimum = "1"
                Maximum = "7" />
```

Basically, in this code segment, this extender was associated with a TextBox control, and the Minimum and Maximum properties were set with the lower and upper bound of the permissible values for the text box. The next sample is similar except that it defines a set of values for months for the NumericUpDown control to iterate through instead of the default +/-1 increment/decrement behavior:

```
<ajaxToolkit:NumericUpDownExtender ID="NumericUpDownExtender2" runat="server"
                TargetControlID="TextBox2"
                Width="120" RefValues="January;February; March;April;May;June;
                July;August;September;October;November;December"
                ServiceDownMethod=""
                ServiceUpMethod=""
                TargetButtonDownID=""
                TargetButtonUpID="" />
```

Not much notable here other than the 12 months listed in the RefValues property. However, when the RefValues property is used, Minimum and Maximum values are empty. The next example gets its data from a web service that just picks a random integer between 0 and 1000, either higher or lower than the existing value in the text box:

```
<ajaxToolkit:NumericUpDownExtender ID="NumericUpDownExtender3" runat="server"
                TargetControlID="TextBox3"
                Tag=""
                Width="120"
                ServiceUpPath="NumericUpDown.asmx"
                ServiceDownPath="NumericUpDown.asmx"
                ServiceUpMethod="NextValue"
                ServiceDownMethod="PrevValue"
                RefValues=""
                TargetButtonDownID=""
                TargetButtonUpID="" />
```

Because the NumericUpDown extender allows you to specify different web services for the increment and decrement functionality, there are also different properties in which to state them. ServiceUpPath and ServiceDownPath each define the necessary web services, whereas the ServiceUpMethod and ServiceDownMethod define the desired web method for providing the data for incrementing or decrementing the value of the target TextBox. Here is an example of using the NumericUpDownExtender with images for Up and Down buttons:

```
<ajaxToolkit:NumericUpDownExtender ID="NumericUpDownExtender4" runat="server"
                TargetControlID="TextBox4"
                Width="80"
                TargetButtonDownID="img1"
```

```
TargetButtonUpID="img2"
RefValues=""
ServiceDownMethod=""
ServiceUpMethod="" />
```

Lastly, the preceding code segment demonstrates how to have image buttons replace the plain up and down arrows for incrementing or decrementing the value inside the `TextBox`. You can use the `TargetButtonDownID` and `TargetButtonUpID` properties to specify desired images to replace the standard buttons, but keep in mind that there are no references to image files but rather ASP.NET `ImageButton` controls. Figure 8-9 shows the *NumericUpDown.aspx* file containing all four samples.

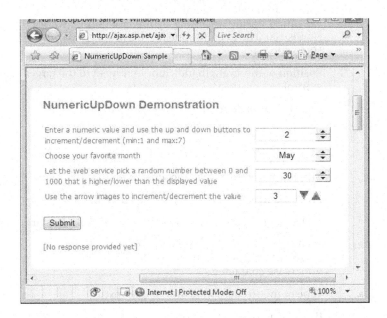

Figure 8-9. *Four samples of using the* `NumericUpDown` *extender for incrementing/decrementing values*

PasswordStrength **Extender**

At times, security is of particular concern in your web application, and you may need to consider enforcing a password policy, most commonly in a login page. Although it's possible to do so today with existing validation controls and/or custom code, it can be somewhat tedious to enforce a password policy along with responsive user feedback without postbacks. The `PasswordStrength` extender is associated with a `TextBox` control and is highly configurable as to what constitutes a strong or weak password. Before looking at an example, let's view the properties of the `PasswordStrength` extender as shown in Table 8-10.

Table 8-10. `PasswordStrength` *Extender Properties*

Property Name	Description
BarBorderCssClass	CSS class used for the border of the bar.
BarIndicatorCssClass	CSS class used for the bar indicator.
CalculationWeightings	Calculation weightings for determining the strength of the password. This semicolon-delimited list must contain four values (length weighting, numeric weighting, casing weighting, symbol weighting) whose sum is 100. The default value for this property is 50;15;15;20.
DisplayPosition	Position of the strength indicator in respect to the target control.
HelpHandleCssClass	CSS class applied to the password help handle.
HelpHandlePosition	Position of the help handle element.
MinimumNumericCharacters	Minimum number of numeric characters.
MinimumSymbolCharacters	Minimum number of symbol characters.
PreferredPasswordLength	Preferred length for ideal password strength.
PrefixText	Prefix text to be displayed before the strength indicator.
RequiresUpperAndLowerCaseCharacters	Boolean value indicating whether or not to force the password to include a mixture of lowercase and uppercase characters.
StrengthIndicatorType	Type of the strength indicator (bar or text).
TargetControlID	ID of the target `TextBox` control.
TextCssClass	CSS class applied to the text used for the strength indicator.
TextStrengthDescriptions	List of semicolon-delimited values used to display the strength indicator (can range from 2 to 10 values).
TextStrengthDescriptionStyles	List of semicolon-delimited style classes applied to the descriptions. This could be used to apply different styles to each of the indicator descriptions.

Suppose you need to recommend the user to create a password of at least ten characters without regard to case sensitivity. You can use the `PasswordStrength` extender to provide instant feedback to the user about the strength of the password as it is being typed in. Consider the following markup:

```
<asp:TextBox ID="TextBox1" Width="150" runat="server" autocomplete="off" /><br />
    <asp:Label ID="TextBox1_HelpLabel" runat="server" /><br /><br />
    <ajaxToolkit:PasswordStrength ID="PasswordStrength1"
        runat="server" TargetControlID="TextBox1"
        DisplayPosition="RightSide"
        StrengthIndicatorType="Text"
        PreferredPasswordLength="10"
        PrefixText="Strength:"
        HelpStatusLabelID="TextBox1_HelpLabel"
        TextStrengthDescriptions="Very Poor;Weak;Average;➡
        Strong;Excellent"
        TextStrengthDescriptionStyles= "TextIndicator_TextBox1➡
        Strength1;TextIndicator_TextBox1_Strength2; ➡
        TextIndicator_TextBox1_Strength3;  TextIndicator_TextBox1➡
        Strength4;  TextIndicator_TextBox1_Strength5"
        MinimumNumericCharacters="0"
        MinimumSymbolCharacters="0"
        RequiresUpperAndLowerCaseCharacters="false" />
```

Here a TextBox control and a Label control are used to notify the user of the password's strength level as typed. Because this message is being delivered to this Label control, you can decorate it with a CSS class, skin, or other styling code. The TextStrengthDescriptions property contains a semicolon-delimited list of messages to be displayed to the user as the password goes through the range of predefined strengths (from very poor to excellent). This property is complemented by the PreferredPasswordLength, which specifies the ideal length for the password and what is considered to be excellent strength. TextStrengthDescriptionStyles is used to add styling to the strength description presented to the user. Here you could set background colors for the description so that a weak password can have a red background in the message and an excellent password can have a green background or something to that effect. See Figure 8-10 to see the preceding code in the browser.

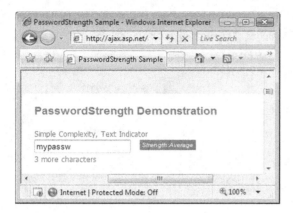

Figure 8-10. PasswordStrength *extender used to recommend a password policy to the user*

While typing in the password, the user will be able to see the number of characters remaining to achieve the excellent strength level desired for the password. The user will also notice the strength description to the right of the password TextBox change as the characters are typed.

PopupControl **Extender**

The PopupControl extender allows you to easily enhance an existing control, such as a TextBox, in your page with richer content that is hosted inside another control (most often a Panel control). An important point to note here is that because most often this richer content contains interactive element(s), using an UpdatePanel is highly recommend to handle postback issues and make a responsive AJAX-style user experience. Table 8-11 displays the main properties of the PopupControl extender.

Table 8-11. PopupControl *Extender Properties*

Property Name	Description
CommitProperty	Additional property settings applied after the pop-up is loaded
CommitScript	Additional script to be executed after the pop-up is loaded
OffsetX/OffsetY	Offset values (in pixels) for the pop-up control from the initial position
PopupControlID	ID of the pop-up control that will be displayed when triggered
Position	Initial position of the pop-up in respect to the target control (Left, Right, Top, Bottom, Center)
TargetControlID	The target control over which the pop-up will display

Figure 8-11 shows a sample page containing two controls with the PopupControl extender. The first control displays a Calendar control as a pop-up when the TextBox is clicked. Clicking the second TextBox control displays a list of radio buttons.

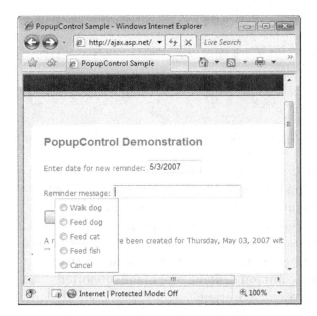

Figure 8-11. *An example of the* PopupControl *extender*

The following segment is the code behind the second TextBox displayed in that sample page shown in Figure 8-11. There is an empty TextBox control along with a Panel control that contains a RadioButtonList control with a few options. There is also an UpdatePanel defined for AJAX-style user interaction when the user makes a selection.

```
<asp:TextBox ID="MessageTextBox" runat="server" Width="200" autocomplete="off" />
<br /><br />
        <asp:Panel ID="Panel2" runat="server" CssClass="popupControl">
            <div style="border: 1px outset white; width: 100px">
                <asp:UpdatePanel runat="server" ID="up2">
                    <ContentTemplate>
                        <asp:RadioButtonList ID="RadioButtonList1" runat="server"➥
                        AutoPostBack="true"   OnSelectedIndexChanged=
                        "RadioButtonList1_SelectedIndexChanged">
                            <asp:ListItem Text="Walk dog" />
                            <asp:ListItem Text="Feed dog" />
                            <asp:ListItem Text="Feed cat" />
                            <asp:ListItem Text="Feed fish" />
```

```
                         <asp:ListItem Text="Cancel" Value="" />
                    </asp:RadioButtonList>
                </ContentTemplate>
            </asp:UpdatePanel>
        </div>
    </asp:Panel>
    <ajaxToolkit:PopupControlExtender ID="PopupControlExtender2" runat="server"
        TargetControlID="MessageTextBox"
        PopupControlID="Panel2"
        CommitProperty="value"
        Position="Bottom"
        CommitScript="e.value += ' - do not forget!';" />
```

The RadioButtonList1_SelectedIndexChanged method commits the selected value from the radio button lists to the underlying TextBox control. Other than that, the only other piece worth noting here is the addition of the PopupControl extender with the MessageTextBox control set as its TargetControlID. The CommitScript property just displays additional text along with the selected value from the RadioButtonList control. And that's all! It's that easy to use the PopupControl extender and associate extra content with a TextBox or other HTML controls. The main common denominator in the supported controls is that they must all have support for a Click event.

Rating **Control**

From various product reviews to feedback forms, songs, and other media online, some variation of a Rating control is becoming common on web sites these days. These controls are often a simple manifestation of a finite rating system and usually appear as a number of stars or other small icons. The Rating control provides very similar functionality by displaying a star-based Rating control with a minimum amount of code while allowing the flexibility of applying various styles to get the intended appearance. Table 8-12 lists the main properties of this control.

Table 8-12. Rating *Extender Properties*

Property Name	Description
AutoPostBack	Boolean value indicating whether or not postback is initiated with a change in ratings
CurrentRating	Current value of the Rating control
EmptyStarCssClass	CSS class used for empty (unselected) stars
FilledStarCssClass	CSS class used for filled (selected) stars

Property Name	Description
MaxRating	Highest possible rating
OnChanged	Client-side event fired when the rating is changed
RatingAlign	General alignment of the starts (Vertical/Horizontal)
RatingDirection	Flow direction of the stars (LeftToRight, TopToBottom, etc.)
ReadOnly	Boolean value indicating whether or not the rating can be changed
StarCssClass	CSS class for stars in the Rating control
Tag	Parameter used to store auxiliary information to pass to the client
WaitingStarCssClass	CSS class for stars in waiting mode

Here we have an example of a Rating control with a max number of five stars (as stated by the MaxRating property) with the initial rating set to two stars:

```
<ajaxToolkit:Rating ID="ThaiRating" runat="server"
                CurrentRating="2"
                MaxRating="5"
                StarCssClass="ratingStar"
                WaitingStarCssClass="savedRatingStar"
                FilledStarCssClass="filledRatingStar"
                EmptyStarCssClass="emptyRatingStar"
                OnChanged="ThaiRating_Changed"
                style="float: left;" />
```

The ThaiRating_Changed method simulates logic processing by 400ms of pause and notifies the user as shown in the following code:

```
protected void ThaiRating_Changed(object sender, RatingEventArgs e)
{
    Thread.Sleep(400);
    e.CallbackResult = "Update done. Value = " + e.Value + " Tag = " + e.Tag;
}
```

Beyond these basic properties, there are a few CSS-based properties such as WaitingStarCssClass and FilledStarCssClass for various states of the control. In addition to that, in the OnChanged event, you can specify a server-side method to implement more custom logic. You can see an example running on the browser in Figure 8-12.

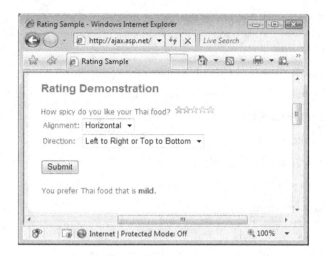

Figure 8-12. Rating *control being used to rate a person's preference of Thai food*

ReorderList **Control**

In many web and desktop applications, you may have come across the typical UI construct for reordering lists that is often done by two buttons (one for Up and another for Down) placed adjacent to the list itself. The user then has to select the item in the list and click the appropriate button enough times to get the selected item in the designated position. It would certainly be nice to be able to simply drag the item to the desired position instead.

You have already seen how easy it is with the controls provided in the ASP.NET AJAX tools to implement dragging and dropping of various controls on the page without page postbacks. However, trying to implement a data-bound list still requires much work to allow the user to reorganize the order of the items. The ReorderList control can be applied to a bound object source, such as an ObjectDataSource control, and provide AJAX-style reordering of the bound items. Table 8-13 lists the main properties of this control.

Table 8-13. ReorderList *Control Properties*

Property Name	Description
AllowReorder	Boolean value indicating whether or not to enable reordering of the items in the list.
DataKeyField	Field containing the primary key for the underlying data source.
DataMember	Designated field name in the specified data source.
DataSource	Data source object used to bind to the ReorderList control.

Property Name	Description
DataSourceID	ID of the data source control used to retrieve the list of items.
DragHandleAlignment	Layout alignment of the drag handle (Top, Bottom, Left, Right).
DragHandleTemplate	Markup/template used for the drag handle. (All template-based properties derive from ITemplate and can be assigned programmatically as well.)
EditItemTemplate	Markup/template used when the item is edited.
EmptyListTemplate	Markup/template used when there are no underlying items.
InsertItemTemplate	Markup/template used to create a new item.
ItemInsertLocation	Location of the newly created item (Beginning or End of the list).
ItemTemplate	Markup/template used to display an individual item.
PostbackOnReorder	Boolean value indicating whether or not to initiate a postback each time an item is reordered.
ReorderTemplate	Markup/template used to show where the new item is being relocated to.
SortOrderField	The key field in the data used to sort the list.
ShowInsertItem	Boolean value indicating whether or not to display the inserted item.

As you can see by the properties, the ReorderList control not only provides the ability to manually drag and drop items to different positions in the list, it can also perform auto sorting if specified in its property, SortOrderField. One classic case for a list of items that can really take advantage of a reordering functionality is a to-do list of tasks including items whose priority can change. The following markup is used to create a to-do list that allows the user to reorganize its members by simply moving the individual items throughout the list.

```
<ajaxToolkit:ReorderList ID="ReorderList1" runat="server"
                PostBackOnReorder="false"
                DataSourceID="ObjectDataSource1"
                CallbackCssStyle="callbackStyle"
                DragHandleAlignment="Left"
                ItemInsertLocation="Beginning"
                DataKeyField="ItemID"
                SortOrderField="Priority">
                <ItemTemplate>
                        . . .
                </ItemTemplate>
                <EditItemTemplate>

. . .
```

```
</EditItemTemplate>
                        <ReorderTemplate>
                <asp:Panel ID="Panel2" runat="server"
CssClass="reorderCue" />
                        </ReorderTemplate>
                        <DragHandleTemplate>
                            <div class="dragHandle"></div>
                        </DragHandleTemplate>
                        <InsertItemTemplate>
                        . . .
                        </InsertItemTemplate>
                    </ajaxToolkit:ReorderList>
```

As you can see, much like many other data-bound controls such as the ASP.NET
DataList control, the ReorderList control has support for ItemTemplate, EditItemplate, and
more, thereby allowing ample flexibility when dealing with lists of data. Figure 8-13
shows the sample page containing this code in the browser.

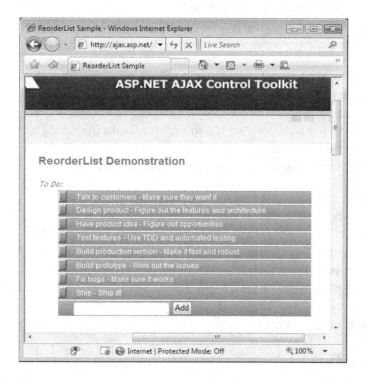

Figure 8-13. *Items of a to-do list can be rearranged using the* ReorderList *control.*

ResizableControl **Extender**

The ResizableConrol extender is a very well implemented and easy to use extender that can be associated with just about any HTML or ASP.NET UI control. The user can then drag the lower-right corner of the control and resize it much like any window. Before looking at how this extender can be used, take a look at its main properties in Table 8-14.

Table 8-14. ResizableControl *Extender Properties*

Property Name	Description
HandleCssClass	CSS class to be applied to the resize handle of the target control
HandleOffsetX/HandleOffsetY	X and Y offsets applied to the resize handle in respect to the target control
MaximumHeight	Maximum allowed height of the target control
MaximumWidth	Maximum allowed width of the target control
MinimumHeight	Minimum allowed height of the target control
MinimumWidth	Minimum allowed width of the target control
OnClientResize	The client event triggered right after the target control has been resized
OnClientResizing	The client event triggered when while resizing the target control
OnClientResizeBegin	The client event triggered when resizing starts to occur on the target control
ResizableCssClass	The CSS class to be applied to the target control during resize
TargetControlID	ID of the target control associated with the ResizableControl extender

So, let's say we have a panel in our web page that contains an image as shown here:

```
<asp:Panel ID="PanelImage" runat="server" CssClass="frameImage">
<asp:Image ID="Image1" runat="server" ImageUrl="~/images/AJAX.gif"
AlternateText="ASP.NET AJAX" style="width:100%; height:100%;" />
</asp:Panel>
```

We could enable this panel to be resizable by using the ResizableControl extender and assigning its TargetControlID property to the ID of this Panel:

```
<ajaxToolkit:ResizableControlExtender ID="ResizableControlExtender1" runat="server"
        TargetControlID="PanelImage"
        ResizableCssClass="resizingImage"
        HandleCssClass="handleImage"
```

```
                    MinimumWidth="50"
                    MinimumHeight="26"
                    MaximumWidth="250"
                    MaximumHeight="170"
                    HandleOffsetX="3"
                    HandleOffsetY="3"
                    OnClientResize="OnClientResizeImage" />
```

The OnClientResize property defines a client-side function to execute when the image is resized, which in this case has the following script:

```
function OnClientResizeImage(sender, eventArgs) {
 $get("lastResize").innerHTML = "Last image resize at " + (new Date()).toString();
}
```

You can use HandleCssClass, HandleOffsetX, and HandleOffsetY to better control the appearance of the lower-right drag handle for the resize. Furthermore, using the OnClientResize property, you can write a client-side JavaScript function to modify the behavior of the extender as the underlying control is being resized. The user can use the small hand icon on the bottom-right corner of the image to resize the image (see Figure 8-14).

Figure 8-14. *An image on a page can be resized by the user using the* ResizableControl *extender.*

Slider **Extender**

Slider controls are excellent UI constructs for allowing the user to change the settings for some entity. This is essentially a graphical way of changing an underlying number value. And as if you couldn't have guessed by now, the Slider extender provides an easy way to implement a slider-type control in your web pages by extending a TextBox control. By default, the range of numbers for this extender is from 0 to 100, but that can certainly be changed using the Minimum and Maximum properties. Some of the main properties of the Slider extender are listed in Table 8-15.

Table 8-15. Slider *Extender Properties*

Property Name	Description
BoundControlID	ID of the Label and TextBox control that displays the value of the Slider control
Decimals	Decimal points used for the value of the slider handle
EnableHandleAnimation	Boolean value indicating whether or not the slider handle will have animation (sliding/gliding effect)
HandleCssClass	CSS class used for the Slider control's handle
HandleImageUrl	URL of the image used for the Slider control's handle
Length	Length of the Slider control expressed as Width/Height
Minimum	Minimum value of the Slider control
Maximum	Maximum value of the Slider control
RailCssClass	Boolean value indicating whether or not to fire the Change event after a left mouse click
Steps	Number of discrete values in the range of the Slider control
Steps	Tool tip text displayed when the user hovers the mouse over the slider handle
TargetControlID	ID of the target TextBox control
TooltipText	Current value of the Slider control

To start using the Slider extender, you just need a couple of TextBox controls: one to be extended by the Slider extender and another to display the current value of the slider. Beyond that you just need the Slider extender itself.

```
<table>
  <tr>
    <td style="width:140px;border:solid 1px #808080">
      <asp:TextBox ID="Slider1" runat="server" style="right:0px"➥
```

```
                Text="0" />
        </td>
        <td style="width:15px"></td>
        <td style="width:auto">
          <asp:TextBox ID="Slider1BoundControl" runat="server"➥
              Width="30" />
          </td>
    </tr>
  </table>
          <ajaxToolkit:SliderExtender ID="SliderExtender1" runat="server"
          TargetControlID="Slider1"
          BoundControlID="Slider1BoundControl"
          Orientation="Horizontal"
          EnableHandleAnimation="true"
          TooltipText="Slider: value {0}. Please slide to change value." />
```

In this case, we have chosen Horizontal for the Orientation property of the Slider extender as opposed to Vertical. In this particular example, the EnableHandleAnimation property is set to True, thus providing smoother slides as the user changes the values. You can also use the ToolTipText property to display a message to the users when they hover over the target TextBox control. Figure 8-15 shows the Slider extender in action.

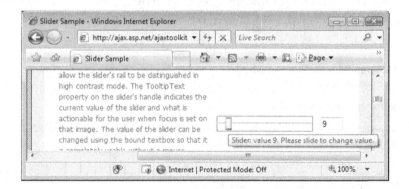

Figure 8-15. *A simple* Slider *extender*

SlideShow **Extender**

Once rare, you don't have to look far on the Internet to find a plethora of sites with slide show elements in them. In addition to large photo-sharing sites, many smaller sites now allow their users to create custom slide shows. With the ASP.NET AJAX SlideShow extender, you too could easily add a simple slide show to your site. This extender uses a web service to get a list of images through which it will iterate. In addition to the configurable delay time between the image transitions, you can also have custom Play, Pause, and Stop buttons for manual control of the slide show. Table 8-16 lists the main properties of the SlideShow extender.

Table 8-16. SlideShow *Extender Properties*

Property Name	Description
AutoPlay	Boolean value indicating whether or not the SlideShow control should automatically start upon launch
ContextKey	A user-defined context key to be used when fetching the list of images from the web service
ImageDescriptionLabelID	ID of the Label control displaying the current image's description.
ImageTitleLabelID	ID of the Label control displaying the current image's title
Loop	Boolean value indicating whether or not the slide show should automatically loop through the list of images
NextButtonID	ID of the ASP.NET Button control for the Next button
PlayButtonID	ID of the ASP.NET Button control for the Play button
PlayButtonText	Text displayed in the Play button to play the slide show
PlayInterval	Slide show interval between image transitions (in milliseconds)
PreviousButtonID	ID of the ASP.NET Button control for the Previous button
SlideShowServiceMethod	Name of the web method used for fetching the images
SlideShowServicePath	Path of the web service used to fetch the images from
StopButtonText	Text displayed in the Play button to stop the slide show
UseContextKey	Boolean value indicating whether or not ContextKey should be used

Now that you've seen the properties of the SlideShow extender, let's see what it would take to actually implement it. Consider the following code snippet used to create a simple slide show with three buttons for manual control on top of the automatic time delay between each image's transition:

```
<asp:Image ID="Image1" runat="server"
           Height="300"
           Style="border: 1px solid black;width:auto"
           ImageUrl="~/SlideShow/images/Blue hills.jpg"
           AlternateText="Blue Hills image" />
<asp:Label runat="server" ID="imageDescription" CssClass= ➥
      "slideDescription" />➥
<br /><br />
```

```
<asp:Button runat="Server" ID="prevButton" Text="Prev" ➥
          Font-Size="Larger" />
<asp:Button runat="Server" ID="playButton" Text="Play" ➥
          Font-Size="Larger" />
<asp:Button runat="Server" ID="nextButton" Text="Next" ➥
          Font-Size="Larger" />

<ajaxToolkit:SlideShowExtender ID="slideshowextend1" runat="server"
              TargetControlID="Image1"
              SlideShowServiceMethod="GetSlides"
              AutoPlay="true"
              ImageTitleLabelID="imageTitle"
              ImageDescriptionLabelID="imageDescription"
              NextButtonID="nextButton"
              PlayButtonText="Play"
              StopButtonText="Stop"
              PreviousButtonID="prevButton"
              PlayButtonID="playButton"
              Loop="true" />
```

The TargetControlID of this extender is set to an ASP.NET Image control, which starts off the slide show with the initial image. The AutoPlay and Loop properties set to True start the slide show immediately and instruct it to loop through the images (as provided by the web service) again and again. Basically, other than the various ButtonID properties used to specify the Play, Stop, and Previous buttons, the only other noteworthy point here is the SlideshowSeviceMethod, which is set to GetSlides, the web method that will feed the extender with a list of images to display as shown here:

```
public static AjaxControlToolkit.Slide[] GetSlides()
{
    return new AjaxControlToolkit.Slide[] {
    new AjaxControlToolkit.Slide("images/Blue hills.jpg", "Blue Hills", "Go Blue"),
        new AjaxControlToolkit.Slide("images/Sunset.jpg", "Sunset", "Setting sun"),
        new AjaxControlToolkit.Slide("images/Winter.jpg", "Winter", "Wintery..."),
        new AjaxControlToolkit.Slide("images/Water lilies.jpg", "Water lillies",
         "Lillies in the water"), new AjaxControlToolkit.Slide(
         "images/VerticalPicture.jpg"  , "Sedona", "Portrait style picture");
    }
```

Figure 8-16 shows the SlideShow extender in the browser.

Figure 8-16. *A slide show with three control buttons using the* SlideShow *extender*

TabContainer **and** TabPanel **Control**

Tabs are fundamental and useful UI elements that are becoming increasingly popular in web applications. The highly extensible duo controls TabContainer and TabPanel provide for a highly functional and AJAX-style tab support in your web application. The TabContainer control is a host control that can contain one or more TabPanel controls. These tabs can be customizable because just about any HTML markup can exist in the Content-Template or HeaderTemplate sections of the TabPanel control. Tables 8-17 and 8-18 list the properties of the TabContainer and TabPanel controls, respectively.

Table 8-17. *Main Properties of the* TabContainer *Control*

Property Name	Description
ActiveTabChanged	The server-side event triggered when the user switches to another tab.
ActiveTabIndex	Index of the selected tab.
CssClass	CSS class used to decorate the Tab control with custom settings. You can define the header, outer, inner, and body of the tab as well as other behavior settings such as when a tab becomes active.
Height	Height of the individual tab body.
OnClientActiveTabChanged	The client-side event triggered when the user switches to another tab.
ScrollBars	Display mode for scrollbars in the body of the tabs. The possible values are None, Horizontal, Vertical, Both, and Auto.

Table 8-18. *Main Properties of the* TabPanel *Control*

Property Name	Description
Enabled	Boolean value indicating whether or not the tab is enabled
HeaderText	Title text of the tab
OnClientClick	The client-side event triggered when the tab is clicked

Let's change our focus once more to the sample pages included with the ASP.NET AJAX Toolkit under *Tabs.aspx*. Here we find a TabContainer control with three TabPanels. For the sake of brevity, the details of the ContentTemplates with the TabPanel controls has been removed in the following code snippet:

```
<ajaxToolkit:TabContainer runat="server" ID="Tabs" Height="138px"➡
    OnClientActiveTabChanged="ActiveTabChanged" ActiveTabIndex="0"➡
    Width="402px">

<ajaxToolkit:TabPanel runat="server" ID="Panel1" HeaderText="Signature and Bio">
    <ContentTemplate>
        <asp:UpdatePanel ID="updatePanel1" runat="server">
            <ContentTemplate>
                . . .
```

```
            </ContentTemplate>
        </asp:UpdatePanel>
    </ContentTemplate>
</ajaxToolkit:TabPanel>

<ajaxToolkit:TabPanel runat="server" ID="Panel3" HeaderText="Email" >
    <ContentTemplate>

        . . .
    </ContentTemplate>
</ajaxToolkit:TabPanel>

<ajaxToolkit:TabPanel runat="server" ID="Panel2" OnClientClick=➥
            "PanelClick" HeaderText="Controls">
    <ContentTemplate>

        . . .
    </ContentTemplate>
 </ajaxToolkit:TabPanel>

</ajaxToolkit:TabContainer>
```

But as you can imagine, the ContentTemplate tags can contain any desired HTML markup as well as ASP.NET controls and functionality. Also, two event handlers are defined here: the OnClientClick for the TabPanel (which fires when the tab is clicked) and OnClientActiveTabChanged (which fires when the user switches to another tab). These events are handled via JavaScript on the client and can be used to deliver further customization to the behavior of the tabs such as UI changes. The following script snippet is for the OnClientActiveTabChanged event handler, ActiveTabChanged:

```
function ActiveTabChanged(sender, e) {
var CurrentTab = $get('<%=CurrentTab.ClientID%>');
CurrentTab.innerHTML = sender.get_activeTab().get_headerText();
Highlight(CurrentTab);
}
```

In this script, the ClientID and the header text of the current tab are fetched, and the selected tab is highlighted. Lastly, you can use the CssClass property to make vast UI changes to the appearance of the tabs, including such things as having images as tab headers. Figure 8-17 shows the Tabs Sample page for the aforementioned code snippet.

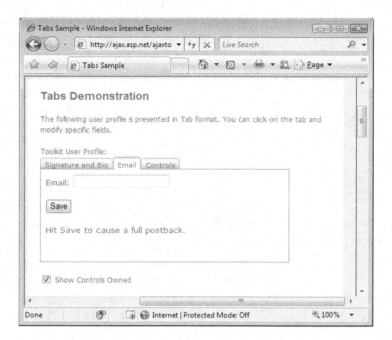

Figure 8-17. *A sample page with a* TabContainer *control and three* TabPanels

Summary

In this chapter as well as the previous one, you were introduced to most of the controls in the ASP.NET AJAX Control Toolkit. And as you have seen, these controls can bring about tremendous gains in development effort because they provide some advanced effects and client UI functionality with very little code and near drag-and-drop ease. Also, this toolkit is available with its source code and thus customizable.

Finally, due to a large number of script files that are often generated, the performance of your ASP.NET page may at times be somewhat sluggish. Therefore, it's important to use good judgment when deciding to use a number of the toolkit extenders on heavy (containing lots of content and dynamic controls) pages with lots of traffic.

■ ■ ■

CHAPTER 9

AJAX-Style Mapping Using the Virtual Earth SDK

One of the first mainstream uses of AJAX in web applications was mapping. AJAX-enhanced maps are significantly more user friendly because they enable the user to have a much richer, smoother, and interactive experience with the maps. Mapping functionality based on Virtual Earth packaged in script files was shipped with some of the earlier beta bits of ASP.NET AJAX (also known as Atlas) but was removed from the final release of the product. Microsoft Virtual Earth, which is now part of the Windows Live family of products, provides a comprehensive SDK (available at `http://dev.live.com/virtualearth/sdk/`) for developers to integrate AJAX style maps right into their web applications. This includes support for all the cool features, including 3D maps and bird's eye view (where available). In this chapter, we will examine the Virtual Earth SDK along with some of its basic functionality and discuss how you can leverage it in your own applications.

Introduction to Microsoft Virtual Earth (VE)

Mapping is a major part of the new Windows Live Local web application, which is essentially powered by Virtual Earth (VE), the core of Microsoft's online mapping offering. On top of support for traditional map views in road, aerial, or hybrid, VE also includes 3D maps and bird's eye views. 3D maps often contain textured 3D models of key buildings or landmarks, whereas bird's eye view images were harvested by flying an actual plane over the area. This is why at the time of this writing, bird's eye view is only available in major cities, but coverage for more cities seems to be constantly growing.

You can use VE to look at what businesses and services are available at a particular location and have them all mapped out for you in addition to the classical location and direction search typically done when using an online mapping application. You can access this online application by visiting `http://local.live.com`.

Figure 9-1 shows an example of this; you can search for a company name such as *Barnes and Noble* in the context of a city such as Chicago, Illinois, and you get all the

Barnes and Noble locations in the Chicago area along with their addresses, phone numbers, and other information.

The search results appear in the left pane, and their numbered icons appear on the map. These icons are called *pushpins*, and they simply enumerate the search results while showing their location on the map. You'll see how to implement them in the "Using Pushpins" section a bit later in this chapter, as well as how to use the same mapping libraries for your own applications.

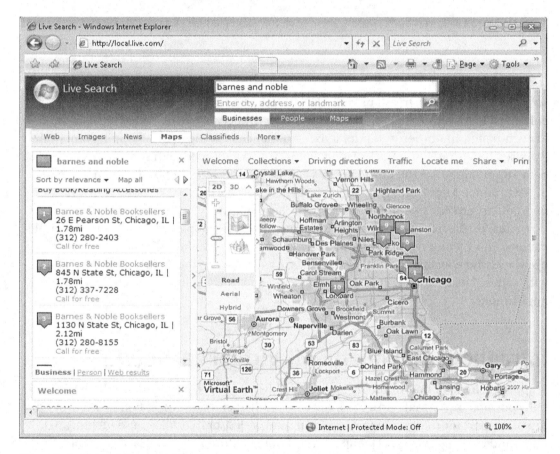

Figure 9-1. *Using Microsoft Live Local*

Programming the VEMap Control

VE is an entirely hosted online application and as such doesn't require any extra component on the client to function properly. External script inclusion on top of your page is all that is needed to open the doors to the rich functionality of VE. One exception to this fact is the use of 3D maps. 3D maps are implemented via an ActiveX plug-in that needs to be installed on Internet Explorer before you can view any of the 3D maps/landscapes. If the plug-in is not installed when the user attempts to switch the map mode to 3D, the user will be prompted to download it. With that in mind, let's take a look at what is involved in incorporating a basic map in your page and explore some of the key API features of the VE SDK.

Creating a Simple Map

As mentioned earlier, all that's needed to include support for VE maps in your page is the inclusion of an external script file that is hosted on Microsoft servers. VE maps are intrinsically AJAX enabled, meaning that no extra effort is required at your end. By simply including the VEMap control in your page, users get the full AJAX experience and are able to view and move the map around and change various viewing options without any page refresh. At the time of this writing, the current version of the VE SDK is 5.0 and can be referenced in your page by adding the following line to the top of the page:

```
<script src="http://dev.virtualearth.net/mapcontrol/mapcontrol.ashx?v=5"></script>
```

With that, we can now use the VE API. One of the first things to do when adding a map to your page is to create a host container for the map. For our purposes a simple <div> tag will suffice as shown here:

```
<div id='MapPane' style="position:relative; width:800px; height:600px;"></div>
```

Here, the width and height of the <div> tag have been set to 800 by 600 pixels but can certainly be any size you need. Now, the VE control itself should be instantiated with the ID of the <div> tag, and the map should be initialized with the right parameters as shown in this code snippet:

```
<script language=javascript type="text/javascript">
function DisplayMap()
{
    var newMap;
    newMap = new VEMap('MapPane');
    newMap.LoadMap(new VELatLong(48, -122), 9 ,'r' ,false,VEMapMode.Mode2D,
    true);
}
</script>
```

The VEMap control takes in the ID of the <div> tag as the host container in its constructor. VEMap is at the heart of the VE API, and as the core component, it handles most of the functionality. Take a moment to look at some of the methods in the VEMap control shown in Table 9-1.

Table 9-1. *Methods of the* VEMap *Control*

Method Name	Description
AddControl	Adds a custom control to the map.
AddPolygon	Renders a Polygon object (VEPolygon) on the map.
AddPolyline	Renders a Polyline object (VEPolyline) on the map.
AddPushpin	Adds a pushpin to the map.
AddShape	Adds a shape object (VEShape) object to the map.
AttachEvent	Wires up an event of the map control with a client-side event handler.
Clear	Clears all added layers such as pushpins and other search results from the map.
ClearInfoBoxStyles	Clears out all default VE info box CSS styles.
DeleteRoute	Clears the current route (VERoute object) from the map.
DeleteTileLayer	Deletes a tile layer from the map.
DetachEvent	Removes an event handler from an event of the VEMap control.
EndContinuousPan	Stops continuous map panning on the VEMap control.
Find	Returns an array of found search results.
GetAltitude	Returns the altitude (in meters) above a specified location (only available in 3D mode).
GetBirdseyeScene	Returns the current VEBirdseyeScene object (only available in bird's eye view mode).
GetCenter/SetCenter	Gets or sets the location of the center of the current map (VELatLong object).
GetHeading/SetHeading	Gets or sets the compass heading of the current map (only available in 3D mode).
GetLeft	Returns the pixel value of the left edge of the map.
GetMapMode/SetMapMode	Gets or sets the current map mode (Mode2D, Mode3D).
GetMapStyle/SetMapStyle	Gets or sets the current map style (Road, Aerial, Hybrid, Birdseye).
GetMapView/SetMapView	Gets or sets the current map view object as a VELatLongRectangle object.
GetPitch/SetPitch	Gets or sets the pitch of the current map view with values ranging from 0 for level to -90 (only available in 3D mode).
GetRoute	Returns the specified VERoute object and draws the route on the map.
GetTop	Returns the pixel value of the top edge of the map control.
GetVersion	Returns the current version of the map control.

Method Name	Description
GetZoomLevel/SetZoomLevel	Gets or sets the zoom level of the map.
HideAllShapeLayers	Hides all of the shape layers on the map.
Hide3DNavigationControl	Hides the default user interface for controlling the map in 3D mode (only available in 3D mode).
HideDashboard	Hides the compass and the zoom control from the current map.
HideFindControl	Hides the find control from the map.
HideMiniMap	Hides the mini map from view.
HideTileLayer	Hides a tile layer from view.
ImportShapeLayerData	Imports data from Live Search Maps or a GeoRSS feed collection.
IncludePointInView	Changes the map view so that it includes both the specified VELatLong point and the center point of the current map.
IsBirdseyeAvailable	Boolean value indicating whether or not the bird's eye map style is available in the current map.
LatLongToPixel	Converts a VELatLong object (latitude/longitude pair) to the corresponding pixel on the map.
LoadMap	Loads the specified map. All parameters are optional as explained later in this chapter.
Pan	Moves the map the specified amount (only available in 2D mode).
PanToLatLong	Pans the map to a specific latitude and longitude.
PixelToLatLong	Converts a pixel to a VELatLong object (latitude/longitude) on the map.
Resize	Resizes the map based on the specified width and height.
SetAltitude	Sets the altitude (in meters) above the current position on the map (only available in 3D mode).
SetBirdseyeOrientation	Sets the orientation of the existing bird's eye image (VEBirdseyeScene object) to the specified orientation.
SetBirdseyeScene	Sets the bird's eye image specified by the VEBirdseyeScene ID.
SetCenterAndZoom	Centers the map to a specific latitude and longitude and sets the zoom level.
SetDashboardSize	Sets the dashboard size.
SetDefaultInfoBoxStyles	Sets the info box CSS styles back to their default classes.
SetScaleBarDistanceUnit	Sets the distance unit (kilometers or miles) for the map scale.
SetTileBuffer	Sets the number of map tiles that are loaded outside of the visible map view area.
Show3DNavigationControl	In 3D mode, shows the default user interface for controlling the map in 3D mode. By default, this control is shown.

Continued

Table 9-1. *Continued*

Method Name	Description
ShowDashboard	Shows the default user interface for controlling the map (the compass-and-zoom control). By default, this control is shown.
ShowDisambiguationDialog	Specifies whether the default disambiguation dialog box is displayed when multiple results are returned from a location query.
ShowFindControl	Shows the find control, which enables users to enter search queries.
ShowInfoBox	Shows a shape's custom or default info box.
ShowMessage	Displays the specified message in a dialog box on the map.
ShowMiniMap	Displays the mini map at the specified offset from the top-left corner of the screen.
ShowTileLayer	Shows a tile layer from view.
StartContinuousPan	Moves the map in the specified direction until the EndContinuousPan is called.
ZoomIn	Increases the map zoom level by 1.
ZoomOut	Decreases the map zoom level by 1.

The LoadMap method is responsible for actually initiating the rendering of the map onto the page. Basically, the latitude and longitude (which will be discussed in greater detail in the next section) of the Seattle, Washington area (used here as an arbitrary location) is passed into the method along with a few other display properties such as zoom level and map view mode. It has six optional parameters without which the default map of the United States would be rendered. Therefore, the map is loaded with latitude of 48 and longitude of -122 with zoom level 9 in road view. To see a complete list of the LoadMap method's parameters with descriptions, refer to Table 9-2.

Table 9-2. *Parameters of the* LoadMap *Method*

Property Name	Description
VELatLong	The latitude/longitude value pair (VELatLong object) representing the center of the map.
zoom	Zoom level used to display the map (ranges from 1-19). The default zoom level is 4.
style	The map rendering style. Possible values are a for aerial, h for hybrid, o for oblique (bird's eye), and r for road. The default style is r.
fixed	A boolean value indicating whether or not the map is fixed so that the user cannot change the selected position of the map. By default, the map is not fixed.

Property Name	Description
mode	A VEMapMode enumeration value that indicates whether to load the map in 2D or 3D mode. The default mode is 2D.
showSwitch	(Optional) A boolean value indicating whether or not to show the map mode switch on the dashboard control. By default, the map mode switch is displayed.

The only thing left to do is to call the DisplayMap function somewhere on the page. You could set this to an event handler for a button or some other control on the page. In this case, you could simply set it to the onload event of the <body> tag:

```
<body onload='DisplayMap();'>
```

And when the page loads, the map is displayed as depicted in Figure 9-2.

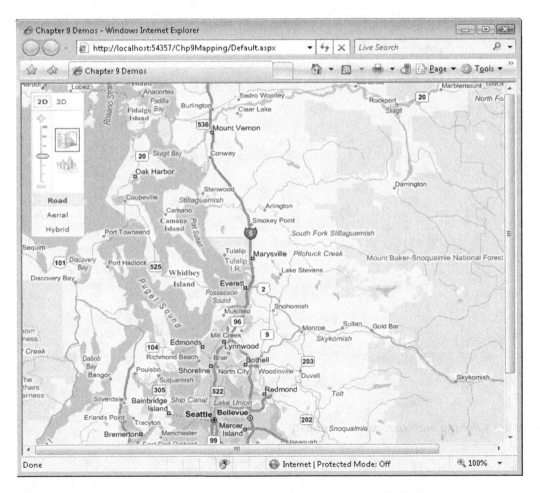

Figure 9-2. *Map of the Seattle, Washington area hosted in an ASP.NET page*

The VEMap control contains all the code necessary to handle mouse interaction. If you hold the mouse button down on the map, you can drag the map in any direction with the map being updated in a completely AJAX manner. This is an excellent showcase of AJAX and its importance in web applications, namely that asynchronous updates can significantly improve the user experience. In this case, the map you are viewing consists of a number of tiles. As you are viewing the map surface, the tiles for the surrounding areas are downloaded and cached. If you drag the map around, another download for these tiles isn't necessary. However, if you drag really fast to see areas that are far away, you'll see that VE is working to catch up, caching the tiles as it goes. During this time, you often notice blank tiles or sometimes tiles with an icon. See Figure 9-3 for an example of this.

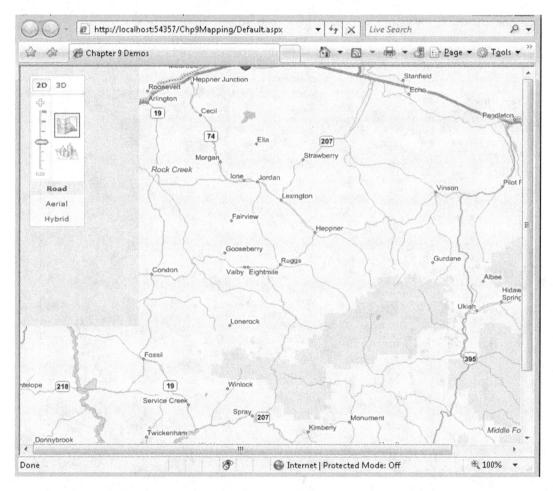

Figure 9-3. *Caching map tiles asynchronously*

If you look at an HTTP trace (using any HTTP tracing utility) of what is happening as you run this application, you'll see the following. (Much of this has been removed for brevity.) Take note that the VE service implements the mapping functionality, returning the correct map tiles upon requests from this client library.

First the browser issues the initial request to a page:

```
#1  10:34:27.328  127.0.0.1:4611
GET /chapter9/Default.aspx HTTP/1.1
Accept: */*
Accept-Language: en-us
Accept-Encoding: gzip, deflate
Connection: Keep-Alive
```

Then the server responds with this:

```
#2  10:34:27.390  127.0.0.1:4611
HTTP/1.1 200 OK
Server: ASP.NET Development Server/8.0.0.0
Date: Mon, 21 May 2007 18:34:27 GMT
X-AspNet-Version: 2.0.50727
Cache-Control: private
Content-Type: text/html; charset=utf-8
Content-Length: 1624
Connection: Close
<!DOCTYPE html PUBLIC "-//W3C//DTD XHTML 1.0 Transitional//EN"
    "http://www.w3.org/TR/xhtml1/DTD/xhtml1-transitional.dtd">
...
```

After the initial download of the page, the map control kicks in and starts making the asynchronous requests for the map tiles using XMLHttpRequest. You can see the request, issued by the map control:

```
#11  10:34:28.656  65.55.241.30:80
GET /tiles/r021230000.png?g=15 HTTP/1.1
Accept: */*
Referer: http://localhost:4611/chapter9/Default.aspx
Accept-Language: en-us
Accept-Encoding: gzip, deflate
User-Agent: Mozilla/4.0 (compatible; MSIE 7.0; Windows NT 5.1; SV1; .
NET CLR 2.0.50727; WinFX RunTime 3.0.50727)

Host: r0.ortho.tiles.virtualearth.net

Connection: Keep-Alive
```

This is the response from the VE map server:

```
#12  10:34:28.859  65.55.241.30:80
HTTP/1.1 200 OK
Content-Length: 17055
Content-Type: image/png
Expires: Sat, 24 May 2008 01:39:58 GMT
Server: Microsoft-IIS/6.0

Srv: 31300
Date: Mon, 21 May 2007 18:34:28 GMT
```

As you pan around the map, you see the same functionality—the images being requested, downloaded, and cached asynchronously.

In addition to panning around the map, you can zoom in and out because VE also caches images when you zoom, providing what is effectively a smart multilevel cache of the current map context. In other words, the VEMap control looks at the current context of the map and caches the area outside the current view in the current zoom context as well as a zoom-in context and a zoom-out context.

If you have a mouse with a wheel, you can roll the wheel to zoom in and out. You can see this for the current application in Figure 9-4.

Now that you've gotten a feel for the functionality of the map, you'll see some more of the programmatic features for further controlling the map that are available to application developers.

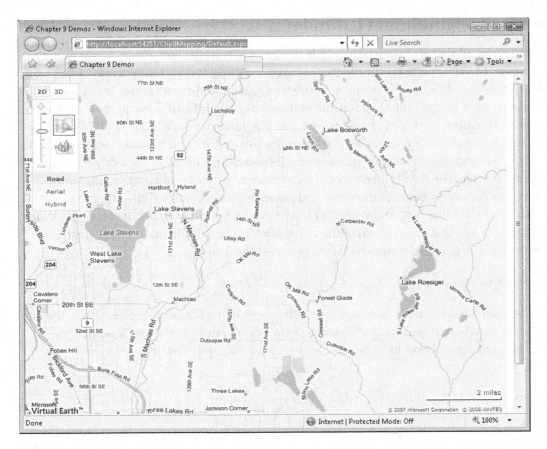

Figure 9-4. *Zooming into the map*

In the previous section, you saw how to create a simple page that hosts the VEMap control, which probably whetted your appetite for some juicy APIs that you can use to finely control the map. So, without further delay, let's explore a few of them.

Setting Longitude and Latitude

As you know, places on a map have a latitude and a longitude. Longitude values range from –180 to +180, whereas latitude values range from –90 to +90. Using these values, you can calculate and locate any position in the world. Longitude determines how far east or west a location is, and latitude determines how far north or south a location is. To determine any location, you need only these two values. Locations at a latitude of 0 are on the equator; locations with a latitude of 90 are at the North Pole; and locations with a latitude of –90 are at the South Pole. Locations with a longitude of 0 are either directly north or directly south of the Royal Observatory in Greenwich (a suburb of London, England), with negative values being to the west, and positive values being to the east.

If you look at the map shown earlier in Figure 9-1, you will see that it is specified with a latitude of 48 (48 degrees north of the equator) and a longitude of –122 (122 degrees west of Greenwich, England), which brings you to the Seattle area:

```
LoadMap(new VELatLong(48, -122), 9 ,'r');
```

You don't have to use whole numbers when specifying longitude and latitude; the latitude/longitude numbers can be floating-point "style" values that provide some fine-grained control over locations. So, you can quite happily control your location like this:

```
LoadMap(new VELatLong(47.7512121212, -122.43234), 9 ,'r');
```

You can see this in Figure 9-5; notice that the map is now more centered around the Seattle/Bellevue area.

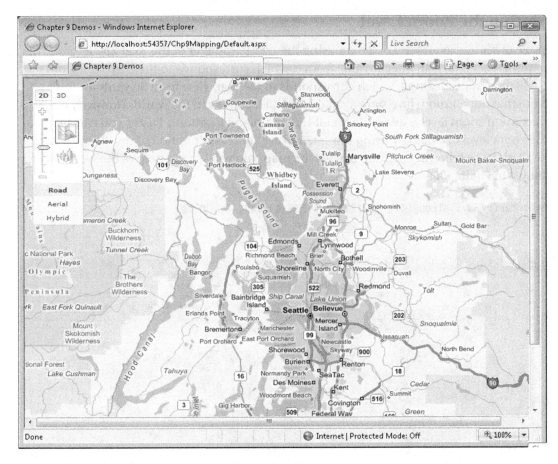

Figure 9-5. *Map using detailed latitude and longitude*

Setting the Zoom Level

You can set the zoom level of a map using the zoom parameter of the LoadMap method. This parameter can take an integer value from 0, which corresponds to the map view from 5,000 miles altitude, to 19, which corresponds to the map view from 30 yards altitude. Note that not all zoom levels are available for all locations in the world. However, the maximum zoom level is available for all U.S. mainland locations. Lastly, you can also set the zoom level of a map by using the SetZoomLevel accessor method of the VEMap control.

Using the following method call for the map, you will see the map of the world as shown in Figure 9-6:

```
LoadMap(new VELatLong(47.7512121212, -122.43234), 0 ,'r');
```

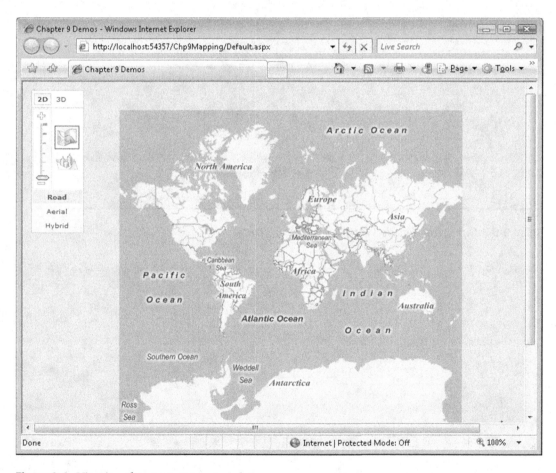

Figure 9-6. *Viewing the map at* ZoomLevel 0

Choosing a Map Type

In addition to setting the location of the map, you can also specify the map type. At the time of this writing, four types are available:

Road(r): This gives the typical road-type map. All the examples used so far in this chapter use this type.

Aerial(a): This gives you a photograph of the location from above.

Hybrid(h): This gives you a combination of the previous two—an aerial photograph of the location with roads, names, and locations superimposed on it.

Bird's Eye(o): This gives you a much closer and clearer aerial shot of the location. These images were acquired via an actual flying airplane.

You set the map style type using the `style` parameter of the `LoadMap` method. In all the previous sections of this chapter, this attribute was set to r for Road, and as such, all the maps so far in this chapter have been road maps. Hybrid and aerial maps can be a little slower to load due to the extra processing required, but the load times are still quite reasonable. Specifying a map as a hybrid is equally simple and straightforward. Here's the script:

```
LoadMap(new VELatLong(47.7512121212, -122.43234), 9 ,'h');
```

You can see the results in Figure 9-7.

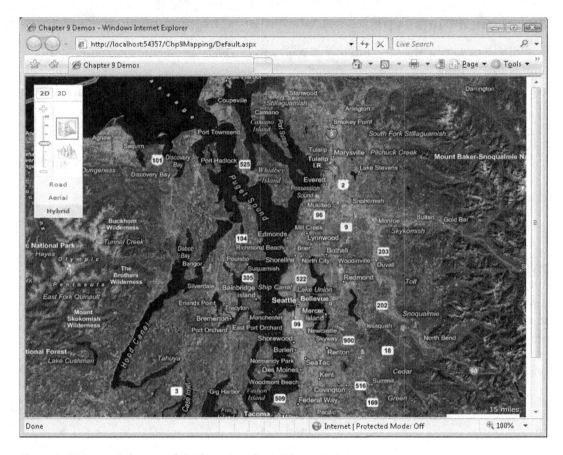

Figure 9-7. *An aerial map of the location from Figure 9-2*

Specific or Relative Panning

You can programmatically pan the map to a specific location as specified by longitude and latitude or relative panning by using X and Y pixels. Let's first look at how you can use the VE API to map a specific location. You can use the PanToLatLong method of the VEMap control to pan the map to a specified latitude and longitude. This information is passed in via a VELatLong object as you saw in the earlier example in this chapter. You cannot set the zoom level with this method, so you will be panning across the current zoom level. Consider the following <script> block:

```
<script>
    var newMap=null;

    function DisplayMap()
```

```
    {
        newMap = new VEMap('MapPane');
        newMap.LoadMap(new VELatLong(47.7512121212, -122.43234), 9 ,'r');
    }

    function PanLatLong()
    {
        newMap.PanToLatLong(new VELatLong(txtLat.value, txtLong.value));
    }

    function PanXY()
    {
        newMap.Pan(txtX.value, txtY.value);
    }
</script>
```

In addition to the DisplayMap function you've seen already, there are two functions here: PanLatLong and PanXY. PanLatLong pans the map to a specific latitude and longitude (as provided in two text boxes) by creating a new VELatLong object. Now we have to create a few HTML input fields in the page and be sure to call the DisplayMap method in the onload event of the <body> tag as shown here:

```
<body onload="DisplayMap();">
    <div id='MapPane' style="position:relative; width:600px; height:400px;"></div>
    Pixels X:
    <input id="txtX" style="width: 50px" value="100" />  | 
    ;  Pixels
    Y:
    <input id="txtY" style="width: 50px" value="100" />  
    <input id="btnPanPixels" type="button" value="Pan by X/Y pixels"
      name="btnPanXY" onclick="PanXY()" />
    <br />
    Lat:
    <input id="txtLat" value="47.757014822032184" />  |   Long:
    <input id="txtLong" value="-122.4300390625" />  
    <input id="btnPanLL" type="button" value="Pan to Lat/Long"
      name="btnPanLatLong" onclick="PanLatLong()" />
</body>
```

With this markup, when the PanLatLong button is clicked, the map will pan to the specified coordinates as shown in Figure 9-8.

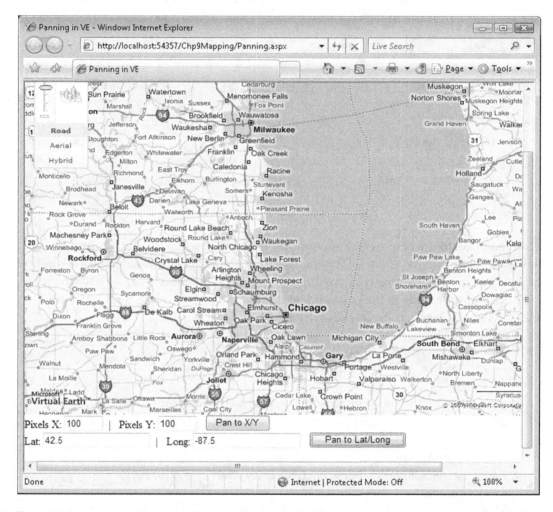

Figure 9-8. *Example of panning by location (set by latitude/longitude to the Chicago area)*

In addition to panning to a particular location, you can pan relative to the current location by a number of pixels using the PanXY method. It takes two parameters, X and Y, with which you specify the direction. For X, negative values pan to the left of the map, and positive values pan to the right. For Y, negative values pan toward the bottom of the map, and positive ones pan to the top. The PanXY JavaScript function you saw in the preceding code segment reads the X and Y coordinates from the text boxes on the page and pans the map accordingly using the Pan method of the VEMap control.

Using Pushpins

Maps are all very nice, but without any kind of attribution and labeling, they lose their usefulness after a while. Fortunately, VE maps support graphical pushpins that allow you to highlight specific locations on the map. You have already seen pushpins in Figure 9-1 when searching for Barnes and Noble bookstores in the Chicago area. In version 5.0 of the VE SDK, pushpins are now specified as an enumeration of the VEShapeLayer class. This class contains rich functionality around rendering various shapes and objects, including images on the VEMap control. The VEShapeType enumeration includes Pushpin, Polyline, and Polygon. For the purposes of this chapter, only pushpins are discussed. Let's view a simple example of using pushpins. Consider the following script and markup:

```
<script>
    var newMap=null;

    function DisplayMap()
    {
        newMap = new VEMap('MapPane');
        newMap.LoadMap(new VELatLong(47.7512121212, -122.43234), 9 ,'r');
    }
    function AddPin()
    {
        var loc = new VELatLong(47.75, -122.43);
        var pin = newMap.AddPushpin(loc);
        pin.SetTitle(txtTitle.value);
        pin.SetDescription(txtDescription.value);
    }
</script>

<body onload="DisplayMap();">
    <div id='MapPane' style="position:relative; width:600px; height:400px;"></div>
    Title: <input id="txtTitle" value="" /><br />
    Description <input id="txtDescription" value="" />
    <input id="btnAddPin" type="button" value="Add Pushpin" onclick="AddPin()" />
</body>
```

Here, the VEMap control is instantiated with the coordinates of the Seattle area. The AddPin function uses the AddPushPin method of the VEMap control and passes in a VELatLong object, which simply stores a latitude, longitude value pair. After that, the title and the description of the pin are set using the SetTitle and SetDescription based on values from the HTML input boxes on the page. So as you can see, all that is needed to create a pushpin is basically values for latitude and longitude. You can also assign images to the pushpin by adding the URL of an image. Then, at render time, the specified image will be placed on the map at the specified location. You can see the preceding code segment running on Figure 9-9.

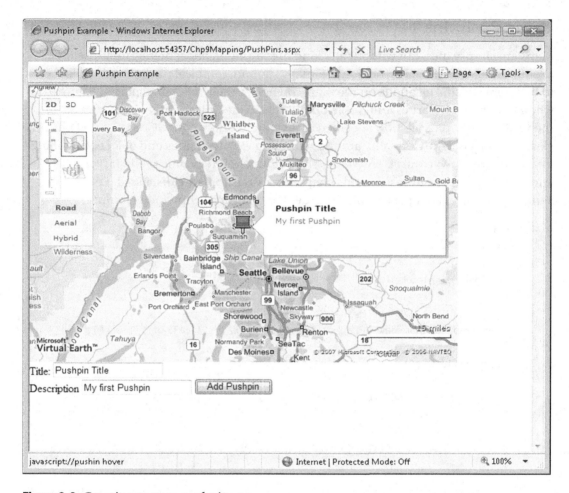

Figure 9-9. *Creating custom pushpins on a map*

Summary

In this chapter, you looked at the VE SDK and how you can use it to build your own mapping applications. You looked at how to create and invoke a map on a page and how you can set its location using latitude and longitude. You learned how to zoom in and out of a page programmatically and how to use the object model of the VE control to move the map pane from place to place. Finally, you learned how to annotate the map using the built-in pushpin technology. We just scratched the surface of the capabilities of the feature-rich VE SDK because more in-depth coverage of the entire API would have quickly gone beyond the scope of this chapter.

CHAPTER 10
■ ■ ■

Building a Sample Application Using ASP.NET AJAX

Throughout this book, you've been exploring some of the underpinning technologies of ASP.NET AJAX, including the client-side JavaScript libraries, which are object-oriented additions to JavaScript. You've also seen the power of ASP.NET AJAX server controls and the ease with which they can be used to add asynchronous update functionality to an ASP.NET page. In addition, we explored the rich set of UI controls and extenders offered as part of the ASP.NET AJAX Control Toolkit. Lastly, we reviewed the Virtual Earth SDK, and you saw how to add AJAX-style mapping functionality to your web applications.

In this chapter, you'll go through, in detail, what it takes to build an application that makes the most of these features to deliver a real-world application. The application you will build is a very simple financial research tool that delivers stock quotes, extended stock information, and some price history analytics. This sort of information is typically used in *technical analysis* stock trading. Stock traders use a number of methodologies to determine a good buying or selling price of a stock, including *fundamental analysis,* where you look at company fundamentals such as dividends, profits, earnings per share, gross sales, and more—usually a good methodology when investing in a company for medium- to long-term investments. Day traders, who are looking for a quick in and out, typically use technical analyses where they want to look at the momentum of the stock based on how it has performed in similar situations recently. The closing price for a stock over time is called the *price history*, and by applying various mathematical transforms to it, a day trader can guess where it is going to go. It's an inexact science, but when carefully applied, it can be effective.

We will also use Bollinger band–based analysis of price history and see how to deliver it in an ASP.NET AJAX application. You'll see how technical traders use this to determine potential times to get in and out of a stock. This should not be construed as investment advice; it is provided for informational use only and as a demonstration of the ASP.NET technology. You can see a snapshot of this application in Figure 10-1.

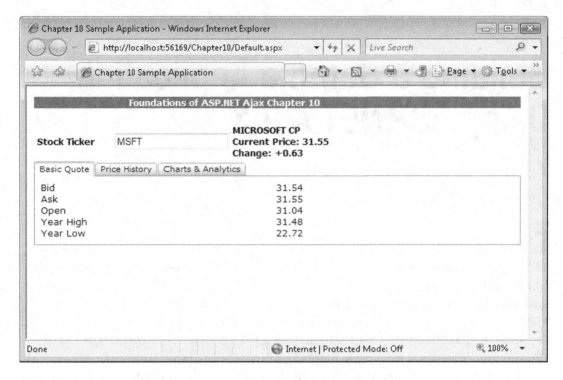

Figure 10-1. *An ASP.NET AJAX-based stock application*

Understanding the Application Architecture

The application is built as a typical logical *n*-tier application comprising a resource tier that contains the back-end resources. In this case, the resources are the Company Information web service (courtesy of Flash-db.com, a provider of a number of useful and free web services) and the Price History web service that provides comma-separated values (CSV) over HTTP from Yahoo!. You can see the architecture in Figure 10-2.

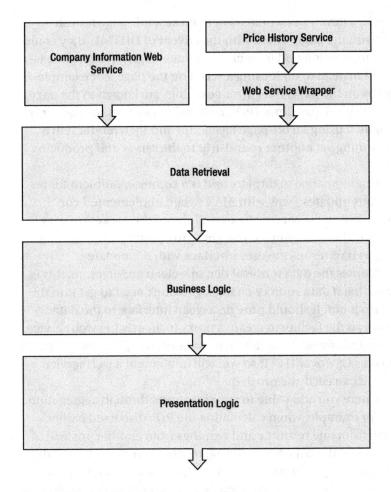

Figure 10-2. *Application logical architecture*

In a multitiered architecture like this, the information that drives your service comes from the resource tier. In many applications, and this one is no exception, the information is read-only—you are simply presenting the resources to the end user. However, the raw resources are rarely presented. Some value has to be added to show how you visually present them and also how you enhance them for presentation using business logic. Many applications blur the distinction between business logic and presentation logic, but it is important to distinguish these. When using ASP.NET AJAX, the ability to distinguish them becomes a lot easier.

This is because before AJAX, a developer would have to make a full-page refresh whenever the user interacted with the page. Then, with the advent of DHTML, they could make a decision—for a simple interaction and for a bit of business logic, it might be easier not to do it on the server but instead to do it using a script on the page. For example, if the current price for the stock is on the page, the current earnings are known to the page, and the user wants to display the profit/earnings (P/E) ratio (which divides the former by the latter), why not just calculate it using an on-page JavaScript and then render it in a <div> element instead of performing yet another round-trip to the server and producing a "blink" as the page refreshes?

This can quickly lead to a maintenance nightmare and is a common problem that has been solved by asynchronous updates. Now with AJAX (when implemented correctly), despite making a round-trip to the server, the overall size of the packets of data getting passed will be a lot smaller because you are just going to update part of the page; the entire page will not "flash" as it refreshes the user interface with the update.

Beneath the resource tier comes the data retrieval tier. In a clean architecture, this is kept separate from the logic so that if data sources change, you don't need to get into the business logic plumbing and rip it out. It should provide a clean interface to the data layer. Visual Studio 2005 offers you the facility to create a proxy to an existing web service, which you can use to implement a data retrieval tier. In this application, the Price History web service from Yahoo! provides CSV over HTTP, so you will implement a web service that wraps this functionality and can easily be proxied.

The business logic tier is where you add value to your resources through aggregation, integration, and calculation. For example, when calculating the P/E, discussed earlier, with price information coming from one resource and earnings from another, instead of integrating and calculating these on the page level, you aggregate the information in the business logic tier where the function performing the calculation calls the data retrieval tier to get the information from both resources and then performs the calculation. It then provides the resultant information to the presentation tier as a response to the original request for the P/E analytic.

The presentation tier is typically server-side logic that provides the markup and/or graphics that will get rendered in the browser. This can be anything from a C-based CGI service that generates raw HTML to an advanced control-based ASP.NET server application. In this case, the example will use a variety of technologies, from ASP.NET controls that will render HTML that is generated by server-side C# code to advanced graphics functionality that renders the time series chart (you can see these charts in Figure 10-1).

Finally, what appears to the user is the output of this presentation tier, which is a document that contains HTML, graphics, JavaScript, style sheets, and anything else the browser needs to render.

As you see how to construct the application, you'll see each of these tiers in a little more detail.

Creating the Application

As you saw in Figure 10-1, this application consists of a top header where the stock ticker and company information is displayed, followed by three tabs in a TabContainer control that host the extended quote information, price history, and Bollinger band analytic charts. Let's start by creating a new ASP.NET AJAX-enabled web site. Create the basic layout of the application along with the corresponding TabContainer and TabPanel controls from the ASP.NET AJAX Control Toolkit. After creating the basic UI shell, we'll look into the data tier and explore how data is obtained and consumed in this application.

This application requires a stock ticker as the only source of user input. As such, upon creating the ScriptManager, UpdatePanel, and Timer control (all of which are fully discussed later), an ASP.NET Label control and a TextBox control are necessary. Another Label control is also needed to host the basic stock information such as company name, current price, and price change on the top header. The top section of the page should look similar to Figure 10-3.

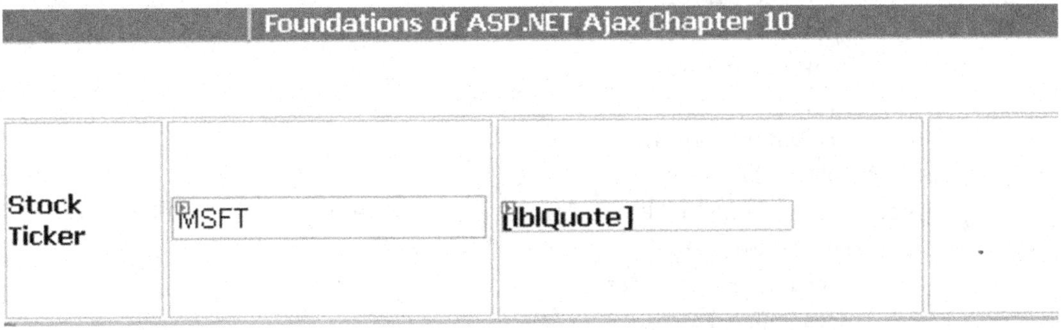

Figure 10-3. *Creating the top section of the application*

As mentioned earlier, this application will have three tabs that contain much of its functionality. The back-end processing and rendering for each tab should only occur when the user clicks the tab. This way, additional overhead of recreating everything is avoided, and also the user is presented with the most up-to-date information for the selected stock ticker.

To create the tabs, from the ASP.NET AJAX Control Toolkit tab on the Toolbox in Visual Studio, drag and drop a new TabContainer control onto the page with the <ContentTemplate> tag of the main UpdatePanel. You can then use the designer window to add three tabs (TabPanel controls) to the TabContainer control and name them "Basic Quote", "Price History", and "Charts & Analytics", respectively. Lastly, specify an event

handler for the ActiveTabChanged event. This, of course, can also be done in code as
shown in the following segment:

```
<cc1:TabContainer ID="TabContainer1" runat="server"  ActiveTabIndex=0 ➡
AutoPostBack=true OnActiveTabChanged="TabContainer1_ActiveTabChanged">
        <cc1:TabPanel ID="TabPanel1" runat="server" HeaderText="TabPanel1">
            <HeaderTemplate>
                Basic Quote
            </HeaderTemplate>
            <ContentTemplate>
                <asp:Label ID="lblBasicQuote" Text ="Label" runat="server">
                </asp:Label>
                </ContentTemplate>
        </cc1:TabPanel>
        <cc1:TabPanel ID="TabPanel2" runat="server" HeaderText="TabPanel2">
            <HeaderTemplate>
                Price History
            </HeaderTemplate>
            <ContentTemplate>

                . . .

                </ContentTemplate>
        </cc1:TabPanel>
        <cc1:TabPanel ID="TabPanel3" runat="server" HeaderText="TabPanel3">
            <HeaderTemplate>
                Charts & Analytics
            </HeaderTemplate>
            <ContentTemplate>
. . .

                </ContentTemplate>
        </cc1:TabPanel>
    </cc1:TabContainer>
```

You can see the created tabs in design view in Figure 10-4.

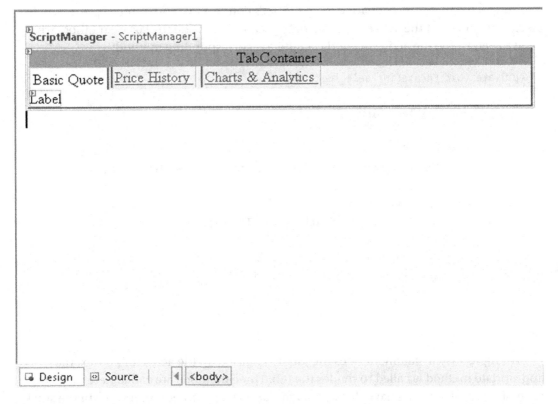

Figure 10-4. *Three* TabPanel *controls in a* TabContainer *control*

That's basically all there is to the outer shell of the UI. A bit later, we will add an
UpdateProgress control to notify the user when postbacks are occurring. As mentioned
earlier, we wanted to only execute code for each pane when it becomes active. In other
words, we do not want all panes rendered at all times. Therefore, in the ActiveTabChanged
event handler, the specific rendering code for each pane must be stated as shown here:

```
protected void TabContainer1_ActiveTabChanged(object sender, EventArgs e)
{
    Update(TabContainer1.ActiveTabIndex);
}
```

To specify rendering code for each pane, let's define a method named Update, which takes in the index of the active tab as its only parameter. Inside the Update method, we need to determine the active tab and execute the corresponding method:

```
private void Update(int selectedTabIndex)
{
    switch (selectedTabIndex)
    {
        case 0: //Basic Quote
            lblBasicQuote.Text = GetBasicQuote(txtTicker.Text.Trim());
            break;
        case 1: //Price History
            GetPriceHistory(txtTicker.Text.Trim());
            break;
        case 2: //Analytics
            GetAnalytics(txtTicker.Text.Trim());
            break;
    }
}
```

A simple switch statement does the job here. Based on the active tab index, the appropriate method is called to render the tab. Three methods are called here, one for each of three tabs that all have the same signature: one parameter that takes in the stock ticker entered by the user in the TextBox control. The individual methods, GetBasicQuote, GetPriceHistory, and GetAnalytics, are covered a little later in this chapter.

With that out of the way, let's take a closer look at how to obtain the required data and implement the individual sections of this application.

Creating Basic Company and Quote Information

Flash-db.com provides several hosted web services free of charge. One of these services is the excellent Company Information web service, which provides basic and extended stock price information, as well as the name of the company associated with a stock ticker. Accessing this from a Visual Studio 2005 application is straightforward. The WSDL (Web Services Description Language) for the web service is hosted at the following location:

http://www.flash-db.com/services/ws/companyInfo.wsdl

To create a proxy to this WSDL, right-click your project in Solution Explorer, and select Add Web Reference (see Figure 10-5).

Figure 10-5. *Adding a web reference*

A dialog box appears in which you specify the WSDL of the service you are referencing. In the URL text box, enter `http://www.flash-db.com/services/ws/companyInfo.wsdl` (see Figure 10-6).

When you enter a valid WSDL here, the description pane updates with the supported functions on the web service, as well as the services that are available to this WSDL (multiple services can be published to a single WSDL). In the Web Reference Name field, you should enter a friendly name, such as companyInfo, because this is the name that will be generated for the proxy that talks to the web service on your behalf. Click the Add Reference button to generate the proxy class for the web service.

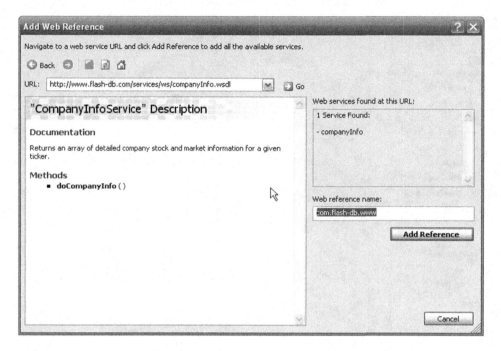

Figure 10-6. *Specifying the WSDL*

The Company Information web service is used in the application to present the name of the company as well as the current price information. Now there needs to be a method called GetCompanyInfo in which we write the code to use a few of the properties to get the actual company data. After that, this information needs to be assigned to the lblQuote control as shown in the following code snippet:

```
private void GetCompanyInfo(string strTicker)
{
    companyInfo.CompanyInfoService service = new
                                        companyInfo.CompanyInfoService();
    companyInfo.CompanyInfoResult result = service.doCompanyInfo("anything",
                                        "anything", strTicker);
    lblQuote.Text = result.company + "<BR>Current Price: " + result.lastPrice
                            + "<BR>Change: " +result.change;
}
```

This function updates the company information pane as well as the price history text and graphs. Also, because this is the one piece of information that does not reside within the tabs, it should be rendered and updated without the user clicking on the individual tabs. Furthermore, the user should be able to enter a new stock ticker in the main

TextBox and have the data updated. So to address these points, we need to first call the GetCompanyInfo method during the Page_Load event and then create a Timer control. In the control's Tick event handler, we call the method shown here:

```
protected void Page_Load(object sender, EventArgs e)
{
if (!Page.IsPostBack)
    {
        GetCompanyInfo(txtTicker.Text.Trim());
        //Default to first tab
        Update(0);
    }
}
```

This way, the ticker information is updated in regular intervals, and if the user enters a new stock ticker, the changes are reflected as soon as the GetCompanyInfo method is called again (in 5 seconds).

To create a timer for this page, drag and drop the ASP.NET AJAX Timer control from the Toolbox onto the page, and set its Interval property to 5000ms, so that the page updates every 5 seconds. Also, don't forget to set the event handler for the Tick event as shown here:

```
<asp:Timer ID="Timer1" runat="server" Interval="5000" OnTick=➡
    "Timer1_Tick"></asp:Timer>
```

Lastly, for the timer functionality to work properly, you must call the GetCompanyInfo method in the Timer1_Tick event handler as such:

```
protected void Timer1_Tick(object sender, EventArgs e)
  {
      GetCompanyInfo(txtTicker.Text.Trim());
  }
```

You can view the company information and Quote section on the top of the page for a specific stock ticker such as MSFT for Microsoft Corporation (see Figure 10-7).

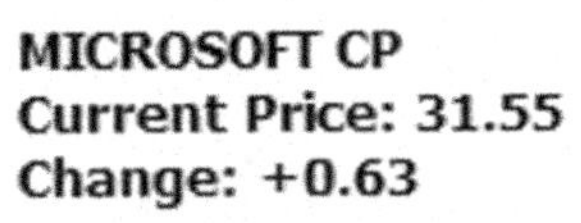

MICROSOFT CP
Current Price: 31.55
Change: +0.63

Figure 10-7. *The company name and current price information*

With the brief quote information on top of the page, we need to create the more extended quote information in the first tab. This extended price information includes the bid and ask prices. These are, respectively, the current price that is being bid on the stock by prospective buyers and the one that is being asked for by sellers. When you make a purchase at the current market price, it is usually between these two values, provided you are buying a large amount of shares in the stock. It also provides the opening price for the day, as well as the year's (52 weeks) high and low.

Now let's take a look at the code that implements this. First, create a new TabPanel control with one ASP.NET Label control in the <ContentTemplate> section. The following code snippet shows the markup for that section:

```
<cc1:TabPanel ID="TabPanel1" runat="server" HeaderText="TabPanel1">
    <HeaderTemplate>
        Basic Quote
    </HeaderTemplate>
    <ContentTemplate>
        <asp:Label ID="lblBasicQuote" runat="server"></asp:Label>
        </ContentTemplate>
</cc1:TabPanel>
```

As you can imagine, much of the implementation logic is going to be in content generation for the lblBasicQuote Label control because that is where all the quote information will reside. To do this, we have a method with a similar signature to the GetCompanyInfo method called GetBasicCode, which calls the CompanyInfoService web service to provide data for this Label control. Here's the code for that method:

```
private string GetBasicQuote(string strTicker)
{
    companyInfo.CompanyInfoService service = new
                companyInfo.CompanyInfoService();
    companyInfo.CompanyInfoResult result =
                service.doCompanyInfo("UID", "PWD", strTicker);
    StringBuilder theHTML = new StringBuilder();
    theHTML.Append("<table width='100%' cellspacing='0'
            cellpadding='0'  style='border-width: 0'>");
    theHTML.Append("<tr><td  width='40%'>");
    theHTML.Append("Bid ");
    theHTML.Append("</td><td  width='40%'>");
    theHTML.Append(result.bid);
    theHTML.Append("</td></tr>");

    theHTML.Append("<tr><td  width='40%'>");
    theHTML.Append("Ask ");
    theHTML.Append("</td><td  width='40%'>");
```

```
        theHTML.Append(result.ask);
        theHTML.Append("</td></tr>");

        theHTML.Append("<tr><td  width='40%'>");
        theHTML.Append("Open ");
        theHTML.Append("</td><td  width='40%'>");
        theHTML.Append(result.open);
        theHTML.Append("</td></tr>");

        theHTML.Append("<tr><td  width='40%'>");
        theHTML.Append("Year High ");
        theHTML.Append("</td><td  width='40%'>");
        theHTML.Append(result.yearHigh);
        theHTML.Append("</td></tr>");

        theHTML.Append("<tr><td  width='40%'>");
        theHTML.Append("Year Low ");
        theHTML.Append("</td><td  width='40%'>");
        theHTML.Append(result.yearLow);
        theHTML.Append("</td></tr>");

        theHTML.Append("</table>");
        return theHTML.ToString();
    }
```

This function is similar to what you saw earlier in that it creates an instance of the proxy to the Flash-db.com web service and an instance of the object type that contains the results to the doCompanyInfo() web method call. It then generates HTML for a table using a StringBuilder and places this HTML into the Text property of the Label control. Obviously, populating a Label control is not the most ideal way to represent some data on the screen, but it suffices just fine for the purposes of this sample. In such scenarios, it's best to bind a typed data structure to one of the more sophisticated ASP.NET data-bound controls, such as GridView or DataList.

The proxy to the Flash-db.com web service is called CompanyInfoService. An instance of this proxy is first created, called svc. This exposes an object of type CompanyInfoResult, which is used to store the returned information from the service. The second line creates an instance of this type, called rslt, into which the results of a doCompanyInfo web method call are loaded. This web method takes three parameters; the first two are username and password. The web service is open, so you can put anything in for the username and password parameters. The third parameter is the ticker for which you are seeking the company information.

The company name (result.company) is then appended to a string containing text (Current Price:), which in turn is appended to the last traded price for the stock (result.lastPrice). You can see this in Figure 10-8.

Basic Quote	Price History	Charts & Analytics

Bid	31.54
Ask	31.55
Open	31.04
Year High	31.48
Year Low	22.72

Figure 10-8. *Extended quote information in the first tab pane*

Creating the Price History Pane

The price history pane renders the 20-day price history (the closing price for the stock over the past 20 days) in a simple text table. Of course, the number 20 is completely an arbitrary number. You could really configure it to be any number of days you want so long as historical data is available for that particular ticker. After we get the data for this period, a GridView control is used to display the information. You can see this in Figure 10-9.

Basic Quote	Price History	Charts & Analytics

Date	Open	High	Low	Close	Volume	Adj Close
2007-07-18	30.51	30.97	30.50	30.92	64414400	30.92
2007-07-17	30.02	30.88	30.01	30.78	77526500	30.78
2007-07-16	29.76	30.24	29.72	30.03	48007000	30.03
2007-07-13	29.94	30.02	29.66	29.82	42166500	29.82
2007-07-12	29.56	30.11	29.44	30.07	54296500	30.07
2007-07-11	29.24	29.65	29.21	29.49	47970400	29.49
2007-07-10	29.70	29.99	29.18	29.33	66013500	29.33
2007-07-09	29.86	29.95	29.81	29.87	33831400	29.87
2007-07-06	29.91	30.04	29.66	29.97	57541000	29.97
2007-07-05	30.05	30.22	29.83	29.99	47838500	29.99
2007-07-03	29.79	30.22	29.78	30.02	35202600	30.02
2007-07-02	29.67	29.80	29.49	29.74	47316000	29.74
2007-06-29	29.87	29.93	29.04	29.47	71183900	29.47
2007-06-28	29.86	29.97	29.68	29.83	46055200	29.83
2007-06-27	29.36	29.95	29.36	29.87	53468600	29.87
2007-06-26	29.55	29.80	29.50	29.52	48337500	29.52
2007-06-25	29.47	29.77	29.38	29.49	53905800	29.49
2007-06-22	30.00	30.10	29.45	29.49	86219900	29.49
2007-06-21	29.98	30.30	29.91	30.22	56564800	30.22
2007-06-20	30.44	30.51	29.96	30.01	46861600	30.01

Figure 10-9. *The price history pane*

This information is ultimately sourced from Yahoo! as CSV over HTTP. This CSV file is returned from a call to the iFinance server at Yahoo! using a URL call similar this:

```
http://ichart.finance.yahoo.com/table.csv?s=MSFT&d=2
       &e=4&f=2007&g=d&a=2&b=1&c=2006&ignore=.csv
```

This returns a CSV file with the following format:

```
Date,Open,High,Low,Close,Volume,Adj. Close*
3-Mar-06,26.81,27.16,26.74,26.93,45218800,26.93
2-Mar-06,27.02,27.10,26.90,26.97,41850300,26.97
1-Mar-06,26.98,27.20,26.95,27.14,53061200,27.14
```

Each data item is separated by a comma, and each line is separated by a carriage return. To make this data easier to consume by the data retrieval and business logic tiers, a web service consumes this HTTP service and exposes it as a structured DataTable. You'll see this in the next section.

Creating the Wrapper Web Service

This web service provides a web method that makes a call to the Yahoo! iFinance server on your behalf, takes the CSV that is returned from it, and serializes it as a DataTable. It is designed to be consumed by a .NET-based client, so using a DataTable object works nicely. If you want to expose a web service that is easily interoperable with other platforms, you should serialize the returned data using straight XML that can be parsed on the client side. To do that, we have a web method called GetFullPriceHistory, which takes in a stock ticker and an integer value representing the number of days. Here is the code for this web method:

```
[WebMethod]
public DataTable GetFullPriceHistory(string strTicker, int nDays)
  {
    WebClient client = new WebClient();
    StringBuilder strURI = new
        StringBuilder("http://ichart.finance.yahoo.com/table.csv?s=");
    strURI.Append(strTicker);

    strURI.Append("&d=1&e=22&f=2007&g=d&a=8&b=28&c=1997&ignore=.csv");
    Stream data = client.OpenRead(strURI.ToString());
    StreamReader reader = new StreamReader(data);
    string s = reader.ReadToEnd();
```

```
      DataTable theTable = CsvParser.Parse(s);
      if (nDays > 0)
      {
        int i = nDays + 1;
        while (theTable.Rows.Count > i)
        {
          theTable.Rows.RemoveAt(i);
        }
      }
      data.Close();
      reader.Close();
      return theTable;
    }
```

This makes the connection to the Yahoo! server to fetch historical data of about 10 years by using an object derived from the WebClient class, which is defined in the System.Net namespace. To use this, you use its OpenRead method, which is pointed at a URI. This returns a stream, which can be read by a StreamReader. The contents of this can be parsed into a string using a CsvParser abstract helper class.

This helper class provides the parsing functionality that reads the CSV information and returns it as a DataTable. The Source Code/Download area of the Apress web site (www.apress.com) includes a version of this class that was derived from one published in the excellent blog from Andreas Knab at http://knab.ws/blog/.

The call to the Yahoo! iFinance server provides the entire price history for the stock, which can be thousands of days' worth of information. It provides an additional layer that allows you to crop this data to the specified number of days by iterating through the DataTable and removing rows beyond what you are interested in. So if you want to pull 10 days' worth of data, you can modify the query to Yahoo! iFinance accordingly or simply remove all rows beyond number 10.

That's about it. This web method is present in a web service called DataTier.

Consuming the Web Service

As mentioned earlier, an ASP.NET GridView control will be used to display the historical price data. So, in the <ContentTemplate> section of the second TabPanel, add a GridView control named grdPriceHistory, and change a few properties as shown in the following markup:

```
<asp:GridView ShowHeader=False  ID="grdPriceHistory" runat="server" BackColor=➥
"White" BorderColor="#CCCCCC" BorderStyle="None" BorderWidth="1px" CellPadding="3"
Height="119px" Width="470px" Font-Size="9pt">
    <RowStyle ForeColor="#000066" />
```

```
<SelectedRowStyle BackColor="#669999" Font-Bold="True" ForeColor="White" />
    <PagerStyle BackColor="White" ForeColor="#000066" HorizontalAlign="Left" />
</asp:GridView>
```

Figure 10-10 shows the design for the price history pane.

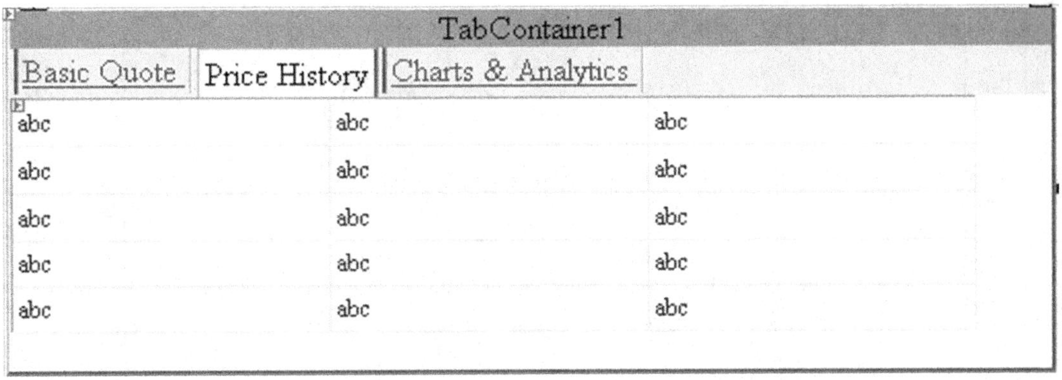

Figure 10-10. *Designing the price history pane*

With the GridView control in place, we need a helper method to populate the GridView with the historical price information obtained from the web service. So similarly to previous methods on this page, create a method called GetPriceHistory as shown here:

```
private void GetPriceHistory(string strTicker)
{
    DataTier data = new DataTier();
    DataTable priceData = data.GetFullPriceHistory(strTicker, 20);
    grdPriceHistory.DataSource = priceData;
    grdPriceHistory.DataBind();
}
```

Here we just instantiate the data tier and invoke the GetFullPriceHistory web method, passing the stock ticker and the number of days for which we would like price history. After that, the DataSource and DataBind properties of the GridView are used to display the data.

Creating the Charts & Analytics Pane

You are no doubt familiar with seeing price history graphs on business TV shows on CNN or the Bloomberg channel. Figure 10-11 and Figure 10-12 show the price history charts for companies such as Microsoft (MSFT) and Starbucks (SBUX) for the past 100 days.

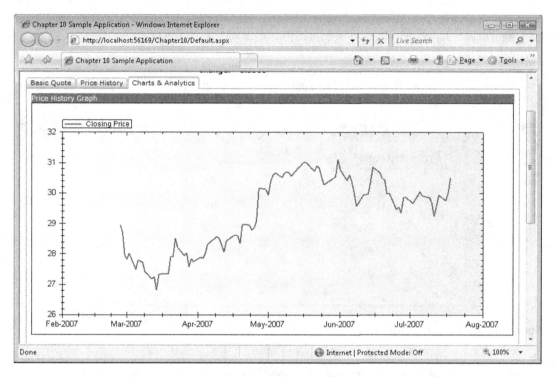

Figure 10-11. *The 100-day price history for MSFT*

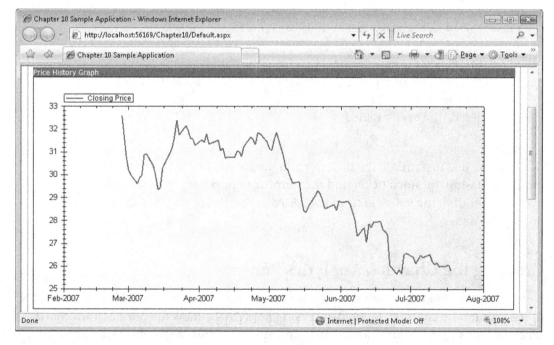

Figure 10-12. *The 100-day price history for SBUX*

These charts are useful in determining where a stock is going, its recent trends, and its long-time trends. Many stocks move between high values and low values in what sometimes looks like a sine wave; this is typically called its *trading envelope*. This is apparent in Figure 10-11, which shows a cycle from 26 to 28 indicating that March 2007 had been a good point to purchase the stock on a short-term basis because it is at the lower end of the trading envelope. This is no guarantee that the stock will not break from the trading envelope and fall far below 26. Also, typically when a stock breaks from its trading envelope, it tends to move quickly outside the trading range, which can lead to the stock rocketing either upward or downward. A more reliable methodology for using price history analysis is to use the Bollinger band method, which you'll see a bit later.

But, let's get back to the technology—how is this implemented?

The resource and data retrieval tiers are the same as for the text-based price history pane you saw previously. If you've skipped ahead, you should return to the "Creating the Price History Pane" section, which describes the DataTier web service and how you can use it to retrieve the price history of a stock.

To implement the charts, the example uses the ZedGraph open source library.

Using the ZedGraph Library Charting Engine

ZedGraph (http://zedgraph.org) is an open source set of classes, written in C#, that enable the creation of various 2D graphs of arbitrary datasets. Because the set is class-based, it has a high degree of programmatic flexibility, and you can modify almost every aspect of a graph, including features such as scale ranges, scale types, step sizes, and so on, to be overridden from their defaults. It also allows for multirange, multitype, multiaxis graphs to be overlaid in a single chart. See Figure 10-13 for an example of a single chart that includes stacked bars, transparent overlays, filled lines, legends, and annotations.

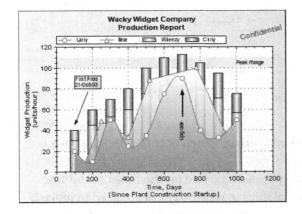

Figure 10-13. *Sample ZedGraph chart*

As such, ZedGraph makes an excellent choice for use in an ASP.NET AJAX-based project and is easy to implement in your applications. You simply make a reference to the *ZedGraph.DLL* in your solution and add the ZedGraph tools to your Toolbox in the standard way.

Drawing the Price History Graph with ZedGraph

To implement the price history graph, you can use a new web form. The Source Code/Download area on the Apress web site (www.apress.com) contains the web form in a file called *PH.aspx*. This web form contains a single ZedGraph control.

When you place a ZedGraph control from your Toolbox onto a web form, it draws the default chart you saw in Figure 10-13. You can see the *PH.aspx* page in the web form designer in Figure 10-14.

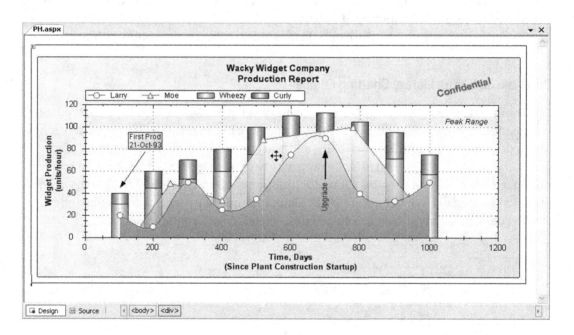

Figure 10-14. *Placing the* ZedGraph *on a web form*

The ZedGraph control fires an event upon rendering, which occurs when the page is loaded or refreshed. This event is called RenderGraph.

In this case, the page is going to take two parameters, one for the ticker of the stock to be rendered and the other for the number of days to render. These are used to make a call to the DataTier web service to get the DataTable back. The DataTable then loads the graph with the appropriate data.

The following code segment shows the full code for the ZedGraphWeb1_RenderGraph event handler:

```
protected void ZedGraphWeb1_RenderGraph(
    System.Drawing.Graphics g, ZedGraph.MasterPane mPane)
{
  int nDays = 0;
  int nRows = 0;
  GraphPane pane = mPane[0];
  PointPairList pt = new PointPairList();
  double nx;
  double ny;

  string days = (string)Page.Request.Params["days"];
  string ticker = (string)Page.Request.Params["ticker"];

  if (ticker != null)
  {
    ticker = ticker.Trim();
    DataTier theDataTier = new DataTier();
    if (days == null)
      nDays = 0;
    else
      nDays = Convert.ToInt32(days);

    DataTable dtTable =
      theDataTier.GetFullPriceHistory(ticker,nDays);
    nRows = dtTable.Rows.Count;


    for (int i = 1; i < nRows; i++)
    {
      ny = Convert.ToDouble(dtTable.Rows[i].ItemArray[1]);
      XDate tmpDate = new XDate(
        Convert.ToDateTime(dtTable.Rows[i].ItemArray[0]));
      nx = (double)tmpDate;
      pt.Add(nx, ny);
    }
    pane.XAxis.Type = AxisType.Date;
    pane.XAxis.GridDashOff = 0;
    LineItem priceCurve = pane.AddCurve(
      "Closing Price", pt, Color.SlateBlue,
```

```
        SymbolType.None);
      priceCurve.Line.Width = 2.0F;
      pane.AxisFill = new Fill(Color.White, Color.AntiqueWhite);
      pane.XAxis.MinGrace = 0;
      pane.XAxis.MaxGrace = 0;
      pane.YAxis.MinGrace = 0;
      pane.YAxis.MaxGrace = 0;
      pane.AxisChange(g);
  }
}
```

This event handler takes two parameters. The first is the base System.Drawing. Graphics object. To render the graph, right at the bottom of the event handler, the System.Drawing.Graphics object is passed to the AxisChange method of a ZedGraph pane to refresh and redraw the graph. The second parameter is a reference to the ZedGraph master pane, which is the collection of drawing surfaces that the ZedGraph exposes. Check out the ZedGraph documentation for information about how to use the panes to create different drawing surfaces. This graph is a simple line chart that uses only one pane, which is the one at the zero index of this collection.

You refer to the pane with this line:

```
GraphPane pane = mPane[0];
```

The subsequent graphical operations are then performed on this pane object.

To draw a line curve, you should use the PointPairList collection that the ZedGraph library provides. This allows you to create a single collection of data items that correspond to the X and Y values of a chart. The PointPairList supports many data types, including dates, so it's perfect for the example's needs.

After the input parameters (ticker and days) have been read in and sanitized, the DataTier service is called to return a DataTable containing the results of the query for that stock and the number of days of price history you want for it.

You then iterate through the DataTable and pull this information out like this:

```
for (int i = 1; i < nRows; i++)
    {
      ny = Convert.ToDouble(dtTable.Rows[i].ItemArray[1]);
      XDate tmpDate = new XDate(
        Convert.ToDateTime(dtTable.Rows[i].ItemArray[0]));
      nx = (double)tmpDate;
      pt.Add(nx, ny);
    }
```

The closing price for the stock should go on the y axis, so it comes from .ItemArray[1] and is converted to a Double value. The original source from Yahoo! and the column on the DataTable encode the value as a string. This is retrieved and loaded into the ny variable.

The date for the closing price should go onto the x axis. This uses the XDate class (also part of the ZedGraph library), which is the data type used by ZedGraph to store dates in a chart and automatically generate axes from them. When using a PointPairList, you encode the XDate into a Double. You can see this being encoded in the variable nx.

Finally, you add the values for nx and ny to the PointPairList (called pt).

To finalize drawing the chart, you load the PointPairList, set the visual configuration of the chart, and call the AxisChange method, which refreshes it. First set the XAxis to be date encoded so that it recognizes the Doubles as dates:

```
pane.XAxis.Type = AxisType.Date;
```

Then load the PointPairList onto the chart. You do this using the AddCurve method of the pane. This method takes four parameters. The first is a string with the name of the data range. In this case, it is Closing Price. If you were superimposing data ranges on the chart (as shown later in Figure 10-15), you would give them their distinct names here. The second parameter is the PointPairList. The third is the color for this range, which in this case is Color.SlateBlue, and the final parameter is the SymbolType used to indicate a point on the line. If you refer to Figure 10-14, you'll see that some points are indicated with triangles or diamonds. You specify these here. Because the graph has a lot of points that would cause it to look cluttered, you won't use a symbol type for this example.

```
LineItem priceCurve =
    pane.AddCurve("Closing Price", pt,
      Color.SlateBlue, SymbolType.None);
```

Next, set the line width to 2 pixels to make the chart stand out a little more clearly, and fill the background for the pane with a graded fill between white and antique white:

```
priceCurve.Line.Width = 2.0F;
pane.AxisFill = new Fill(Color.White, Color.AntiqueWhite);
```

Finally, call the AxisChange event to render the graph:

```
pane.AxisChange(g);
```

Rendering the Charts within the `TabPanel`

For rendering the chart, we simply create a server side ASP.NET `Image` control, `imgPriceHistory` within the `<ContentTemplate>` of the third `TabPanel`, and set the `ImageUrl` property of the `Image` control to the corresponding *PH.aspx* page. This should all be done in an asynchronous manner because all these controls reside within an `UpdatePanel` control (as discussed later). Here's the markup:

```
<cc1:TabPanel ID="TabPanel3" runat="server" HeaderText="TabPanel3">
    <HeaderTemplate>
        Charts & Analytics
    </HeaderTemplate>
    <ContentTemplate>
      <table width="400" cellspacing="0" cellpadding="0" style="border-
        width: 0">
      <tr>
        <td style="background-color: #1077ad"><span class="style2">
            Price History Graph</span></td>
      </tr>
      <tr>
        <td><asp:Image ID="imgPriceHistory" Width="800px" Height="400px"➥
                runat="server" />
        </td>
      </tr>
      </table>
...</ContentTemplate>
< /cc1:TabPanel >
```

The graph is then generated by the *PH.aspx* page and set as the source of the `imgPriceHistory` `Image` control to be rendered within the body of the `TabPanel`. Also to ensure a consistent image size, dimensions of 800 x 400 are specified for the image. As expected, another helper method is needed to programmatically do just that; we can call this one `GetAnalytics` and have the same signature as the previous helper methods used here. Here's the code for that method:

```
private void GetAnalytics(string strTicker)
{
    imgPriceHistory.ImageUrl = "PH.aspx?ticker=" + strTicker + "&days=100";
}
```

Once again, this just sets the source of the `Image` control here to the image generated from *PH.aspx*. This includes the ticker that had been entered in the text box, and the "days=100" are also passed onto the *PH.aspx* page, which results in the price history chart you saw earlier in Figure 10-11 and Figure 10-12.

Generating an Analytics Graph

A methodology for determining good buy and sell prices for a stock comes from a technical analysis of the stock's trading envelope through the use of *Bollinger bands*. These bands are based on a calculation of the moving average of the stock—the moving average being the average price of the stock over a number of periods preceding the current one. For example, a 30-day moving average on any day is the average of closing prices for the stock over the previous 30-day period. Thus, today's average is slightly different from yesterday's, which is slightly different from the day before; hence, it's called a *moving average*.

Bollinger bands are calculated from this value. The "upper" band is the average over the preceding period plus two times the standard deviation. The "lower" band is the average over the preceding period minus two times the standard deviation. Figure 10-15 and Figure 10-16 show the price history overlaid with Bollinger bands for MSFT and SBUX.

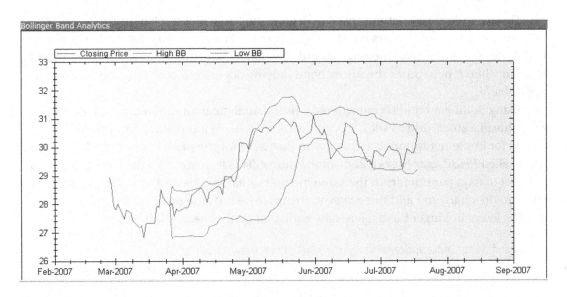

Figure 10-15. *Bollinger bands for MSFT over 100 days*

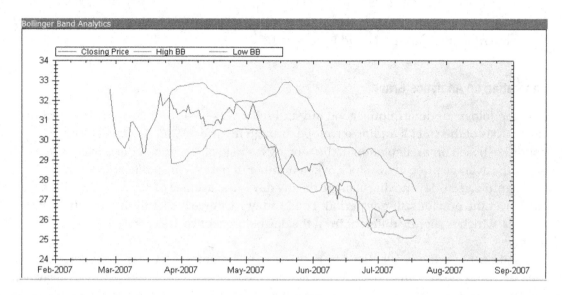

Figure 10-16. *Bollinger bands for SBUX over 100 days*

These bands are sometimes used to predict the value of a stock based on a projection of its future value based on its past behavior. A typical rule is to buy the stock when it penetrates the lower band moving upward or when it "bounces off" the lower band, and to sell it when it penetrates the upper band moving downward or when it bounces off the upper band.

Using Bollinger bands is considered a useful analytical methodology for assessing the value of a stock, and as such this application includes a Bollinger band graph.

As for implementation, it's identical to that used for the price history graph. A web form called *PHBB.aspx* hosts a ZedGraph control. This form accepts the stock ticker and number of days parameters in the same manner as earlier. Instead of adding a single curve to the chart, you add three curves: the price history, the upper Bollinger band, and the lower Bollinger band. Here's the code that generates the Bollinger bands:

```
protected void ZedGraphWeb1_RenderGraph(System.Drawing.Graphics g,
                                        ZedGraph.MasterPane mPane)
{
int nDays = 0;
int nRows = 0;
GraphPane pane = mPane[0];


string days = (string)Page.Request.Params["days"];
string ticker = (string)Page.Request.Params["ticker"];
```

```
if (ticker != null)
{
  ticker = ticker.Trim();
  DataTier theDataTier = new DataTier();
  if (days == null)
    nDays = 0;
  else
    nDays = Convert.ToInt32(days);

  DataTable dtTable = theDataTier.GetFullPriceHistory(ticker, nDays);
  nRows = dtTable.Rows.Count;
  double[] nx = new double[nRows-1];
  double[] ny = new double[nRows-1];
  double[] bbh = new double[nRows-1];
  double[] bbl = new double[nRows-1];
  double[] pht = new double[20];
  int nIndex = 0;
  for (int i = nRows-1; i > 0; i--)
  {
    ny[nIndex] = Convert.ToDouble(dtTable.Rows[i].ItemArray[1]);
    XDate tmpDate = new
        XDate(Convert.ToDateTime(dtTable.Rows[i].ItemArray[0]));
    nx[nIndex] = (double)tmpDate;
    if (nIndex > 20)
    {
      int x = 0;
      for (int n = nIndex - 20; n < nIndex; n++)
      {
        pht[x] = ny[n];
        x++;
      }
      bbh[nIndex] = GetAverage(pht)
          + (2 * GetStandardDeviation(pht));
      bbl[nIndex] = GetAverage(pht)
          - (2 * GetStandardDeviation(pht));

    }
    else
    {
      bbh[nIndex] = ny[nIndex];
      bbl[nIndex] = ny[nIndex];
    }
```

```
      nIndex++;
    }
    pane.XAxis.Type = AxisType.Date;
    pane.XAxis.GridDashOff = 0;
    pane.AddCurve("Closing Price", nx,
        ny, Color.SlateBlue, SymbolType.None);

    pane.AddCurve("High BB", nx,
        bbh, Color.Red, SymbolType.None);

    pane.AddCurve("Low BB", nx,
        bbl, Color.Red, SymbolType.None);

    pane.AxisFill = new Fill(Color.White, Color.AntiqueWhite);
    Axis.Default.MinGrace = 0;
    Axis.Default.MaxGrace = 0;
    pane.AxisChange(g);
}
```

The GetAverage and GetStandardDeviation helper functions that the application uses
are as follows:

```
public double GetAverage(double[] num)
{
  double sum = 0.0;
  for (int i = 0; i < num.Length; i++)
  {
    sum += num[i];
  }
  double avg = sum / System.Convert.ToDouble(num.Length);

  return avg;
}


public double GetStandardDeviation(double[] num)
{
  double Sum = 0.0, SumOfSqrs = 0.0;
  for (int i = 0; i < num.Length; i++)
  {
    Sum += num[i];
    SumOfSqrs += Math.Pow(num[i], 2);
  }
```

```
    double topSum = (num.Length * SumOfSqrs) - (Math.Pow(Sum, 2));
    double n = (double)num.Length;
    return Math.Sqrt(topSum / (n * (n - 1)));
}
```

To display this in the Analytics pane directly below the price history chart, an extension is made to the `<ContentTemplate>` of the third `TabPanel` with the following markup:

```
<table width="400" cellspacing="0" cellpadding="0" style="border-width: 0">
  <tr>
    <td style="background-color: #1077AD; height: 5px;">➡
      <span class="style2">Bollinger Band Analytics➡
      </span></td>
  </tr>
  <tr>
    <td>
        <asp:Image ID="imgAnalyticGraph" Width="800px" Height="400px"
        runat="server" />
    </td>
  </tr>
</table>
```

Nothing new here, just like the previous chart, an ASP.NET `Image` control, `imgAnalyticGraph`, is created to act as a placeholder for the Bollinger band chart generated by the *PHBB.aspx* page. This `Image` control must be accompanied by an additional line of C# code in the `GetAnalytics` method in the code behind:

```
imgAnalyticGraph.ImageUrl = "PHBB.aspx?ticker=" + strTicker + "&days=100";
```

And with that, the Bollinger band is integrated into the Analytics pane just like the price history chart. Lastly, let's looks at the most important and yet simple part of this sample, AJAXifying the form so that all updates occur without doing any page refresh.

Applying ASP.NET AJAX

By now, you know that the easiest and fastest way to add AJAX functionality to an existing ASP.NET application is to use the ASP.NET AJAX server controls, mainly the `UpdatePanel`. For the purposes of this chapter, we assume that the project itself has already been ASP.NET AJAX-enabled, and the appropriate changes have been made to the *Web.Config* file as shown in the earlier chapters.

As you know all too well, if you have not created an AJAX-enabled ASP.NET web site/project, the very first step before the addition of any ASP.NET AJAX server controls is to add a ScriptManager component to the page, which you can do by either dragging and dropping the component from the Toolbox or simply adding the markup to the page:

```
<asp:ScriptManager ID="ScriptManager1" runat="server">   </asp:ScriptManager>
```

Because most of the markup for this project resides in the TabContainer control, we can easily encapsulate almost the entire application in the ContentTemplate of the UpdatePanel control without even having to create manual triggers. To do so, create an UpdatePanel control right before the markup for the Timer control. This would also be before the stock ticker TextBox.

```
<asp:UpdatePanel ID="UpdatePanel1" runat="server">
<ContentTemplate>
<asp:Timer ID="Timer1" runat="server" Interval="5000" OnTick=➡
    "Timer1_Tick"></asp:Timer>
<table width="100%" cellpadding="2" style="border-width: 0">
  <tr>
    <td style="width: 117px" class="style1"><b>Stock Ticker</b></td>
    <td style="width: 133px">
      <asp:TextBox ID="txtTicker" runat="server" MaxLength="4" >➡
          MSFT</asp:TextBox>
    ...
</ContentTemplate>
</asp:UpdatePanel>
```

With that simple addition, we have added AJAX capabilities to this application, and the page will not blink as it obtains data and renders the updates.

You can see that there is no explicit coding for a partial-page update for all content, including price information and analytic charts. Everything is handled under the hood by the ASP.NET AJAX runtime. You concentrate on building your application, and by wrapping standard ASP.NET controls with an UpdatePanel, you can enable the asynchronous functionality.

One last item to complete is a way of notifying the user when the page is being updated. Because all updates are done asynchronously with no page refresh, the user may be confused at times during page updates when nothing is happening. Just like an UpdatePanel, you can create this either from the left Toolbox or by manually typing the markup as shown here:

```
<asp:UpdateProgress runat="server" ID="prog1" DisplayAfter="300"➡
    AssociatedUpdatePanelID="UpdatePanel1">
  <ProgressTemplate>
    <span style="color: #ffff00; background-color: #3300ff">
      Loading...</span>
  </ProgressTemplate>
</asp:UpdateProgress>
```

This can be placed just about anywhere within the page, but in this case, we have it as one of the first elements in the UpdatePanel. The DisplayAfter property is set to 300 so that the UpdateProgress renders 300 milliseconds after a postback. Because we have only one UpdatePanel on this page, setting the AssociatedUpdatePanelID property isn't required but is usually a good practice to do so anyway as done here. Also quite often, a circular animating GIF image is used to show updates taking place as used in some of the earlier chapters. In this case, however, we are simply specifying "Loading…" with bright yellow colors and a blue background. Figure 10-17 shows UpdateProgress in action.

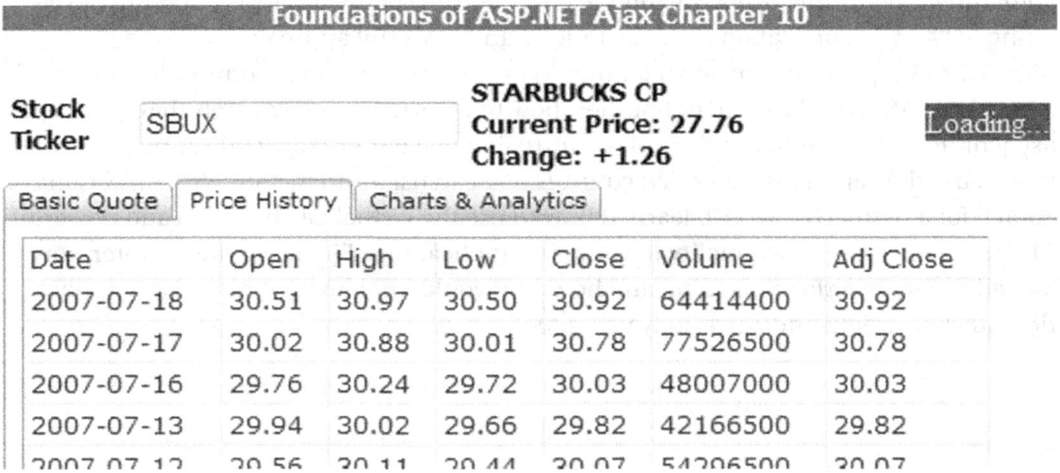

Foundations of ASP.NET Ajax Chapter 10

Stock Ticker	SBUX	STARBUCKS CP Current Price: 27.76 Change: +1.26	Loading…

Basic Quote	Price History	Charts & Analytics

Date	Open	High	Low	Close	Volume	Adj Close
2007-07-18	30.51	30.97	30.50	30.92	64414400	30.92
2007-07-17	30.02	30.88	30.01	30.78	77526500	30.78
2007-07-16	29.76	30.24	29.72	30.03	48007000	30.03
2007-07-13	29.94	30.02	29.66	29.82	42166500	29.82
2007-07-12	30.56	30.11	30.44	30.07	54296500	30.07

Figure 10-17. UpdateProgress *used to notify users during asynchronous updates*

Summary

This chapter covered a typical real-world ASP.NET application and showed how you could drastically enhance it using the ASP.NET AJAX server and client libraries. It demonstrated a logical *n*-tier architecture, with diverse resource tiers exposed via web services; a data retrieval layer that abstracted the complexity of talking to the resources; a business logic tier that applied business logic such as the calculation of financial analytics; and a presentation tier that implemented the presentation logic. The code that was written to implement this functionality was straight ASP.NET and C#.

You then enhanced this application using ASP.NET AJAX server-side controls. You used UpdatePanel controls to wrap the various page panes that get updated to provide partial asynchronous page updates. A button on the page provided a drill down into some more advanced analytics of the historical stock ticker data, which demonstrated how you could add an update to the page without triggering a full-page refresh and the associated "blink."

The example showed how to embed graphics—generated using a third-party control, the open source ZedGraph—within the page by hosting them on external pages and generating the HTML markup that would reference them on the main page. This HTML was embedded within an UpdatePanel, so again it didn't cause a full-page refresh when the graphic was downloaded and rendered on the page.

The example implemented two graphics: first, a basic line graph containing the price history of the stock, and second, a compound line graph containing three lines (the price history, the lower Bollinger band, and the upper Bollinger band).

With that, this book comes to an end. I hope you have enjoyed learning about the *Foundations of ASP.NET AJAX*, including a tour of some of the basic principles in developing AJAX-style applications and the unique and powerful approach to this that ASP.NET AJAX gives you. You looked through how JavaScript has become object oriented when using ASP.NET AJAX client libraries; how to use server-side controls that empower asynchronous functionality with as little intrusion on your existing code as possible; and how to use the various value-added controls and extensions in the ASP.NET AJAX Control Toolkit for a better UI. You also learned how to use the Virtual Earth SDK to add powerful AJAX style mapping functionality to your web applications. Finally, in this chapter, you looked at a real-world application and how you would implement it as an AJAX application quickly, simply, and powerfully using ASP.NET AJAX.

Index

<%@ WebService %> attribute, 53
4WD property, 43

A

abstractMethod property, 46
AcceptAMPM property
    MaskedEdit extender, 175
    MaskedEditValidator control, 177
AcceptNegative property, 175
Accordion control, 133–135
AccordionPane control, 133–135
<AccordionPane> tag, 134
ActiveTabChanged event, 230, 231
ActiveTabChanged property, 202
ActiveTabIndex property, 202
add method, 56
Add Reference button, 233
addComponent method, 69
AddControl method, 208
addCssClass method, 72
AddCurve method, 247
addHandler method, 75, 77
$addHandler shortcut, 77
addHandlers method, 75
$addHandlers shortcut, 77
AddPin function, 223
AddPolygon method, 208
AddPolyline method, 208
AddPushpin method, 208
AddPushPin method, 223
addRange method, 56
AddShape method, 208
Aerial(a) type, 219
AJAX, 1, 16–17, 29
    applications
        coding, 40–41
        creating, 32–34
        running, 40–41
    ASP.NET 2.0, 23
        AJAX Extensions, 28–29
        server controls, 17
    JSON, 28
    Microsoft AJAX Library
        overview, 26–27
        web services, 27
    overview, 7–10
    Script Manager server control, 37–38

synchronous versus asynchronous
    web applications, 24
    XMLHttpRequest object, 10–11
AJAX core classes, 41
AJAX Library. See Microsoft AJAX Library
AJAXBook namespace, 36, 41, 44
AJAXBook.Car object, 43
AJAXBook.Car.registerClass method, 43
AJAXBook.IStickShift.isImplementedBy( )
    method, 49
AJAXBook.js, 35
AJAXBook.SUV class, 44
AjaxControlToolkit.dll, 132
AjaxToolKit, 132
AllowPaging property, 120
AllowReorder property, 192
AllowSorting property, 120
altKey parameter, 76
AlwaysVisibleControlExtender control,
    135–136
animation
    discrete, 144
    fade, 138–140
    length, 140–142
Animation control, 137
AnimationExtender control, 137–144
    discrete animation, 144
    fade animation, 138–140
    length animation, 140–142
AnimationTarget property, 141
App_Data folder, 32
append method, 79
appendLine method, 79
Application class, 67, 68
ApplicationLoadEventArgs class, 67
argument method, 60
argumentNull method, 60
argumentOutOfRange method, 60
argumentType method, 60
argumentUndefined method, 60
Array extension, 55–58
.asmx file, 53
<asp:AsyncPostBackTrigger> trigger, 111,
    120
<asp:BoundField> tag, 120
<asp:Calendar> tag, 21

You Need the Companion eBook

Your purchase of this book entitles you to buy the companion PDF-version eBook for only $10. Take the weightless companion with you anywhere.

We believe this Apress title will prove so indispensable that you'll want to carry it with you everywhere, which is why we are offering the companion eBook (in PDF format) for $10 to customers who purchase this book now. Convenient and fully searchable, the PDF version of any content-rich, page-heavy Apress book makes a valuable addition to your programming library. You can easily find and copy code—or perform examples by quickly toggling between instructions and the application. Even simultaneously tackling a donut, diet soda, and complex code becomes simplified with hands-free eBooks!

Once you purchase your book, getting the $10 companion eBook is simple:

❶ Visit **www.apress.com/promo/tendollars/**.

❷ Complete a basic registration form to receive a randomly generated question about this title.

❸ Answer the question correctly in 60 seconds, and you will receive a promotional code to redeem for the $10.00 eBook.

THE EXPERT'S VOICE™

2855 TELEGRAPH AVENUE | SUITE 600 | BERKELEY, CA 94705

Offer valid through 5/19/08